Emancipation Day

CELEBRATING FREEDOM IN CANADA

Natasha L. Henry

NATURAL HERITAGE BOOKS
A MEMBER OF THE DUNDURN GROUP
TORONTO

Edited by Jane Gibson
Copy-edited by Jennifer McKnight
Designed by Courtney Horner
Printed and bound in Canada by Marquis

Library and Archives Canada Cataloguing in Publication

Henry, Natasha L.
    Emancipation Day : celebrating freedom in
Canada / by Natasha L. Henry.

Includes bibliographical references and index.
ISBN 978-1-55488-717-0

    1. Emancipation Day (Canada). 2. Black
Canadians--Social life and customs. I. Title.

FC106.B6H457 2010   394.263   C2009-907479-6

1   2   3   4   5   14   13   12   11   10

We acknowledge the support of **The Canada Council for the Arts** and the **Ontario Arts Council** for our publishing program. We also acknowledge the financial support of the **Government of Canada** through the **Canada Book Fund** and **The Association for the Export of Canadian Books**, and the **Government of Ontario** through the **Ontario Book Publishers Tax Credit** program, and the **Ontario Media Development Corporation**.

Care has been taken to trace the ownership of copyright material used in this book. The author and the publisher welcome any information enabling them to rectify any references or credits in subsequent editions.

J. Kirk Howard, President

www.dundurn.com

Published by Natural Heritage Books
A Member of The Dundurn Group

Cover image courtesy of Library and Archives Canada, Q4-54997.
Back cover image shows Elanor Roosevelt posing with the Hour-A-Day Study Club. Courtesy of the North American Black Historical Museum, FS-33. See page 201.

Dundurn Press	Gazelle Book Services Limited	Dundurn Press
3 Church Street, Suite 500	White Cross Mills	2250 Military Road
Toronto, Ontario, Canada	High Town, Lancaster, England	Tonawanda, NY
M5E 1M2	LA1 4XS	U.S.A. 14150

Table of Contents

Foreword

by Afua Cooper

On August 1, 1851, Black Canadians in Sandwich (now a suburb of Windsor), Canada West,[1] and their allies commemorated Emancipation Day. Festivities included speeches, musical and cultural performances, and a dinner. The initiative was led by Henry and Mary Bibb, a Black abolitionist couple who had become leaders in the Black communities of the province, and who had founded the *Voice of the Fugitive*, Canada's first Black newspaper. Here is how an article published in the *Voice* described the event:

> The friends of freedom in Sandwich will celebrate the abolition of chattel slavery in the British West Indies, in A.D. 1837 at the Stone Barracks where there will be speaking, singing, etc.[2] Several distinguished speakers from abroad are expected, among whom are Samuel R. Ward, of Boston, Mr. Johnson, of Ohio, J.J. Fisher of Toronto, George Cary, of Dawn Mills. A general Invitation is hereby extended to all persons friendly to the cause.
>
> Dinner will be furnished by the ladies for twenty-five cents per ticket. Refreshments may be had during the day and supper in the evening. The proceeds will be appropriated towards erecting a Baptist church.

It was Mary Bibb, a publisher in her own right, who wrote the article. She also listed her name and the names of several women who were part of the women's Emancipation Day Committee. On that day in 1851, the Bibbs were continuing the tradition of Emancipation Day celebrations and the renewal of the Black community spirit through such commemorations. It is instructive to note that the Bibbs and the rest of the community had a specific objective for the use of the funds garnered from the celebrations, and that was to concretely aid in the development of the Black community through the building of a church. That objective was realized in the founding and erecting of the First Baptist Church, which is still in operation today.

West Indian Emancipation Day, or August First as it was popularly referred to, has been celebrated by African Canadians since 1834 when the British Parliament passed the Act a year earlier to free all the enslaved Africans in the overseas slave colonies. Some slave colonies like Barbados and Antigua received complete emancipation in 1834, while others, like Jamaica and British Guiana, had to wait for a period of "apprenticeship" between 1834 to 1837–38 when they were granted full freedom. Nonetheless, the Act and the subsequent freeing of the enslaved people were momentous events because close to one million Africans who were held in bondage in the British overseas colonies, mainly in the West Indies, were freed. The Emancipation Act was a milestone in the annals of Black freedom not only in the Americas but globally as well.

Canada was part of the British Empire, and though it was not a slave society as we understand it, it was a society with slaves. Africans had been enslaved in Canada since 1628 and though the institution declined significantly by the 1820s, there were still enslaved people in the colonies who were freed by the Emancipation Act. On the other hand, in the United States slavery had grown by leaps and bounds by the time of British Emancipation. Therefore, the end of slavery in Canada made this country the only genuine free soil on the continent. The creators of August First celebrations were African Americans who had migrated to Canada during the first part of the nineteenth century in their quest for a free life.

These African Americans, runaway slaves and free persons, first began arriving in Canada after the War of 1812. They came as war refugees from the Chesapeake Region to New Brunswick and Nova Scotia. Later, other immigrants, mainly associated with the Underground Railroad experience, started coming primarily to the provinces of Ontario and Quebec after 1818.³ Likewise, beginning in 1858 a stream of Black immigrants from California made an exodus to British Columbia. It is these Blacks who collectively began to memorialize August First. The reason for this is three-fold. First, these Canadians were grateful to the British Crown for providing them with refuge and the opportunity to build new lives in Canada. Second, these Africans were abolitionists who made it their life's work to fight for the end of slavery in the United States, and saw the commemoration of "British freedom" as one way to signal to the slaveholding American Republic their intention. Finally, their commemoration of August First was an exercise in solidarity with Black Caribbean people in their struggle and success to win emancipation for themselves and their communities. The August First event marked the internationalization of the Black freedom struggle and the awareness of Black Canadians that "we are our brothers and sisters keeper."

The Emancipation Act is usually seen as a manifestation of British philanthropy, and as a "handing down of freedom" to disenfranchised Blacks. But this is only a partial truth. Black enslaved Caribbean people had fought in diverse ways for their freedom. The Haitian Revolution sheds much light on this. In this instance, enslaved Africans in Haiti fought a thirteen-year war with France (and also Britain and Spain) for their freedom. The Haitians won. Their victory sent a shock wave throughout the world especially to the slaveholding empires.

It was felt by many in the political elite in Britain that it was best to avoid another Haiti in the British colonies by abolishing slavery by peaceful means. However, like the Haitians, the enslaved people in the British Caribbean had been engaged in a long struggle for their freedom. Ever since Britain became a colonizing and slave power in the Caribbean, enslaved Africans have led numerous rebellions and revolts against British slaveholding and colonial rule. Historian Michael Craton has noted that British rule in the Caribbean can be seen as a protracted 250-year war between the colonizing slaveholders and the enslaved Africans.⁴ In Jamaica, for example, in 1831 a slave revolt convulsed the island. In December of that year the "Baptist War" as it was called (because so many of the leaders were Baptist deacons) was started by the enslaved masses in their desire to throw off slavery and its attendant dehumanization.

The British Army and government responded ferociously. They hanged at least four hundred freedom fighters and put the country under martial law. Alarmed by the desire and intention of enslaved Blacks to free themselves, less than two years later, the British proclaimed West Indian Emancipation. The point is that enslaved Africans themselves had agency and exercised that agency in their quest to be the architects of their own lives and freedom. But in a Eurocentric interpretation of the Emancipation Act, it is the British government that has received the full credit for "giving freedom to the Blacks." While I am not discounting the significant work done by the British Anti-slavery Movement and of such stalwarts like Granville Sharpe, I must point out that when the British passed the Emancipation Act they were well aware that the Caribbean enslaved masses had begun the struggle for their own freedom long before the British Anti-slavery Movement came into being, and that some of these enslaved people, like the Haitians, had already seized their freedom.

Likewise, the African Canadians who created Emancipation Day commemorations showed tremendous agency in originating these celebrations. They also realized, I believe, that in launching these commemorations they were sinking into the collective psyche and memory the significance of Black struggle and freedom. Emancipation Day was a vehicle used by the Black community to express their collective identity as New World Africans, a ritual in which they articulated their personhood, and further as a site in which they locate their struggle against racism. Emancipation Day celebrations began in 1834 and are still commemorated today. That is a phenomenal accomplishment. The Emancipation of Black people in Euro-American societies during the nineteenth century sits at the centre of Western discourse on freedom, human rights, and citizenship. Black Canadians have contributed greatly to this discourse and its praxis through memorials of Emancipation Day. The August First events have even given birth in 1967 in Toronto to the Caribana Festival and street parade which also takes place on August First weekend. Caribana today attracts a crowd of over one million and is the largest street festival in all of North America. It is instructive to add that Caribana brings annually upwards of five hundred million dollars to the City of Toronto.

Despite its integral place in Canadian history, the August First history has not yet been told in its fullest. That is about to change.

Educator and historian Natasha Henry has written what will become, for the foreseeable future, the definitive book on the Emancipation Day history in Canada. She cogently explores the origins and evolution of the commemoration in the older Canadian provinces (Ontario, Nova Scotia, Quebec, New Brunswick), how the celebrations were articulated throughout the nineteenth and twentieth centuries, and the spread of the Emancipation Day initiatives to the rest of the country, in particular to British Columbia.

Henry reveals how the communities used the cultural arts as an integral part of Emancipation Day memorialization and sheds light on the Canadian Black community's outreach efforts to the international Black community, their links with the White communities (mainly in Canada itself and the United States), the crucial role of the Black churches, inter-gender initiatives, and the role of women in August First events.

Henry's research shows that the Emancipation Day celebration creators were astute, politically savvy, and committed to the advancement of Black community life. In her insightful analysis Henry also underscores the fact that while Black Canadians were grateful to the British Crown they were still mindful of the fact that Black people as a whole had not yet achieved full citizenship in either the British West Indies or Canada. Moreover, the creators of the celebrations often used the events to illuminate these issues of Black freedom and to further articulate solutions. Put another way, Emancipation Day events in Canada were a space in which culture, politics, religion, and history intersected and intertwined.

Henry has conducted in-depth research in several archives, libraries, and museums across Canada in order to write this outstanding book. She has brought to light what for us in the twenty-first century is a little-known story, but which for the years following 1834 was a major event in the Black and Canadian community. We learn, for example, that famed boxer Jack Johnson participated in Emancipation Day Celebrations in Windsor in 1909, and we also learn that music superstar Diana Ross cut her teeth in the music business at August First celebrations in Canada. Further, we discover that the Chatham Black community used the commemoration in 1895 to alert and inform both observers and participants about their struggle against segregated schooling and their fight for their children to get an education. In addition, we gain knowledge of the fact that by 1931, over twenty thousand people attended the commemoration which was dubbed "The Greatest Freedom Show on Earth," and that the 1948 events in Windsor attracted a massive crowd of 275,000! By this date, Windsor had begun hosting the largest commemorations in North America.

Through her efforts, Henry has made a vast contribution to the history of Black Canadians, the abolitionist movement, festivals in Canada, African-Canadian traditions, Caribbean history, African-American history, and that of the African Diaspora. By filling the gaps in these narratives, Natasha has restored to all of us our shared and collective history. For this, we owe her a debt of gratitude.

Afua Cooper
Spring 2010

Afua Cooper, Ph.D., is the leading historian of the African Diaspora in Canada. She has researched widely in the field and has published groundbreaking and award winning books, including *The Hanging of Angélique: The Untold Story of Slavery in Canada and the Burning of Old Montréal* and *We're Rooted Here and They Can't Pull Us Up: Essays in African Canadian Women's History*. Afua recently held the Ruth Wynn Woodward Endowed Chair in Women's Studies at Simon Fraser University. She is also the recipient of the Harry Jerome Award for Professional Excellence.

Acknowledgements

I am grateful to Denise Stern for her research assistance and to Raulandre Thompson and Breanna Henry for their help. I would like to express sincere gratitude to the people and organizations that assisted me with this project:

Ann Marie Langlois, Archives of Ontario, archivist at Osgoode Hall Library; Afua Cooper, Adrienne Shadd, and Karolyn Smardz Frost; the Chatham-Kent Museum; Anne Jarvis, historical interpreter of Griffin House/Fieldcote Museum and Memorial Park; the St. Catharines Museum; the Norval Johnson Library Collection at the St. Catharines Central Library; Karen Foster, archivist, Grey Roots Archives and Museum, Owen Sound; Chatham-Kent Historical Society; Buxton Museum; Dr. Delta McNeish, Beth Emanuel BME Church; University of Western Ontario; London Public Library; British Columbia Archives; Gary Shutlak, Nova Scotia Archives and Record Management; Margaret Houghton, archivist, Hamilton Public Library; Toronto Public Library; Janie Cooper-Wilson, executive director of the Silvershoe Historical Society; Nancy Mallett, archivist, The Cathedral Church of St. James; the Marsh Collection Society; John Hennigar-Shuh, Maritime Museum of the Atlantic; David States, Parks Canada Atlantic Service Centre; the Oakville Historical Society; the Oakville Museum at the Erchless Estate; the Canadian Caribbean Association of Halton; the Elmira Public Library; the Doon Heritage Crossroads; the York University Clara Thomas Archives and Special Collections; Lezlie Wells of Niagara Bound Tours; and O'Neil and Marlon McLean of Kaimera Design.

Special thanks also goes to Kenn Stanton, curator of North American Black Historical Museum; Dr. Henry Bishop, executive director of the Black Cultural Centre of Nova Scotia; Justice Beth Allen, Justice Romain Pitt, and Justice George Strathy, all of the Superior Court of Justice; Marcus Snowden; Dennis and Lisa Scott of Owen Sound; Melinda Mollineaux; and the many others I contacted for providing invaluable information, photos, and other resources and for providing research leads and suggestions. A special thank you goes to Hilary Dawson, historical researcher of Toronto, Ontario, for the background on Joshua Glover.

I would like to thank Barry Penhale and Jane Gibson of Natural Heritage Books for approaching me with this project, for their confidence in my abilities, and for providing encouraging editorial support. Thanks also to my copy editor, Jennifer McKnight, for her thorough work and helpful feedback.

The support, patience, time, understanding, and encouragement of my family and close friends helped me through this project. Thank you to Rawle Thompson, my sisters Simone and Nicole, my brothers Desroy and Gary, my nephews and nieces, and other extended family members. Finally, I would like to extend a heartfelt appreciation to my mother Nancy Whynter, my daughter Jamaya Dixon, and my life partner Fitzroy Dixon.

Introduction

Background on an African-Canadian Celebration

The moment of freedom is finally at hand.
The patience, the faith, the journey, the battle! Oh yes, that mighty
stand.
No more bondage. No more captivity.
No more being contained and confined, for it's all faded away as
we look ahead with utmost anticipation to be free once again.
— Fitzroy E. Dixon, "The True Essence of Freedom," 1996.[1]

The end of the horrific, inhumane practice of African slavery in all British
colonies was the result of the determination of enslaved Africans in the New
World, including Canada, along with Black and White abolitionists in the
Western Hemisphere and in Europe. The passage of the 1833 Abolition
of Slavery Bill was a victory for those who advocated fervently, but most
importantly, for the people who were emancipated. In recognition of their
newly acquired freedom, which came into effect in most British territories on
August 1, 1834, former slaves quickly created a venue from which to express
their allegiance, elation, and gratitude. The first day of liberation was a joyous
occasion, for with emancipation came freedom and much cause for great
celebration. Emancipation Day observances arose spontaneously throughout
the colonies of Britain, as well as those in Canada, to commemorate the
piece of legislation that led to the abolition of slavery throughout the British
Empire and to rejoice in the possibilities new freedom would bring.

Emancipation Day celebrations of freedom have been held in many towns across Ontario and Quebec since 1834, in the Maritime provinces of Nova Scotia and New Brunswick from around 1846, and in British Columbia since 1858. The locations of these events throughout each province included a range of Black settlement sites. Celebrations spread across Ontario from Amherstburg on the Detroit River, to Owen Sound and Collingwood on Georgian Bay, and Niagara on the Niagara River. Larger centres such as Brantford, Toronto, Hamilton, London, and Windsor held major celebratory days. Long-settled communities such as Buxton, Chatham, Dresden, and Sandwich — all pivotal in the days of the Underground Railroad — also hosted annual events. Areas in Nova Scotia and New Brunswick with significant Black Loyalist and Black Refugee populations such as Halifax, North Preston, and Saint John also conducted freedom festivities, but seemingly not ever in Yarmouth County, Nova Scotia, despite the extensive Black population that has been there for generations.

People of African descent immigrated to Canada at different times throughout the country's early history, arriving as slaves, fugitives, Black Loyalists, Black Refugees, or individuals with free status, all of them in pursuit of a better life. Documents indicate that Mathieu da Costa was the first African slave to set foot on Canadian soil in New France (later Quebec) in 1605, and the first recorded sale of an African slave was in New France in 1628. The eastern Canadian provinces of Nova Scotia, New Brunswick, and Prince Edward Island, including Acadia, and places in Ontario like Amherstburg (formerly Fort Malden), the Niagara area, Toronto, and Brantford, among others, had been slave-holding territories since the early 1700s, continuing through much of the 1800s. The enslaved Blacks in these regions created the beginnings of African-Canadian communities, which soon became centres of anti-slavery activity for abolitionists, both Black and White, who were committed to the liberation of enslaved Africans in Canada, the West Indies, and the United States. Supporters of anti-slavery efforts included former slaves, free Blacks, sympathetic Whites, and White church ministers who assisted hundreds of fugitive slaves with clothing, food, transportation, and shelter along the final stages of the Underground Railroad.

Abolitionist and legendary Underground Railroad conductor Harriet Tubman used St. Catharines as her last "station" for the runaways whom she helped to escape. Adolphus Judah, an African-American immigrant, was one of the founders of two organizations that assisted incoming fugitive slaves to Toronto and lent his support to the development of the Elgin Settlement when he moved to Chatham. Captain Charles Stuart,[2] a White British officer, helped to secure land grants for refugees in Amherstburg. In Pictou, Nova Scotia Reverend Dr. James MacGregor, a Presbyterian minister from Scotland, purchased the freedom of a young enslaved girl and published an anti-slavery pamphlet, "Letter to a Clergyman Urging Him to set Free a Black Girl He Held in Slavery."[3]

The headquarters of two of the African-Canadian newspapers, primarily read by fugitive slaves, were in Sandwich, Windsor, Chatham, and Toronto in Canada West (later renamed Ontario). The founders of both newspapers were also escapees. Samuel Ringgold Ward, who had escaped slavery in Maryland with his parents in 1820 and moved to Canada West in 1851, started the *Provincial Freeman* in Windsor in 1853. Shortly after, the paper was moved to Toronto and finally to Chatham when Mary Ann Shadd became editor in 1854. The *Voice of the Fugitive*, founded and edited by Henry Bibb and his wife Mary Bibb, was published out of Sandwich and Windsor between 1851 and 1853. These newspapers were very important for the times. Both fugitive slaves and anti-slavery supporters obtained valuable, detailed information from these early papers, and used this data to help mobilize anti-slavery efforts.

Religious mission settlements were established in several of these Ontario locations to assist newly arriving Black refugees become self-sufficient and prosperous through acquiring land, and obtaining education and practical training. The idea for the Dawn Settlement was created in Colchester Township near Amherstburg, the Refugee Home Society was set up in Sandwich, the Free Coloured Mission was established in London, and The Elgin Settlement (Buxton Mission) was formed in the Chatham area.

In the Maritimes, all-Black settlements populated with former slaves, free Blacks and their descendants, Black Loyalists, and Black Refugees developed into self-sufficient communities. Close-knit neighbourhoods founded in Nova Scotia included Africville and other parts of the city of Halifax, North Preston, and Birchtown. In New Brunswick, Saint John, Fredericton, and St. Andrews also had independent African-Canadian communities. In addition, these places became northern termini on the Underground Railroad, attracting many fugitive slaves escaping enslavement in the United States. These areas with their proximity to the northern states, closeness to fresh water sources, and fertile land for farming were obvious targets for settlement. Other Black Loyalists and free Blacks also migrated to these areas where early African-Canadian communities were already established.

British Columbia experienced an influx of African American and Black Caribbean immigrants in the late 1850s, all hoping for a better, freer life through prospecting opportunities in the Fraser River Gold Rush. A few hundred African Americans emigrated from California, wishing to remove themselves from the Jim Crow laws[4] that denied them basic rights, increased legislated segregation, and protected the rights of slaveholders. They settled primarily in Victoria on Vancouver Island and on Salt Spring Island.

In the late 1800s and continuing through to the turn of the twentieth century, many of these rural and urban centres in Canada were sites of entrenched racial discrimination and persistent racial protest. The town of Dresden, Ontario, was well-known for practices similar to Jim Crow laws in the southern United States. African Canadians were barred from restaurants and theatres in Saint John in 1915, and, in Owen Sound, Blacks were discouraged from seeking political office. In Toronto in 1929, visiting Blacks were turned away from local hotels. During Canada's own civil-rights movement, African Canadians confronted racism at all levels. Once "described as a stronghold of racial discrimination,"[5] Dresden became a testing ground for new human rights legislation beginning in 1954[6] and segregated schooling was dismantled in Chatham, St. Catharines, and Halifax.

When new waves of immigrants of African origin, including West-Indian students in the 1920s and West-Indian women on the Domestic Scheme of 1955,[7] they would choose cities such as London, Hamilton, Montreal, and Toronto as their homes. These settlers brought with them the influences of carnival which inspired the establishment of Caribana in Toronto. Therefore, it is not surprising that early August celebrations quickly took root in these particular communities, beginning in 1834, and grew to include numerous activities and events. Emancipation Day observances were established and continued by generations of African-Canadian descendants and recent Black immigrants throughout various time periods in Canadian history.

Abundant primary sources such as newspaper articles, personal journals, and diaries, event literature, interviews, stories, anecdotes, correspondence, and photographs accumulated over the years provide detailed, vivid accounts of Emancipation Day observances throughout its 175 years of commemoration in Canada. *Emancipation Day: Celebrating Freedom in Canada* is the first extensively researched book on Emancipation Day commemorations in Canada. It provides descriptive historical accounts and comprehensive background into the establishment of this significant cultural event through an examination and analysis of the political, social, cultural, and educational characteristics of this international annual observance.

Locations of Emancipation Day Celebrations in Canada

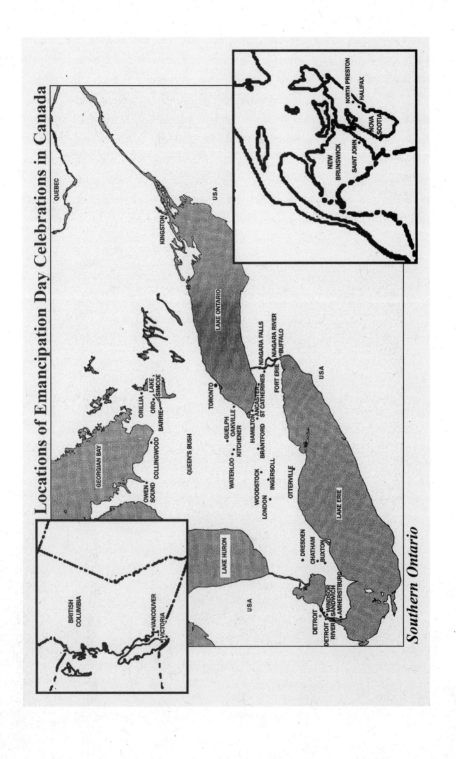

QUEBEC

KINGSTON

USA

LAKE ONTARIO

NIAGARA FALLS
NIAGARA RIVER
BUFFALO
ST CATHERINES
FORT ERIE

USA

ORILLIA
ORO · LAKE SIMCOE
BARRIE

TORONTO

GUELPH
OAKVILLE
WATERLOO
KITCHENER
HAMILTON
ANCASTER
BRANTFORD

GEORGIAN BAY

OWEN SOUND
COLLINGWOOD

QUEEN'S BUSH

WOODSTOCK
LONDON
INGERSOLL

OTTERVILLE

LAKE ERIE

DRESDEN
CHATHAM
BUXTON

LAKE HURON

USA

DETROIT
DETROIT RIVER
SANDWICH
WINDSOR
AMHERSTBURG

NORTH PRESTON
HALIFAX
NEW BRUNSWICK
NOVA SCOTIA
SAINT JOHN

BRITISH COLUMBIA

VANCOUVER
VICTORIA

Southern Ontario

Part I

Interpreting Emancipation Day Celebrations

1

Exploring the Meaning of Emancipation Day

Let me be a free man — free to travel, free to stop, free to work, free
to trade where I chose, free to choose my own teachers, free to follow
the religion of my fathers, free to think and talk act for myself.
— Highn'moot Tooyalaket (Chief Joseph) of the Nez Perces,
"An Indian's View of Indian Affairs," 1879.

With Emancipation Day celebrations in Canada attracting hundreds
and thousands of people annually, extensive preparations were required
to ensure a smooth-running event. Planning began months in advance.
Commemorative events were very large in scale and drew a huge number
of people from all facets of society. Attendees were of all ages and from
different social groups, many of whom travelled long distances to attend.

Guests of various Emancipation Day events came from across the
provinces, including Ontario, Nova Scotia, New Brunswick, Quebec,
and British Columbia. During the nineteenth century, participants from
surrounding locales travelled by horse and carriage, ferry, steamboat,
train, and later by car, alternating visits to different Emancipation Day
celebrations to show support. More visitors came from neighbouring
American cities such as Detroit, Michigan, Cincinnati, Ohio, and cities
in New York State such as Buffalo, Utica, and Rochester, and generally
from across North America, from as far as Louisville, Kentucky, and
Chicago, Illinois, as well as the states of Georgia and Alabama. All travelled

primarily by steamboat or train. Those from America used this time as an opportunity to visit with family who lived in the host town and other nearby areas while showing solidarity with their brothers and sisters in the north. Generally, the numbers of attendees were quite large, often greater than the total number of the Black population in the host town. While the majority of the attendees were Blacks, celebrations were also supported by a considerable number of Whites.

Local mainstream and Black newspapers provided elaborate coverage of Emancipation Day celebrations from their inception throughout the early twentieth century. The reporters would give in-depth descriptions of the social events, quote the speeches delivered by Black and White luminaries, and highlight how well the gatherers conducted themselves. Advertisements for Emancipation Day events were posted in regional newspapers and letters to editors and commentary from the general public relating to Emancipation Day were published. The African-Canadian press often used the occasion of Emancipation Day to discuss the challenges faced by its community and to bolster support and strength to tackle these issues.

Although Emancipation Day events were celebratory in nature with many social functions, several serious themes were consistently part of the event. First and foremost was the theme of liberation for enslaved Africans in British colonies in the West Indies and North America, including Canada, and the ongoing fight for freedom for those who remained in bondage in the United States and other parts of the Caribbean. Another issue was the change in the status that had been forced upon Blacks for hundreds of years. With the passing of the Slavery Abolition Act in 1833, people of African descent in British territories were no longer chattel property, but were now officially recognized as persons entitled to the same rights and privileges as White European citizens. A third theme was appreciation and gratitude for Canada's assistance to Black refugees and other Black colonists. Allegiance was pledged to Britain for the civil rights and privileges bestowed upon Blacks. Remembrance was also a strong theme — not forgetting the past experiences of those who were enslaved and carrying the torch to continue the struggle for equality. An equally important element of emancipation Day observances was the importance of charting a course for the future of Canada's Black citizens.

The invention of this African-Canadian tradition occurred at the same time that the creation of the Dominion of Canada was in the making. Black men and women were seeking to forge a new individual and collective identity and create a unique sense of heritage within early Canada's British-influenced society. This vision of a new identity and heritage meshed African, British, Caribbean, and American elements together with their new citizenship. Throughout the years, Emancipation Day celebrations were used to make statements about the African-Canadian collective identity to the Blacks themselves, to the province, and to the nation. In the mid-1800s, issues of equal rights and discrimination quickly surfaced for some of British North America's Black settlers, causing Emancipation Day traditions to become not only a form of cultural expression but a political demonstration as well.

The celebrations became important to the African-Canadian community for various reasons and served many functions, which changed over time. There was a mix of the traditional celebration components such as historical commemoration, education for all participants, community development, and entertainment. As noted, the most central themes of these events were freedom and change, which in and of themselves would come to mean different things at different times. The "first freedom" celebrated was the emancipation from chattel slavery. Freedom, and its pursuit, was at the core of understanding the historical viewpoint of people of African descent; they had been legally held as property for over 330 years in the Caribbean, over 240 years in the United States, and over 220 years in Canada. The attainment of freedom meant new possibilities. African Canadians believed they could pursue any opportunity they wanted, travel freely within Canada, reunite with their families on free soil, legally marry, vote, and obtain an education for their children. They celebrated the ideas of equality and justice that not only were they entitled to under British law for themselves in the present, but also the same ideals that meant universal rights for all people in the future.

However, African Canadians would soon see that emancipation was just the beginning of the fight for the full rights and privileges that came along with their new-found citizenship. Over the decades, freedom remained a recurring theme and would take many forms and hold different meanings. Each new generation would engage in a liberation struggle because they felt they were still held in bondage by the daily realities of racial discrimination — the lack of job opportunities, the reality of less pay for equal work, the denial of housing and public education, their being banned from public facilities, and other injustices because of their race. Therefore, full emancipation remained a constant pursuit in their ongoing efforts to remove these barriers to equality.

On one hand, Emancipation Day commemorations were a serious time, a moment to reflect on the experience of the enslaved African in the Western world and the triumphs over slavery, and to place the history of Africans in the larger context of Canadian historical narrative. On the other hand, it was also an opportunity to strengthen the growing African-Canadian communities through shaping the social, political, racial, and economical consciousness of African Canadians needed to advance the agenda of civil rights. However, over time entertainment increasingly became a main component partially because Blacks in some areas were barred from visiting certain public attractions. The designated time, a day or weekend, provided the opportunity for leisure-time interaction for a large group of African Canadians who were not often able to socialize freely in a recreational setting. The event also became a time to promote the meaningful cultural rituals, which became key components in all Emancipation Day celebrations.

Church Attendance and Religious Services

The day began with giving thanks to God for deliverance from bondage and to express gratitude for the rights they were always entitled to under the law of the Bible. Many African Canadians held strong Christian beliefs and interpreted their experience with Biblical connections. People of African descent related their plight from enslavement in the New World to the Jews who were brought out of slavery in Egypt, and felt that they were a chosen people selected by God to make the pilgrimage to Canada. Canada was labelled as Canaan, the land promised by God to his children, also known as the land of milk and honey. In another biblical comparison, Harriet Tubman, the famous Underground Railroad conductor, was referred to as Moses because she delivered God's people out of captivity.

Attendees of Emancipation Day church services also wanted to acknowledge that the persistent appeals to individuals' morality, pressing the fact that slavery was an evil against Christian teachings, were rewarded with the abolition of slavery. Thanksgiving services provided an opportunity to educate the masses through sermons. Church ministers also played the role of teachers as many members of their congregation could not read or write. Sermons focused mainly on freedom and taught about the atrocities of slavery. Messages also discussed how to approach the future and how to take advantage of their free life in the north. The hymnals sung in church were equally important as a musical expression of the feelings of African Canadians, joy for their freedom from bondage and an enduring perseverance towards the difficulties of this life.

Parades

Parades became a significant civic ritual during the Victorian era and members from all facets of society were involved. On August First people took time off work, places of employment closed, and notable members of the community, such as government officials and leaders of social, religious, and political organizations, became engaged participants and observers. Emblems were displayed. Some individuals marched through the streets while others observed. Essentially, Emancipation Day parades were ceremonial processions used to express African-Canadian traditions and cultural beliefs through public demonstration. This grand official ceremony demonstrated unity within the African-Canadian community as well as the appreciation of fugitives towards their adopted country. At times however, the street marches were also used to publicly protest acts of racial discrimination committed against African Canadians.

The participation of the female members of benevolent societies and male members of fraternal orders in Emancipation Day parades showed evidence of Black Canadians helping one another to strengthen their community. These social organizations provided food, clothing, shelter, and employment assistance to escapees who were steadily pouring into the provinces. Many anti-slavery groups, with Black and White members, played an active role in the organization of Emancipation Day events, also using the celebrations to continue the push for abolition in the United States. Processions represented freedom from an array of discriminatory social structures and racism in general, a rejuvenation of the mind, body, and soul, and a moment of social cohesion.

Emancipation Day Parade Symbols

The flags, banners, ribbons, and emblems always on display at Emancipation Day parades were designed to make a strong visual impact on observers. Flags included national flags, military flags, and the flags of fraternal orders. The Union Jack was shown to represent Britain, the former enslaver and now liberator of slaves, and to acknowledge allegiance to Britain. Red, blue, and white streamers used in street marches and other events also symbolized the Union Jack. The American flag was displayed in remembrance of life in bondage and of what was left behind, and to represent the new anti-slavery battleground.

Banners were central to parades as distinctive decorations publicizing the collective identity and historical presence of a particular group, the

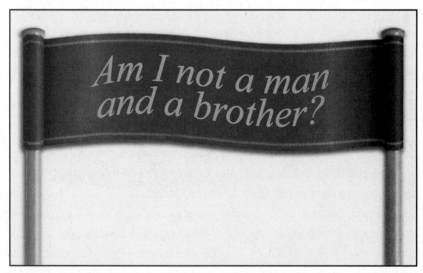

Designed by Kaimera Media Inc.

A depiction of the "Am I not a man?" banner displayed during the Emancipation Day parade in Windsor in 1852. The banner was carried to bring public awareness to the conditions of slaves. On the back was an image of a man breaking free from shackles and chains, symbolizing the thousands of emancipated British slaves.

Designed by Kaimera Media Inc.

A depiction of another banner — "God, Humanity, the Queen and a free country" — that was carried in the 1852 parade by members and supporters of the North American League.

Designed by Kaimera Media Inc.

The original banner, representing the "Sons of England," was carried by the Forest City Band during the Emancipation Day parade in London in 1896.

name of the organization, its location, and particular affiliations being prominently displayed. The presence of the diverse participating groups also publicized the existence of an identifiable African-Canadian community. Additionally, banners were used to reveal relevant themes of a particular year's celebration. In Windsor in 1852, a banner was displayed where on one side it showed a Black man, kneeling in chains looking up and asking, "Am I not a man and a brother?" On the other side of the banner stood a Black, tall and erect with broken shackles, symbolic of the condition of the slave and liberation. Another banner in Windsor, also on parade in 1852, read, "God, Humanity, the Queen and a free Country."[1] In London in 1896 a banner displays the words, "Sons of England."[2] The emblems of the Masonic lodges that were participating were displayed for similar reasons as the banners and flags.

Military Marching Bands

The use of military bands to lead the processions symbolized the long history of service that African Canadians have had in the British, and later Canadian, military. Blacks served in the British and Canadian military during the American Civil War, the War of 1812, the Rebellions of 1837, the First World War, and the Second World War, as well as in numerous other battles overseas. Initially, military service provided hundreds of Black men the chance for a new life with the promise of freedom, free passages to British colonies, income support, and land. While some were employed as soldiers, they also served in various positions such as labourers, boatmen, cooks, and doctors. They served in all-Black militias and in racially mixed regiments. Men of African descent answered the call to take up arms in defence of Britain because it was their ticket to freedom. Once slavery was abolished in British territories, African-Canadian men enlisted in large numbers because any American victory during the 1800s meant the horrors of a possibility of the return to enslavement. Thus, the presence and participation of Black army veterans in the parades made a statement of loyalty, patriotism, and sacrifice for freedom and peace. It also kept the actions of African-Canadian troops in the public memory and paid tribute to those Black heroes. Unfortunately, these men remained on the "battlefront" when they returned home from active duty, this time fighting prejudice and discrimination.

Annual Feasts

Various forms of communal meals during Emancipation Day festivities included luncheons, picnics, and formal dinners. While fulfilling the basic human need for food, these celebratory meals also served as focal point for social functions marked with symbolic meanings. Obviously, Emancipation Day feasts were a time for fellowship among African Canadians, with some people living considerable distances away from other Blacks or others coming from villages or towns that were scattered over a large territory. Shared meals provided the casual means of strengthening the African-Canadian community. They also signified the abundance and bounty similar to a harvest festival. Furthermore, there was a level of resistance symbolized by the act of eating at these banquets. Sharing meals was another way of freeing themselves from the legacy of slavery as former slaves could now buy and eat a range of foods they wanted instead of receiving small weekly rations and undesirable parts of meats from their slave masters. Feasts that were hosted on August First, like other important group meals, also contained Biblical symbols such as food binding people of faith together in God and the blessings of God being extended through the feeding of His people. These festive dinners were another means in the building of African-Canadian identity and values.

Toasts and Resolutions

The toasts given and resolutions passed served a number of meaningful purposes. Proposed to demonstrate patriotism towards Britain and the Queen (Victoria), they illustrated how African Canadians embraced their new citizenship and the rights and privileges that came along with it. The salutations also expressed messages to fellow White citizens that they, the African Canadians, were appreciative of the opportunities afforded to them such as free soil, security from slavery, as well as education, and communicated that Blacks in Canadian provinces were good, productive citizens. Homage was always paid to the ancestors who had gone before them through toasts that recognized their sacrifices. Proclamations and resolutions invoked the future and declared new beginnings. Resolutions would be passed to chart the course of political or social action for the year to come, reflecting the issues that were important to Black cultural organizations and to the community.

Speeches

Oral tradition, which has always been an integral element of African culture, was particularly maintained as part of Emancipation Day. Public addresses were extremely significant because they were used to educate attendees. Speeches were used to educate participants about the atrocities of slavery. The very early events featured storytelling by former slaves who shared their experiences of slavery and escape, and here the memories of older generations were also used to educate the general public. Black speakers stressed the importance of education for future generations of African-Canadian children, deemed as crucial to ensuring personal and community success.

Speeches also served to inspire and motivate members of the crowd to become involved in the fight against slavery, to instill racial pride through education about Black history and Black accomplishments, and to encourage self-determination. During the nineteenth century many of the individuals attending Emancipation Day celebrations could not read and were unable to get information from the newspapers, pamphlets, or other publications. Thus, speeches were very important tools of outreach, mobilization, and communication throughout the Black community. The presence of scholarly, articulate speakers of African descent, such as Henry Bibb, Frederick Douglass, and Josephus O'Banyoun further legitimized African Canadians' pursuit for equal rights and justice.

While all speakers praised Britain for dismantling the institution of slavery and gave adulation to Canada for being a safe haven, there was a notable divergence of views between Black speakers and White speakers on the status of African Canadians. White speakers noted that Blacks had good, equal opportunities in Canada and that it was up to them to take advantage of their freedom. On the other hand, Black speakers discussed that African Canadians had not yet achieved equality and that more needed to be done for Blacks, such as the eradication of discriminatory practices. This gap in perspective would widen, especially around the 1880s.

Remembrance

The preservation of a collective memory has always been an important value in the communities of people of African ancestry. Emancipation Day celebrations were utilized to memorialize the experiences of slaves in the United States, the Caribbean, and Canada, and to honour the African continent. West India Day,[3] or August First events, were also used to determine what should be publicly remembered or collectively forgotten. This was particularly crucial just after Emancipation when those who were once enslaved were in the process of acquiring a new identity and developing a new understanding of what it meant to be African.

Emancipation Day provided the opportunity for African Canadians to establish relationships with others in their new communities and new country. It served as a social gathering, a time to bring different classes, genders, and races together. It was a platform from which to memorialize the ancestors, to address the challenges the African-Canadian community faced, to pass on African heritage, and to set goals and expectations for the future. Many cultural and family traditions have been transmitted through this yearly community celebration. In effect, Emancipation Day celebrations became the premiere social event for African Canadians from all walks of life. In a few areas, Blacks commemorated this historic event at home with family, with simple meetings at local churches or community organizations, private parties, or even at a tavern with friends. On other occasions, however, the observances of Emancipation Day were grand public affairs. These well-organized, huge functions served as political platforms, classrooms, networking arenas, places for family reunions, and a dating scene where couples met or wed.

A couple from Detroit, Forest Nathaniel Shelton Jr. and Earlene Lucy McGhee, were married on the stage at Jackson Park in Windsor in 1954 as part of the August First celebrations. This was Windsor's first public wedding.

By the 1850s African Canadians had created a very consistent and well-defined practice of commemoration around the international public observances of British Emancipation which continued to evolve over the decades to address the objectives of the time. The organization of Emancipation Day celebrations also became more complex as its size and importance grew, involving the booking of speakers and the various public and private venues, organizing food availability and preparation, setting up overnight accommodations and transportation, and securing event permits.

However, before an appreciation and understanding of Emancipation Day can be developed, it is important to grasp the history and background leading up to these celebrations.

2

From Enslavement to Freedom

Let us make our own intensions crystal clear. We must and we will be free. We want freedom now. We do not want our freedom fed to us in teaspoons over another one hundred fifty years. Under God we were born free. Misguided men robbed us of our freedom. We want it back.

— Martin Luther King Jr., from a speech given at the Southern Christian Leadership Conference Crusade for Citizenship, February 12, 1958.

The trade in African peoples began in 1441 with the development of the Transatlantic Slave Trade, a complex international economic system operated by European merchants. Portugal was the first European country to establish the trafficking of Africans followed by Spain, Holland, and France. Britain entered the Transatlantic Slave Trade in 1562 and became the leading slave-trading power by the early 1700s. Ships from Europe brought horses, guns, cutlery, fabrics, copper, and alcohol to West Africa to exchange for captive Africans who were then transported across the Atlantic Ocean to the New World, on the horrific Middle Passage, along with African products such as ivory, gold, palm oil, spices, and animal skins. Africans were forced to work as household servants and on plantations and farms to produce massive quantities of sugar, cotton, rice, tobacco, coffee, and rum that were shipped back to Europe and sold. All of these goods

FIVE DOLLARS REWARD.
RAN away from the Subfcriber on Wednefday the 25th. of June laft, a NEGRO MAN fervant named JOHN, who ever will take up the faid negro man and return him to his Mafter fhall receive the above reward and all neceffary charges.   THOMAS BUTLER.
   N. B. All Perfons are forbid harbouring the faid Negro man at their peril.—NIAGARA, 3d July, 1793.

Advertisements were used by slave owners to deter the public from assisting runaway slaves.

traded in the Transatlantic Slave Trade moved across the Atlantic Ocean in the shape of a triangle and became the foundation of the flourishing economies of these European nations — all based on the successful trade in African bodies.

The participating European powers wanted to increase their wealth, power, and size through the expansion of new colonies in the Caribbean, South America, the United States, and Canada, and believed this could be accomplished by utilizing a large pool of cheap labour. Africans were kidnapped, sold, bought, and traded as chattel goods for the purpose of providing free labour as farm hands, domestics, and many other skilled and unskilled positions. By the time the Transatlantic Slave Trade was deemed illegal by Britain in 1807 and the United States in 1808, over twenty million Africans had been captured or purchased from Africa and almost ten million died in the Middle Passage. Although the transportation of Africans across the Atlantic Ocean was banned, the practice of slavery continued, but not without constant opposition from those who were held in bondage. Enslaved Africans resisted their slave status from the moment they were taken from Africa by revolting on slave ships, refusing to eat, and committing suicide rather than suffer along the Middle Passage. Some political leaders on the continent of Africa — kings, queens, and chiefs — also fought against the enslavement of their people by taking various measures to halt the trade of Africans.

In the Western world, slaves protested their conditions in their daily lives including breaking tools, working slowly, leaving for short periods of time, running away, obtaining an education, and practising African cultural

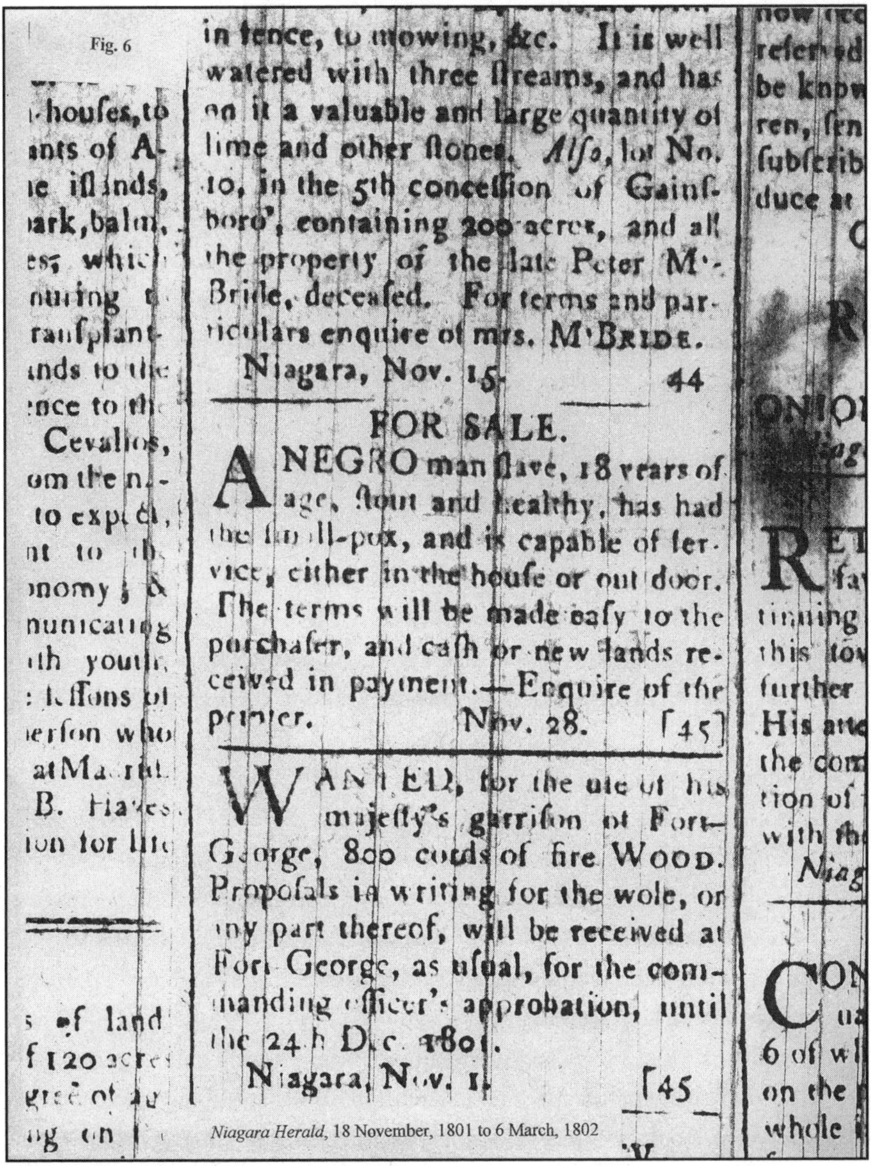

Fig. 6

in fence, to mowing, &c. It is well watered with three ſtreams, and has on it a valuable and large quantity of lime and other ſtones. *Alſo*, lot No. 10, in the 5th conceſſion of Gainſboro', containing 200 acres, and all the property of the late Peter M'Bride, deceaſed. For terms and particulars enquire of mrs. M'Bride.

Niagara, Nov. 15. 44

FOR SALE.

A NEGRO man ſlave, 18 years of age, ſtout and healthy, has had the ſmall-pox, and is capable of ſervice, either in the houſe or out door. The terms will be made eaſy to the purchaſer, and caſh or new lands received in payment.—Enquire of the printer. Nov. 28. [45]

WANTED, for the uſe of his majeſty's garriſon of Fort-George, 800 cords of fire Wood. Propoſals in writing for the wole, or any part thereof, will be received at Fort George, as uſual, for the commanding officer's approbation, until the 24th Dec. 1801.

Niagara, Nov. 1. [45

Niagara Herald, 18 November, 1801 to 6 March, 1802

From the *Niagara Herald*, November 28, 1802.

People of African descent continued to be enslaved after the passage of the 1793 Act to Limit Slavery.

traditions. A dramatic act of resistance was committed by Marie-Joseph Angélique, an enslaved Portuguese woman of African descent in Montreal, who allegedly set fire to her owner's house to protest her pending sale. In total, forty-seven buildings burned down. Immediately after, she was tried, found guilty, tortured, and hanged for her alleged crime of contestation.[1] Taking slave masters to court was another kind of resistance enslaved Blacks employed, which in Canada, with the support of anti-slavery judges, was a key mechanism in the attack and destruction of slavery. For example, in 1899 an enslaved woman in New Brunswick named Nancy Morton legally disputed her masters' ownership rights.[2] Enslaved Africans also engaged in large-scale resistance schemes. In fact, continuous slave-led armed rebellions were instrumental catalysts in the abolition of slavery in the British Empire, largely because slave owners were incurring too many expenses for slave-holding to remain lucrative.

In the Haitian Revolution, hundreds of slaves on the island of Saint Domingue, the portion that is now Haiti, were led by Toussaint L'Overture in an uprising against the French in a fierce, long battle, which lasted from 1791 to 1804. The captive resistors were victorious and Haiti was established, the first independent Black country outside of the African continent. After this long, gruelling fight, colonial powers began to recognize the economical, political, and military threats of such insurrections, a factor that was influential in outlawing the Transatlantic Slave Trade. Revolts also happened in the United States under such leaders as Gabriel Prosser in Virginia in 1800, Denmark Vesey in South Carolina in 1822, and Nat Turner in Virginia in 1831. Caribbean revolts included the four-month long Sam Sharpe Rebellion in Jamaica, also in 1831. Two British Guiana (now Guyana) revolts included the Berbice Slave Rebellion in 1762 and one in Demerara in 1795. Grenada and St. Vincent also had slave uprisings in 1795, and Brazil was the site of the Bahia Rebellion in 1835.

The abolition movement gained momentum and international attention through the persistent agitation of enslaved men and women throughout North America, South America, Europe, and the Caribbean, combined with the varied contributions of Black abolitionists, such as self-emancipated slaves Olaudah Equiano,[3] Harriet Tubman, and Frederick Douglass.[4] White anti-slavery activists such as Toronto newspaper editor George Brown, Belleville doctor and ornithologist Alexander Ross, the St. Catharines politician, architect, and engineer William Hamilton Merritt, the Ohio Quaker Levi Coffin, and British abolitionists William Wilberforce and Thomas Clarkson were also champions of the cause.

ALL perfons are forbidden harbouring, employing or concealing my Indian flave called SAL, as I am determined to profecute any offender to the extremity of the law, and perfons who may fuffer her to remain in or upon their premifes for the fpace of half an hour, without my written confent, will be taken as offending, and dealt with accordingly..

CHARLES FIELD.

Niagara, Auguft 1802.

Niagara Herald August 28, 1802.

Native people comprised a large percentage of the slaves owned in Canada.

Canada was not only involved in the Transatlantic Slave Trade and the enslavement of Africans, but would·eventually be the first British territory to adopt legislation leading to the eradication of slavery. To this day, it is still not common historical knowledge in Canada that Africans were enslaved in both the French and British colonies from as early as 1628.[5] Furthermore, very few Canadians are aware that at one time their nation's economy was firmly linked to African slavery through the building and sale of slave ships, the sale and purchase of slaves to and from the Caribbean, and the exchange of timber, cod, and other food items from the Maritimes for West-Indian slave-produced goods such as rum, tobacco, cotton, coffee, molasses, and sugar.

However, in 1793, the wheels for the abolition of slavery in British possessions starting turning in Upper Canada with the passage of the 1793 Act to Limit Slavery. Lieutenant-Governor John Grave Simcoe, an ardent abolitionist, introduced a bill to end the practice of slavery, but was met by resistance from his slave-holding cabinet members who instead opted for a compromise of a gradual end to this inhumane institution.[6] This first piece of abolition legislation titled, "an Act to prevent the further introduction of slaves, and to limit the term of contract for servitude within this province," outlined that the importation of slaves into Upper

Canada was banned immediately, but those who were enslaved at the time this law was passed would remain the property of their owners for life. Children born after 1793 would be slaves until the age of twenty-five and their children would be free at birth.[7] There were two opposing, simultaneous effects of the Limitation Act. First, enslaved Africans, whose slave status was reinforced by this law, began fleeing Canada for northern American territories such as Michigan, and secondly, Canada became a haven for American slaves who wanted to secure their own freedom. Consequently, a wave of fugitives immigrated to Canada, the new symbol of freedom, especially following the passage of the 1793 Fugitive Slave Law.[8]

Forty years later, abolitionists world-wide claimed victory when the Slavery Abolition Act of 1833 was made law, completely abolishing African slavery in all British colonies and granting freedom to almost one million enslaved Blacks in sixteen British colonies, most in the West Indies but also in South Africa and Britain. As of Friday, August 1, 1834, all enslaved children under six years old and any born after the effective date were free and no longer legally slaves. Celebrations and observances were held in all of the affected areas. For many though, this meant only partial liberation because all charges seven years old and over were to become apprentices of their former owners. Field labourers would have to serve a six-year term and all other former slaves would serve a four-year apprenticeship, after which they would obtain complete emancipation. Former slave masters were to be compensated for the loss of their free labourers from a £20 million fund, but none was allocated to Canadian slaveowners.[9]

Islands such as Bermuda, Trinidad, and Antigua did not implement apprenticeships and instead freed slaves from August 1, 1834. In fact, Trinidad became the first country to declare a national holiday to commemorate the ending of slavery. Although the Act did not mention Upper Canada, it immediately liberated approximately fifty Africans who remained enslaved, including young slaves like Hank and Sukey who were owned by a Mrs. Deborah O'Reilly of Halton County and still considered chattel property. In 1834, they requested and received their freedom.[10] These colonies were the sites of inaugural Emancipation Day celebrations as newly liberated Africans rejoiced, parading through streets, attending church services, and engaging in other festive cultural activities.

Within four years, slaves in the colonies of Barbados, Bermuda, Guyana, Jamaica, and South Africa received their full freedom because the limited apprenticeship system of the Emancipation Act they adopted was brought to an early end. On August 1, 1838, these islands officially ended apprenticeships, granting total emancipation to approximately four hundred thousand indentured servants. This, of course, was an occasion for joyous celebration, because now complete abolition had been achieved in all British colonies. On August 1, 1838 in Spanish Town, then the capital of Jamaica, a hearse containing chains and shackles often used to restrain slaves was driven through the streets and then symbolically buried followed by bonfires and feasts. It was also noted that the soon-to-be ex-slaves climbed the hills and waited for the sun to rise, the dawn of the first day of freedom.[11] Early Emancipation Day celebrations in the British Caribbean began to take place as part of Carnival and integrated numerous elements of other African-influenced cultural rituals such as *jonkunnu* in Jamaica and *canboulay* in Trinidad. These festivities involved the playing of musical instruments, singing and dancing, parading, theatrical acts/shows, and feasts. Over a century later, Caribana, a carnival festival in Toronto, would originate from these roots.

During the next twenty-seven years, Emancipation Day celebrations in the free northern American states, the West Indies, and Canada were used as a platform to petition for the end of American slavery. Participants hoped that the spirit and the momentum towards freedom would continue to spread to the southern United States to free almost ten million still in bondage. Finally, in 1865 the Emancipation Proclamation legislated the manumission of enslaved African Americans. The various slave laws and abolition legislation enacted between 1793 and 1865 heavily impacted the transcontinental and global freedom movements. Likewise, they influenced the tone and the goals of Emancipation Day celebrations in the 1800s. The hard-earned success of the abolition movement culminated in an upsurge of freedom festivals up and down the Atlantic shore and gave birth to a significant African-Canadian tradition. August 1, 1838, was a true Emancipation Day, one that would continue to be celebrated for years to come.

Part II

The Route to Celebrations in Ontario

3

Southwestern Ontario

Freedom is the most precious of our treasures, and it will not be allowed to vanish so long as men survive who offered their lives for it.

— Paul Robeson, valedictory speech, Rutgers University, New Brunswick, New Jersey, 1919.

Essex County

Amherstburg

Amherstburg, along the Detroit River, and Malden are two towns in Essex County that were the sites of large Black communities. Both locales are adjacent and were part of Malden Township until Amherstburg separated from the township in 1851. The earliest African settlers in the area were the slaves owned by French colonists and British Loyalists, such as Colonel Matthew Elliot who owned sixty slaves in 1784 when he arrived in Fort Malden (now part of Amherstburg) to settle on his land grant of eight hundred hectares. Other early Black pioneers included Loyalists like James Fry and James Robertson, who settled on land grants in the area.[1]

The early nineteenth century witnessed an exploding fugitive population in Amherstburg, the most accessible town in Essex County for the fleeing slaves. Situated along the Canadian side of the Detroit River, it was located at the narrowest point that refugee slaves could use to cross the river from the American side. Not surprisingly, at that time Amherstburg was one of the principal terminals on the Underground Railroad. In the 1820s, Black fugitives living in Amherstburg introduced tobacco farming while others ran small businesses such as grocery stores, barbershops, hotels, taverns, and livery stables, or worked various occupations like mechanics and carriage drivers. By 1859 the Amherstburg's Black community numbered about eight hundred while the neighbouring Malden Township's total population was nine hundred.

Blacks embraced their new British citizenship and took measures to secure and exercise their freedoms and rights. African-Canadian troops protected Upper Canada at Fort Malden against American attack during the War of 1812 and the Mackenzie Rebellions in 1837 and 1838. American expansion into Canada, for them, would almost certainly mean a return to slavery.

The development of religious, cultural, and social institutions was central to the survival and success of local Black citizens. A British Methodist Episcopal (BME) church was established in Malden in 1839. The First Baptist congregation, formed around 1840, constructed a church on George Street in 1845–49, and the Nazrey American Methodist Episcopal (AME) Church was established in 1848. These churches also functioned as schools, which was equally important to the community as the local common schools[2] had been segregated since the 1840s and the demand for education by children and adults was steadily increasing. With regards to Black and White children attending common schools, the prevailing sentiment in the Amherstburg area was that "Local trustees would cut their children's heads off and throw them across the roadside ditch before they would let them go to school with niggers!"[3] The school board built the King Street School for African-Canadian students in 1864. It remained segregated until 1912.

Amherstburg was an epicentre of anti-slavery activity carried out by both Blacks and Whites. The Black churches passed anti-slavery resolutions at annual conferences and even joined the Canadian Anti-Slavery Baptist Association, headquartered in Amherstburg. Captain Charles Stuart, a White abolitionist mentioned earlier, helped many of the almost two hundred escapees who arrived between 1817 and 1822 to settle on small plots of land while he lived in Amherstburg. He received a large land grant in the northeastern section of the town for this reason. Presbyterian minister Isaac Rice of the American Missionary Association (AMA) began working among the fugitives in Amherstburg in 1838, giving out clothes and food and running a mission-funded school. Levi Coffin, the Quaker often referred to as "president" of the Underground Railroad, visited Amherstburg in 1844.[4] He stayed with Rice while he toured the province to see how fugitives, some of whom he assisted, were adjusting to a free life.

In 1854, members of the Black community in Amherstburg created the True Band Society to combat discrimination. The group encouraged self-help and community building through economic development and education, and provided financial support for refugees. They promoted unity among Black churches, as well as political involvement and integration throughout the dispersed settlement. The parent group of the fourteen chapters in Canada West, which consisted of six hundred members, later moved to Malden. As well, a number of fraternal organizations were based in Amherstburg in the middle of the nineteenth century. This included societies such as the Prince Hall Masonic Order and the Lincoln Lodge No. 8 F. & A.M., one of the oldest Black Masonic lodges in Canada.[5] Although Blacks in Amherstburg experienced some degree of equality until the 1840s, the arrival of the Irish and other European immigrants resulted in some displacement of African Canadians and an increase in racial prejudice. These fraternal institutions and the Emancipation Day gatherings endeavoured to heighten awareness of these injustices and to eradicate them over time.

According to Dr. Daniel Pearson, a native of Amherstburg, the recognition of Emancipation Day in Amherstburg began in 1834.[6] Given the long history of Africans in the region, it is indeed likely that observances of the abolition of slavery occurred from the inception of Abolition in the British Empire. It was customary, each first of August, for Amherstburg's Black residents to march down to the docks to receive and welcome one thousand or more guests coming over the river from Detroit and from Windsor. People also came from nearby Colchester, Kingsville, and Sandwich, as well as from more distant areas of the province and the United States. With Sandwich, Windsor, and Malden a fairly short distance away, commemorations periodically alternated among these towns or were split between locations. For example, Malden was the selected location for

Courtesy of the North American Black Historical Museum.

Delos Rogest Davis faced discrimination on his path to becoming a lawyer. Like all law students, he was required to article with a practising lawyer for a period of time before taking the entrance exams for admission to the Ontario bar, but for eleven years no White lawyer would hire Davis. He appealed to the Ontario Legislature in 1884 to ask the Supreme Court of Judicature to grant him admission to the Ontario bar providing he pass the exams and pay the required fee. His appeal was granted, and on May 19, 1885, Delos Davis was admitted to the Law Society of Upper Canada.

the 1852 Emancipation Day celebrations in Essex County. In 1875, the day program was held at Walkers Grove near Windsor and in the evening a soiree was held at the Amherstburg Town Hall under the auspices of the local Black Order of Oddfellows. Then, in 1876, Emancipation Day activities occurred at Prince's Grove in Sandwich.[7]

About two thousand individuals assembled in Amherstburg in 1877 to celebrate the abolition of slavery. The procession was accompanied by the Amherstburg Cornet Band and led by the mounted marshals Daniel "Doc" Pearson and Mr. J.O. Johnson to the docks to greet American guests arriving by steamer. The marchers continued through the town to Caldwell's Grove[8] to enjoy an outdoor lunch and hear uplifting speeches. A dance was held in the evening at the Sons of Temperance Hall on Ramsay Street in the old building of the newspaper, the *Amherstburg Echo*, located across from present-day Duby's furniture store.

Caldwell's Grove was the site for the forty-fifth anniversary of the Emancipation Act. In 1879 Daniel Pearson of Amherstburg was appointed the chairman. Over three thousand gatherers paraded through the principal streets of the town and then went to the grove for a picnic lunch, games, dancing, and the anticipated speeches. The first speaker was lawyer Delos Rogest Davis,[9] the son of a former slave. He had grown up in Colchester about twenty kilometres south of Amherstburg. Davis stated that all present should be grateful to be able to assemble on free soil and supported his statement with a legal perspective, saying that any infringements of rights should be blamed on the perpetrator because the laws of Canada did not discriminate. He then went on to identify areas of existing racial discrimination that included denial of access to a good education, of the right to serve in the military, and the right to sit on juries. Davis encouraged African Canadians to demand equality and fair treatment. Other addresses were given by John Richards from Detroit; Mr. Lewis of Toledo, Ohio; and Michael Twomey, the mayor of Amherstburg. An evening program was held at the local BME church to raise money for the church, followed by a dance at the Sons of Temperance Hall.[10]

In 1889, several August First celebrations took place in Essex County, at Central Grove — close to Harrow, Sandwich, Windsor, Chatham, Detroit — and at Amherstburg. Once again, lawyer Delos Davis presided over the day's event in Amherstburg. The recurring theme of the addresses delivered that day was the importance of education. Reverend Josephus O'Banyoun[11] encouraged listeners to "educate their children," Reverend J.S. Masterson of Windsor argued that "education … was the only way to be able to march on,"[12] and Dr. James Brien, Member of Parliament, stated that "the earnest pursuit of education would enable them to take advantage of all opportunities for advancement both moral and material."[13] More messages came from Gore Atkin, a farmer and former warden of Essex County, who pointed out the benefits of knowledge in the abolition movement, because first "the English people were not then ready for it. The people had to be educated to a measure of this kind…."[14] Reverend Mr. Williams from North Carolina, a child of formerly enslaved parents, said that Blacks "in his State, they had forty institutions of learning, yearly sending out 240 thoroughly educated pupils." He further advised the crowd to "love morality education and religion and always look well to the future."[15] Reverend E. North of Colchester South pointed out "the power of education to remove prejudices against their race, as it elevated them in all relations of life and qualified them to fill any position in the land."[16] Lastly, the member of the provincial parliament, W.D. Balfour, remarked that African Canadians "were also being recognized in Government appointments in the country as well as at the seats of Government, and were educating themselves up to the requirements of these positions" and concluded the program "by urging them all to make great sacrifices, if necessary, to enable their children to take advantage of the many educational facilities now at their disposal."[17]

Coincidentally, Emancipation Day was used to promote education when two years later in Chatham speeches were aimed at mobilizing community members to fight against segregated schools, which were still prevalent in some areas of Ontario, including Amherstburg. All Blacks knew that a quality education would afford African Canadians the opportunity for a good life and in turn could be used to dispel racist stereotypes and dismantle the prejudiced school system. Education was a matter close to the hearts of Blacks, largely because of their long history of being denied the right to learn. In spite of the tremendous obstacles, people of African descent persevered throughout the centuries of enslavement in the New World to acquire knowledge, a goal that has remained a constant in African culture. Emancipation Day was an effective instrument in furthering this cause.

The 1894 recognition of August First is immortalized in the famous image presented on the cover of this book. The mounted marshal Moses Brantford Jr., a native of Amherstburg, led the parade. The procession started at the Waterworks lot (now part of the Navy Yard Park) and marched along Dalhousie Street to Caldwell's Grove. The nearly one thousand participants enjoyed an array of foods and the music of the Harrow Brass Band from Detroit who provided the music for the day. While the day was a festive occasion, it was also a sad time because Dr. Daniel Pearson had recently passed away. Thus, the commemoration was also used to honour the man who had played an integral role in the organization of local Emancipation Day celebrations and who had been a prominent community activist. The chairman, Delos Davis, noted "They would all miss the presence of the old man whose delight it was to take part in such proceedings and to begin with the singing the 'Year of the Jubilee.'"[18]

The first speaker, John H. Alexander,[19] also paid homage to Pearson, and spoke to the fact that the community elders such as Bishop Walter Hawkins and men of his stature were disappearing. This was of grave concern to Alexander and others because the past was becoming a distant memory for many, and the younger generation were forgetting the history of their ancestors. He further highlighted the progress that people of African descent had achieved in Amherstburg and in the province, such as serving jury duty, receiving appointments as returning officers and auditors, and becoming teachers and lawyers, all of which was accomplished as a result of education. Subsequent orators included a number of ministers,[20] including a Reverend George Bell of Detroit, and a Thomas Harris. Chairman Davis and Harris talked about the significance of Amherstburg to the history of Blacks in Ontario. Davis said he "was pleased to see the crowd gathered so near the place where so many of the colored race had first stepped upon free ground,"[21] while Harris stated that "Amherstburg was the spot where so many of their race had landed in making their escape from the United States, guided by the north star."[22]

Annual Emancipation Day commemorations also included sports competitions and musical performances. The Jubilee Singers, led by the Reverend O'Banyoun from the local Nazrey AME church, performed regularly. In the evening, the annual ball was held at the Amherstburg Town Hall. In the 1920s and 1930s, fraternal lodges — like the Lincoln

The North American Black History Museum consists of various buildings. It includes the museum and cultural centre, the Nazrey AME Church, and the Taylor Log Cabin, once the home of George Taylor, an escaped slave.

Masonic Lodge, the Damascus Commandery No. 4, and Steven's Lodge of Oddfellows — played important roles in sponsoring Emancipation Day events. Members of these groups also sat on the Emancipation Day committee. Several local and visiting orders such as the Blue Lodges and the Knights Templar led the street parades with their bands and drill squads. As noted, speeches were delivered by political and religious leaders like the member of parliament Eccles. J. Gott for Essex South and the Reverend A.D. Burton of the local AME church.

By the 1930s August First celebrations were more relaxed and less formal. No speeches were given and there was no structured program. The day became a more social affair of getting reacquainted with old friends and extended family members. "With the passing of the years much of old-time formality and ceremony has passed from these emancipation celebrations and they have become big, colourful, informal picnics, attended by both colored and white people in large numbers." "Emancipation Day in Amherstburg has come to be just a happy reunion, with lots to eat."[23] Family and friends barbecued, picnicked, participated in organized games like baseball, and gambled.[24]

Essentially, this more leisurely format of August First celebrations in Amherstburg carried through the next few decades. Citizens of the town who wished to celebrate on a grander scale attended the colossal events held in Windsor between 1931 and 1966. When the Windsor commemorations died down and the revitalization efforts by Edmund "Ted" Powell, Walter

Perry's successor as the organizer for Windsor's Emancipation Day, in the 1970s were unsuccessful, the North American Black History Museum (NABHM)[25] in Amherstburg carried on the tradition of marking August First with a community observance, beginning in 1983.

Emancipation Day celebrations in Essex County moved to Amherstburg's Centennial Park for a four-day festival. Henry White of the NABHM took over the planning of the event with the blessings of Ted Powell. White planned to reintroduce Emancipation Day to Amherstburg with the recreation of the photographed 1894 parade, a move deemed fitting because of Amherstburg's long African-Canadian history. The featured guest speaker for the occasion was Ovid Jackson, the Black mayor of Owen Sound. Since that time, the NABHM has organized annual events on a regular basis and has incorporated a variety of activities to appeal to a wide audience. The holiday weekend includes museum tours, presentations, and special displays, along with the usual family activities at a local park. In 1992, a yearly golf tournament was introduced.[26] The celebrations have continued annually into the twenty-first century.

Sandwich

The first African pioneers in Sandwich (initially known as l'Assomption) were the slaves owned by French and English colonists. Antoine Descomptes Labadie, a French fur trader, held several slaves; a member of the Legislative Council of Upper Canada James "Jacques" Baby considered about thirty slaves as his personal property; and William Dummer Powell, chief justice of Upper Canada, possessed a number of slaves as well.[27] Other Black settlers included Loyalists who were members of Butler's Rangers. They obtained land grants in and around Sandwich, a community about twenty-four kilometres north of Amherstburg. The first major wave of fugitive American slaves to arrive in Upper Canada between 1817 and 1822 chose to settle in Essex County, including the village of Sandwich, now a suburb of the city of Windsor.

By the early 1850s there was a steady influx of escaped slaves coming into the area, many via the Underground Railroad. The village became the site of fugitive settlement and a mission called the Refugee Home Society established in 1851. Under the leadership of Henry and Mary Bibb, the settlement scheme sold land to incoming fugitives and provided support and schooling. The homes of most of the Blacks were found throughout the village, dispersed among the White residents. For the most part they were accepted by their neighbours, except when it came to education. The Sandwich common schools refused to admit African-Canadian children, so the Black community took it upon themselves to secure the future of their children by organizing private schools, such as the small private school Mary Bibb set up in her home to help educate the children of fugitives.

The annual recognition of the freeing of African slaves in British colonies was not always a large group demonstration. Abraham Rex and William Murdoch, both Black men in Sandwich, decided to celebrate the 1st of August at LeDuc's Tavern in 1843, a place regularly visited by White soldiers from the Stone Barracks, a military base.[28] What is interesting about this example is the association of African Canadians with other users of this public space. Some early tavern keepers in Ontario owned Black slaves, primarily women, who worked to keep up the business. In other instances, free Black women were hired as servants to work in bars. In some cases Blacks were denied service or were subject to restricted seating, and so at times the tavern also became as site of resistance when individuals of African descent challenged these unjust practices. Another intriguing aspect is that some well-known taverns in places such as Toronto, St. Catharines, and Chatham were owned by Black men.[29]

Earlier communal Emancipation Day celebrations in Sandwich took place at Park Farm between 1838 and 1856, located on what is now the city-owned Prince Road Park. This property was the estate of Colonel John Prince who had received support from the local Black inhabitants in his successful bid for a seat in the Legislative Council. Apparently they believed he ordered the execution of four American rebel supporters of William Lyon Mackenzie because they killed a man of African descent during the course of an attack in the Rebellion of 1837. Annual festivities ceased being held on his estate after Prince voiced racist beliefs over the steady stream of escapees from American slavery, which estranged his Black voters and contributed to his political defeat.[30]

By this time Sandwich had become a centre of fugitive-led abolition activity. Henry Bibb founded the *Voice of the Fugitive*, Canada's first anti-slavery newspaper, in Sandwich in 1851. Bibb, like hundreds of other self-emancipated slaves, relocated to this area because of the 1850 Fugitive

Slave Act. Along with several community-building initiatives, he and his wife Mary were instrumental in organizing Emancipation Day observances in Sandwich. The celebration in 1851, held at the Stone Barracks, was attended by hundreds "parading up" from Amherstburg, "many of whom were dressed in the red jacket uniform, who marched into Sandwich after a band of military music looking as bold and courageous as John Bull himself."[31] Visitors from Detroit sailed across the Detroit River in the steamboat *Alliance*. Participants in the long parade included the Fugitives Union Society, whose anniversary and annual meeting was held that afternoon. The county's high sheriff opened the assembly, followed by regional speakers including J.J. Fisher of Toronto, George Cary of Dawn, Samuel Ringgold Ward,[32] and other American lecturers. The committee passed two motions, the first being to publish the days' proceedings in the *Voice of the Fugitive* and the second to hold the next year's event in Malden, but it was held in Windsor instead.[33]

Proceeds of the sales of admission tickets as well as the purchases of lunch, dinner, and refreshments went towards the construction of a brick building for the Baptist church on Crown-designated land located on West Peter Street. The building project for the Sandwich First Baptist Church, initially organized in 1840, was completed in 1851. Mary Bibb was one of the fundraising managers: "Dinner will be furnished by the Ladies for twenty-five cents per ticket. — Refreshments may be had during the day and supper in the evening. The proceeds will be appropriated towards erecting a Baptist church."[34]

Sandwich Baptist Church was one of the community institutions that were created by fugitives. The church not only provided spiritual assurance, but physical security as well. Sandwich Baptist was a terminal on the Underground Railroad. There was a secret room beneath the church where escapees were hidden whenever the arrival of bounty hunters was announced by the ringing of a bell. Church parishioners kept lookout during services, as that was when bounty hunters liked to make surprise invasions. If alerted, fugitives escaped through a trap door in the floor of the church. Additionally, a tunnel running from the end of an underground passage connected the secret room to the nearby banks of the Detroit River.[35]

The August First commemorations also exposed the vast network of anti-slavery activists located across the continent. On his 1854 visit to Canada West, Levi Coffin, "president" of the Underground Railroad, attended Emancipation Day celebrations in the Maidstone area, which he described as, "a dense settlement of fugitives about eight miles south of Windsor."[36] He was part of a large group from Windsor, who, along with other guests, gathered at the schoolhouse run by Laura Haviland, a White Canadian-born Quaker, at the request of Henry Bibb and his Refugee Home Society in Sandwich. Invited speakers from Detroit delivered public addresses on a stage set up in a grove near the school. Coffin met and received many thanks from several freedom seekers he had assisted in their flight to Canada.[37] In 1855, an estimated seven thousand people turned out at Prince's Grove, the majority of them fugitives from American slavery, including thirteen who had been assisted to freedom by John Brown, a White revolutionary abolitionist from Kansas, and his son. Colonel Prince delivered remarks along with Eli Ford from Chicago. The evening galas were held in Windsor.[38]

However, by the 1890s, the direction and nature of Emancipation Day observances in Sandwich changed from a celebration of freedom, the maintenance of historic memories, and support of education to merriment and frivolity, so much so that leaders in the Black community, primarily church ministers, were calling for the event to be cancelled. What resulted were two different kinds of celebrations in the Windsor area, as described by the Windsor *Evening Record* in 1895. When celebrants from near and far arrived in Windsor, they split into two distinct groups: the first went to Walker's Grove in Windsor and the second headed for Mineral Springs[39] in Sandwich. The commemoration in Windsor was more serious in tone, focusing on spiritual and community prosperity through a steady schedule of lectures by notable local leaders such as Mayor Clarence Mason and Black alderman Robert Dunn. In contrast, the company in Sandwich did away with some of the traditional aspects of Emancipation Day in favour of having a good time by replacing them with lots of music, sporting activities, and barbecues.[40]

Colin McFarquhar, an assistant professor in the Department of History at the University of Waterloo, suggests that the separation occurred because slavery was in the remote past for too many of the attendees and few survivors were alive to tell the stories. Another reason he identifies is the decrease in speeches that recognized late freedom fighters and staunch abolitionists, resulting in the weakening of the collective memory that had been important in passing on shared historical experiences and cultural values.[41]

In the years immediately following, celebrations in Sandwich saw the introduction and growth of gambling, drinking, rowdy behaviour, and dance halls at Lagoon Park and surrounding venues. All of which became major problems, drawing complaints from both Black and White community leaders. In 1905, the mayor officially banned gambling and extra officers were hired to patrol the park grounds, instructing the police to arrest anyone who attempted to set up a game.[42]

Seven years later an association of Black church ministers appealed to the Sandwich town council to cancel the festivities, but they refused, perhaps because the stream of ten thousand people every summer brought an economic boom to the town. It is also interesting to note the change in tone of the media coverage of events. Previously, sermons and speeches were highlighted first at great length and the conduct of the crowd was always described as orderly. At the turn of the twentieth century the crap games, the arrests, and food were the main topics, with public addresses receiving little if any press, and the decorum that was highlighted favourably for the first sixty years of the celebration diminished greatly. Newspaper editors of the *Windsor Evening Record* joined in the chorus of unhappy Black voices calling for an end to the current trend of observances.

In 1913, the mayor of Sandwich, Edward Donnelly, announced that he would do his best to see that years' celebration be the last because the event organizers refused to pay for the extra police officers that secured the event. His decision seems also to have been influenced by the pressure from the African-Canadian church ministers, coupled with the deterioration of the event.[43]

Interestingly, Mitchell Kachun, author of *Festivals of Freedom*, describes similar protests by African-American leaders about the change in objectives of the August First celebrations in the United States during the early 1900s. These leaders across North America wanted a separation of popular entertainment and commemorative events as the former threatened the spirit of Emancipation Day, and, by extension, the political movements in their respective communities. He argues that the shift was illustrative of a continental trend of increasing "commercialization of leisure," urbanization, and the development of popular culture that was impacting all forms of early culture across Canada and the United States and not just freedom festivals.[44] By 1915, Emancipation Day observances in Sandwich had ceased. Consequently, it appears as though the original meaning of August First as a commemoration of freedom, rights, and opportunities could not be reconciled with the emergence of mass entertainment.

Windsor

By the 1830s and 1840s sizeable Black communities had developed in places such as Windsor, Sandwich, Amherstburg, and the surrounding vicinity. Hundreds of fugitives entered Canada by crossing the Detroit River, taking advantage of the more straightforward access point. Many came to Windsor because the town was a major terminus on the Underground Railroad, and along with Sandwich offered an initial safe haven for fugitive slaves. Dr. Daniel Hill identifies the first influx of refugees as arriving between 1817 and 1822.[45]

By the mid-nineteenth century, Windsor was emerging as a booming commercial and industrial centre. There were over fifty Black families living there by 1851 and seven to eight hundred individuals by 1868. Many of the Black men worked for the Great Western Railway in the construction of the rail lines and later as porters for the trains. Others were employed as labourers, barbers, coopers, draymen, preachers, and sailors. One man was working as an engineer, and another man, named Labalinin Harris, was a postman. Members of the town's African-Canadian community owned an array of businesses including plastering, masonry, and carpentry companies, blacksmith shops, tailor shops, grocery and general merchandise stores, shoemaking shops, a confectionery shop, a paint and varnish store, and several farms. Black women were mainly employed as washerwomen and domestics, while a few were teachers.

Most Blacks in Windsor resided on McDougall, Assumption, Pitt, Pellisier, Church, and Goyeau Streets as well as on Bruce Avenue. With the Black population growing daily, several cultural institutions were established to aid in settlement, provide a sense of solidarity, challenge American slavery, and to help their members weather the increasing racism that punctuated their daily lives.

Although not welcomed in many White churches, Blacks in Windsor actually preferred to worship amongst themselves and several Black churches took root in Windsor. The British Methodist Episcopal Church was constructed on McDougall and Assumption Streets in 1863. The First Baptist Church used two buildings on McDougall Street near Albert in 1856 and 1862, and then in 1915 they relocated to a new location at Mercer and Tuscarora Streets. A Baptist Church formed the Amherst Regular Missionary and the African Methodist Episcopal Church, although in existence for decades, through worship in homes, erected a building at Mercer and Assumption in 1889.

To meet the educational needs of the community, mission schools or private schools were established to serve the children and the adults of the Black community, the African-Canadian children in Windsor having been barred from attending common schools. Before earning the distinction of becoming the first female editor of a newspaper in North America, Mary Ann Shadd was hired as a teacher in a private school for Black children in Windsor. Classes were held in the old military barracks in 1851 until a schoolhouse was built in 1852. A handful of White children also attended this school. When Shadd left in 1853, there were no separate common schools for the growing Black population until 1858 when the Board rented an old, run-down building to serve its purpose. In 1862, the St. George School was built for African-Canadian children at McDougall and Assumption Streets. By 1864, the school was accommodating 150 students.

Blacks in Windsor organized other self-help societies to further strengthen the community like the Temperance Society formed by Robert Ward and Henry Bibb, the Mutual Improvement Society established by Mary Bibb "to hear speeches and improve their minds," and the African Enterprise Society led by William Jones.

Anti-slavery initiatives flourished in Windsor with its high concentration of fugitive supporters. Henry Bibb was appointed as the local vice-president of the Windsor branch for the Anti-Slavery Society of Canada. Bibb's newspaper, the *Voice of the Fugitive*, which began in Sandwich in 1851 and moved operations to Windsor shortly after, played an integral role in the Black community by providing information to local Blacks and attacking the enslavement of Africans in the southern United States. Bibb himself was a fugitive slave from Kentucky and was very active in the abolition movement through his paper and assistance in the settlement of recent escapees. He also managed the Refugee Home Society in Sandwich. White sympathizers active in the movement included John Hurst, who worked with fugitives in

Amherstburg before being assigned to Windsor in 1863. As minister of the All Saints Anglican Church, he attempted to integrate his congregation.

Blacks in Windsor also organized themselves to protest and challenge the many forms of racism they faced on a daily basis. In 1855 they were denied the right to purchase town land lots. Blacks like Clayborn Harris and a Mr. Dunn launched legal challenges against the school board in 1859 and 1884 respectively. Mr. Harris complained that the property rented for the Black school was inadequate, but he lost his case. Mr. Dunn took the school board to court for denying admissions to his child. The superintendents' defence was that it was unsanitary to admit Black children and the courts ruled in favour of the school board. People of African heritage who visited Windsor were refused hotel accommodations. They were not allowed to join Boy Scout troops or the local YMCA. On occasion there were incidents of physical attacks by Whites.

Blacks in Windsor also sought to secure their rights and freedoms through military service. About two hundred Black men defended the Detroit frontier against attacks from Americans during the Rebellion of 1837–38. Josiah Henson, one of the founders of the Dawn Settlement, commanded Black volunteer companies, part of the Essex Militia that commandeered a rebel ship attacking Sandwich. During the First World War, dozens of Windsor's Black men enlisted in the all-Black No. 2 Construction Battalion in 1916, whose duties included logging, milling, and shipping.

Emancipation Day festivities, which have been held in Windsor since the 1830s, were a culmination of these social dynamics. Because the villages of Windsor and Sandwich were only three kilometres apart (Sandwich amalgamated with the City of Windsor in 1935) and Amherstburg about thirty kilometres away, at times the locale for these commemorations alternated among the three locations. These Ontario towns always received support from the African Americans living in nearby American states, which meant many additional participants. In 1852, large numbers of celebrants from Detroit (their city's Emancipation Day event had been cancelled), attended the festivities in Windsor.

Because of proximity, Canada shared a close relationship to Detroit and in fact that city was a part of Upper Canada until 1796 when the British surrendered, transferring British administration to the Canadian side thirteen years after the end of the American Revolutionary War. For some time African Canadians had fostered strong social and economic ties to African Americans in Michigan cities like Detroit and Ypsilanti. People from both sides would attend each other's social events and African Canadians often found employment across the border.

On this day in 1852, as every year, American residents took the ferry across the Detroit River. The street parade began at the military barracks, the present-day site of City Hall Square and Caesar's Windsor. At the time, the barracks also served as temporary shelter for incoming fugitive slaves. Marchers went to meet the Detroit visitors including the Sons of Union, a Black lodge who arrived by ferry and joined the procession. The grand marshal and assistant marshal escorted them on horseback, and participants carried banners with the phrases, "God, Humanity, the Queen, and a Free Country" and "Am I not a man and a brother?" A Black militia from Amherstburg arrived and were "given the right of the line of march."[46] Another group participating in the parade was the Canadian Friends of the North American League who were identified by the badges they wore.[47] The procession continued on to the Pear Tree Grove for a Thanksgiving church service where an anti-slavery song was sung, and Reverend W. Munroe from Detroit delivered an the sermon.

Participants then adjourned to the bank of Detroit River to hear the speeches of the day. Henry Bibb, as Emancipation Day president, extended a warm welcome to all visitors from near and far. Addresses given were directed to the hundreds of African-American freedom seekers in the audience and offered valuable advice on how to benefit from their new, free life. Reverend Munroe recommended that "colored people must work out their own elevation, not trusting the imaginary philanthropy of political rulers."[48] Reverend Samuel May from Syracuse, New York also presented "some noble suggestions to the colored refugee in Canada in relation to how they should get to elevate themselves in the scale of being."[49] The third speaker was Reverend Mr. Culver from Boston, Massachusetts (a White minister), who "urged upon them the necessity of becoming tillers of the soul."[50] Esquire Woodbridge from Sandwich "urged them to go on in well doing, and they would be respected."[51] This comment referred to the way in which the newcomers were understanding and following the laws of the land more, for which they should be commended. He encouraged the crowd to continue to be law-abiding citizens and not to expect special treatment, but equal treatment in all areas including in the enforcement of laws.

After a savoury lunch the assembly resumed and a young girl read a composition she had written and dedicated to Queen Victoria in honour of the occasion. The report in the *Voice of the Fugitive* makes special mention of the speech by the seven-year old that made the audience proud. The inclusion of this story in the newspaper highlights the involvement of children in early Emancipation Day programs and demonstrates the importance of African-Canadian children receiving an education, a recurring theme at these festivals of freedom.

At the end of the program, Reverend John Lyle from Sandwich closed with the pronouncement of ten toasts to parties in Essex County, the United States, and Britain who were involved in some form in the fight against slavery.[52] Indeed, within a short period of time Blacks in Windsor, like their counterparts in other Canadian centres, proved themselves to be industrious and progressive. They succeeded in acquiring ownership of land, exercising voting rights, obtaining an education, and being elected to public office.[53]

Observances in recognition of the sixty-first anniversary of Emancipation Day were held simultaneously in both Windsor and Sandwich, the result of a growing divergence among attendees over the meaning of this special occasion. Events in Windsor continued to focus more on intellectual stimulation and community development while festivities in Sandwich centred more on partying and having a good time. When out-of-town celebrants arrived on August 1, 1895, in Windsor, they divided into two separate groups with one set going to Walker's Grove in Windsor to listen to stimulating speeches by Mayor Clarence Mason and Black alderman Robert Dunn. The other group went to Mineral Springs (later Lagoon Park) in Sandwich.[54]

The ushering in of a new century also symbolized a change in the significance of Emancipation Day and the way in which this notable day was observed not only in Essex County, but in North America as well. Despite the changes, the new kind of celebration seemed to have appealed to many segments of the Black community and Whites, too, as it continued to draw large crowds. Huge celebrations in the first part of the 1900s were hosted at Lagoon Park in the Township of Sandwich, and were attended consistently by several thousand people from Windsor, all points in Ontario, and American states including New York, Ohio, Kentucky, and Indiana. In 1905, five thousand of the attendees were from the United States and in 1909 an estimated ten thousand people converged onto Lagoon Park, including legendary boxer Jack Johnson.[55] It seems to have become a regular practice that there would be two separate celebrations in Essex County, the one at Lagoon Park becoming the most popular: "Lagoon Park drew the larger crowd of the rival celebrations."[56] Many gatherers enjoyed the afternoon activities in Sandwich that consisted of speeches, sports, games, midway rides, and sideshows, then partied in Windsor in the evening. The annual balls included a cakewalk and displays of the latest dance moves including the grizzly bear, the turkey trot, the bunny hug, tangos, two steps, and waltzes.[57]

The Depression era and the war years experienced another marked shift in the event in Windsor, which by far held the grandest and most elaborate Emancipation Day celebrations in Canada for over three decades through the 1930s to 1966. At its zenith in the 1940s to 1950s, the Windsor festival attracted more than two hundred thousand people annually. The August First celebration in Windsor was once the largest outdoor cultural festival in North America, drawing a racially-mixed crowd and receiving ongoing support from like-minded people in the United States.

The ninety-seventh Emancipation Day anniversary celebration was held in 1931 with guests from Ontario and the United States under the auspices of the British-America Association of Colored Brothers (BAACB).[55] Approximately twenty thousand visitors were in attendance. This celebration was particularly historic as it also marked the centenary of the Underground Railroad into Canada. Letters of acknowledgement were received from Prime Minister Robert Borden Bennett, Premier Mitch Hepburn, Toronto's Mayor James Simpson, and Robert Moton of Tuskegee College in Alabama.[59] Honoured guests included Ray Lewis, the track athlete from Hamilton. The growth and popularity of Windsor's Emancipation Day celebrations during this time period can be attributed to Walter Perry,[60] the festival's organizer since 1931 when he launched "The Greatest Freedom Show on Earth." For over thirty years, "Mr. Emancipation," as Walter was kindly known, worked diligently to restore the importance of a sense of community and history to the annual event. He worked tirelessly to revamp the commemoration because he wanted to create a better image. Under Perry's leadership, the festivities expanded to four days, keeping most of the traditional elements while incorporating some newer forms of entertainment.

Courtesy of the North American Black Historical Museum, P84-16-09.

Event organizer, Walter "Mr. Emancipation" Perry, is the man in the white shirt who is shown walking along with the parade at the left of centre in the photograph.

Windsor's yearly parade started from Riverside Drive at the edge of the Detroit River and marched north along Ouellette Avenue. The two-mile long procession, which ended at the Jackson Park grounds at Tecumseh Road West, required three hours to reach its destination. Crowds of Black and White people lined the parade route. Parade participants from Ontario and Michigan towns and cities included drill teams, marching bands, dignitaries, floats of Miss Sepia contestants, community businesses, and fraternal organizations. There was always a mix of entertainment at the park grounds such as fair rides, talent and beauty contests, sporting events, musical performances, speeches, and skill demonstrations that drew elite as well as up-and-coming athletes, singers, and community leaders. World-famous boxer Joe Louis fought in a friendly match. Jesse Owens, a 1936 Olympic gold medallist, demonstrated his track and field abilities. A young Diana Ross competed in a talent contest. Musical acts like the Temptations, the Supremes, Stevie Wonder, Sammy Davis Jr., and numerous gospel choirs performed over the years. Even actress Dorothy Dandridge attended on

Courtesy of the North American Black Historical Museum, FO-3.

Multiple spectators line the street to witness the Emancipation Day parade in Windsor. Parading past is the Union Company No.1, a Black Masonic Lodge from Detroit, Michigan.

one occasion. Homegrown artists and groups also performed, such as the popular North Buxton Maple Leaf Band, formed by Ira Shadd in 1955, who participated in Emancipation Day parades in Windsor beginning in 1960.

Perry returned to the tradition of education and honouring the rich past of Africans in North America and the motherland through the mindful selection of speakers and the publication *Progress*. The magazine included articles about the history of Africans such as the Transatlantic Slave Trade, slavery, resistance, runaways to Canada, abolition, the achievements of Blacks in Windsor and North America, and the fight for equality and justice. It also contained advertisements for local businesses, both Black and White, and the program for Emancipation Day detailing the events and speakers at Jackson Park.

The goals and aims of the civil rights movement were intricately woven into Emancipation Day programming, to heighten awareness and challenge the policies and practices that denied African Canadians their full rights. One such infringement was the denial of the right of Black men to serve in the Canadian military during the Second World War. Other human rights infractions included the ongoing refusal of service in restaurants and bars, barriers to hotel accommodations and housing, and discrimination in employment and education. The BAACB also worked with other community groups in Essex County to address racism. They collectively received reinforcement from various levels in the region. Alvin McCurdy, president of the Amherstburg Community Club and active trade unionist, wrote to the federal government in 1943 expressing that African Canadians "want every single right and privilege to which our citizenship entitles us, no more, no less,"[61] and, in 1947, Walter Perry appealed for "greater understanding of created racial problems."[62] Obviously, this formula was proving successful as the number of participants climbed steadily. In 1947, approximately fifteen thousand assembled at Jackson Park, while the 1948 event saw an astounding 275 thousand attend, and in 1949 about 120 thousand gathered.[63]

As part of the annual program, the BAACB presented awards to various citizens, politicians, and organizations; people such as Walter P. Reuther, the international president of the United Auto Workers–Congress of International Unions (UAW–CIO), and those individuals who had contributed to the betterment of the African race in some way. His brother, in an acceptance speech on Reuther's behalf in 1950, declared, "While Jim Crow may have been kicked off the assembly line, he still lives smugly in many homes and many other places where humans gather."[64] One way the UAW–CIO had contributed to the civil rights movement in Windsor had taken place seven years prior when the union took a position against racial discrimination waged against a Black military officer who was refused service at a local restaurant. The union wrote a letter of support and distributed pamphlets to its members denouncing the racist action.

The 1950s witnessed the height of the American Civil Rights movement aimed at putting an end to Jim Crow laws legalizing the practice of discrimination against descendants of African slaves. But the battle for democracy and equal rights among Blacks and Whites was brewing in Canada as well. The BAACB invited civil rights activists from the United States throughout the mid-1940s to the 1960s, to motivate African

Courtesy of the North American Black Historical Museum, FR-24.

You Are Invited to
the
Rev.-Congressman
Adam Clayton Powell, Jr.
NEW YORK CITY

JACKSON PARK
WINDSOR, ONTARIO

SUNDAY, JULY 29th, 1945

MONDAY, JULY 30th

Featuring
**INTERNATIONAL
SEPIA BEAUTY CONTEST**

Rev.-Congressman
ADAM CLAYTON POWELL, Jr.

Reverend Adam Clayton Powell Jr. was the first African-American to be elected as a city councillor in New York City, in 1941. He was a special guest at Windsor's Emancipation Day celebrations in 1945. A prominent civil-rights activist, he advocated for fair employment and housing for Blacks.

Canadians to act against racism and to show how much they had achieved since the end of slavery. Numerous Black civil rights activists addressed Emancipation Day audiences in Windsor. American congressman and church minister Adam Clayton Powell was a guest speaker in 1945. Mary McLeod Bethune, an African-American female civil right activist,[65] and Eleanor Roosevelt, President Franklin Roosevelt's wife, spoke at Windsor's Emancipation Day festivals in 1954. Twenty-seven-year-old Dr. Martin Luther King Jr. attended in 1956 just after garnering international attention for leading the Montgomery Bus Boycott triggered by the arrest of Rosa Parks. The next decade saw speakers like Daisy Bates,[66] an American civil rights activist; Reverend Fred Shuttlesworth,[67] Baptist minister and civil rights activist in Birmingham, Alabama; and Mrs. Medgar "Myrlie" Evers,[68] wife of civil rights activist Medgar Evers, deliver addresses to the throngs of people at Jackson Park. Emancipation Day had returned to its roots of being an effective political vehicle for the African-Canadian community.[69]

The Miss Sepia International Pageant was a unique feature added to the celebrations in Windsor. This beauty and talent competition,

The 108th Emancipation Day program included
the Miss Sepia Beauty Pageant, which was open to
contestants from both Canada and the United States.

introduced in 1931, provided a platform for young African-Canadian women
who otherwise would not receive such an opportunity. In the early twentieth
century women of African descent were banned from entering mainstream
pageants and women of colour were hardly ever featured in magazine or
television advertisements. Contestants were judged on the basis of evening
gowns, swimwear, and talent competitions. In addition to the honour of
being crowned Miss Sepia, winners also received prizes in the form of cash,
a trophy, and flowers. Local and American contestants took great pride in
representing their cities and their race. Young girls also competed in the Little
Miss Sepia Pageant.[70] Other attractions at Windsor's celebrations included the
anticipated barbecue chicken, one of the most popular foods, and a variety of
captivating forms of entertainment, such as an aviation stunt show.[71]

Preparation for this important annual social event on African-Canadian
calendars required an extensive amount of work. Celebrations had to be
planned months in advance to host hundreds and thousands of observers.
Overnight accommodations needed to be available for the throngs of
people staying in Windsor, and local restaurants had to be prepared to serve
many visitors. According to one person's recollections of the Big Picnic in

Courtesy of York University Libraries, Clara Thomas Archives & Special Collections, *Toronto Telegram*, August 2, 1965, ASC06309.

Janie Cooper-Wilson, born in Collingwood, Ontario, was crowned Miss Sepia
in 1965 at the age of eighteen. During her teenage years she was a competitive
baton twirler, her talent in the Miss Sepia International contest. She is the current
Executive Director of the Silvershoe Historical Society.

St. Catharines, "All of the relatives came to stay. They would sleep anywhere — on the lawn, in a car in the driveway. The police would even put you up for a night until you found accommodation."[72] Cooking and baking had to begin days before the event. It is evident the yearly logistics worked out as Windsor's celebrations remained successful for decades.

Generally during these festivities, Black patrons were not mistreated or denied service because of their race. E.C. Cooper, president of the Chatham Literary Society, remarked that when he visited Windsor he ate "at a first-class restaurant amongst white gentlemen and ladies."[73] However, the same could not be said for attendees of events in Chatham. Throughout the end of the 1800s and early 1900s, African Canadians in Chatham and their guests were refused service in White establishments and could only frequent the few Black-owned businesses.

Three factors led to the end of Emancipation Day celebrations in Windsor in the middle of the twentieth century. Firstly, a fire at Jackson Park in 1957 caused extensive damage to the main event grounds just three weeks before the scheduled event. Secondly, the park was split into two by the construction of an overpass. Then, the 1967 race riots in Detroit led to the refusal of Windsor city council to issue the event permit because of security and safety concerns. No celebrations were hosted in Windsor for the years between 1967 and 1978, but eventually resumed in 1979 at a new location, Mic Mac Park. However, attendance fell dramatically. Shortly after, Windsor's festivities merged with those in Amherstburg.

August First celebrations were revived in Windsor in 2008 by the Windsor Council of Elders and the Emancipation Planning Committee, with the support of several other community organizations and the City of Windsor, in honour of the 175th anniversary of the abolition of slavery throughout British colonies. The organization's aim is to restore an awareness of family unity and identity to the African-Canadians in Windsor. The revitalized four-day event recaptured elements of the past by featuring foods from the African Diaspora, musical concerts highlighting hip hop, gospel, blues, and R&B artists, a sunrise church service and breakfast with a keynote speaker, a boxing demonstration, the Miss Sepia International Pageant, and a parade on Ouellette Avenue. The opening ceremony and reception on the Friday night was co-hosted by the United States Consulate General in Toronto, Mr. John R. Nay. Many provincial

Courtesy of the North American Black Historical Museum, FS-10.

An admission ticket to the Emancipation Day activities at Jackson Park in Windsor on August 5, 1962.

and American dignitaries, along with local dignitaries and community leaders were on hand to lend their support, such as Rosemary Sadlier, president of the Ontario Black History Society. New attractions to appeal to a younger audience included a three-on-three basketball tournament, a graffiti contest, and a tour of some local Underground Railroad historic sites. Many of the festivals events were held at the riverfront.[74]

Kent County

Chatham

During the nineteenth century, Chatham was a developing commercial centre endowed with large export businesses and a series of smaller enterprises, many of which involved local African Canadians. African people have lived in Chatham as early as 1791. A Black man, possibly named Croucher, is recorded as a resident of the town that year. There were seven Black families in 1832, and the population surge as a result of the influx of runaway slaves saw almost two thousand by 1860, a figure that accounted for one-third of Chatham's total population. Refugees were attracted to Chatham as the community with its large, welcoming Black community and ample employment opportunities had gained the distinction of being an ideal place for incoming African Americans. Chatham's Black pioneer community, concentrated primarily on the east side of town, was composed of a mix of free persons, fugitive slaves, and an increasing number of Canadian-born individuals, all with a variety of occupational abilities. Some were skilled workers who operated their own businesses including shoemakers, carpenters, blacksmiths, bricklayers, masons, barbers, cigar makers, cooks, cabinetmakers, watchmakers, ship carpenters, and plasterers. Black labourers were able to find employment on farms, in mills, or lumberyards.

The Black citizenry established cultural institutions that were central to the African-Canadian community. By the 1850s Chatham had three Black churches with a combined membership of about 250 people. The First Baptist Church on King Street was erected in 1853. The Campbell Chapel AME Church, built in 1887 with bricks from Dresden's British American Institute, was also on King Street. The Victoria Chapel became the mother church of the newly formed British Methodist Episcopal church in 1856, following the decision at the AME Conference of that year to split from the main AME body. In 1859, Victoria Chapel moved to Princess Street near Wellington Street with a congregation of about three hundred. These churches, along with several others, not only served religious functions, but social and political purposes, too. For instance, the last session of the John Brown Convention was held at the First Baptist Church on May 10, 1858.[75] Many of these churches supported other anti-slavery campaigns. Schools, such as the Wilberforce Educational Institute constructed in the 1870s with the money raised by the solvency of the Dawn Settlement, were built to meet the needs of Black students who were prohibited from attending the public common schools. The office of the Black newspaper, the *Provincial Freeman*, relocated to Chatham in 1855 at the Charity Block at King and Adelaide Streets under the new ownership of the Shadds: Israel, Isaac, and Mary Ann. The publication, a valuable source of information about African-Canadian institutions in the province, promoted anti-slavery, integration, temperance, and literacy, reported on cases of discrimination, and discussed the concerns of the community.[76]

Dr. Anderson Ruffin Abbott, circa 1900, presented numerous lectures that addressed current issues in science, medicine, education, and social justice, even in his retirement. He was the coroner of Kent County from 1874 until he retired in 1881, at the age of forty-four.

Courtesy of Catherine Slaney, great-granddaughter of Dr. Abbott.

Men of African descent in Chatham coordinated two voluntary militias of eighty men in 1838 to help provide defence during the Mackenzie Rebellion and to practise drills using the guns of the British regular units. They remained active until the corps was disbanded in 1843. Members of the community organized social groups and benevolent societies, such as the Provincial Union Association, the True Band Society, and the Victorian Reform Benevolent Society, to help refugees settle and to provide financial assistance to the sick, destitute, or for funerals. The several Masonic lodges and women's auxiliaries, as well as a temperance group and the Chatham Literary and Debating Society, added to a network of social institutions addressing the demands of a growing fugitive population. As well as providing social support, these groups pushed for American abolition, assisted in the education and betterment of the community, and challenged anti-Black prejudice in Chatham.

Blacks in Chatham fought against slavery in many other ways. The large number of escapees, like Nelson Hackett,[77] attracted bounty hunters to the area. In August of 1857, two White men from the United States came to Chatham in search of a runaway named Joe Alexander. They were confronted by a crowd of Black residents, including Alexander himself who ran them out of town. Chatham hosted the meeting of the Canadian Anti-Slavery Baptist Association in 1854 and an all-faith convention was held in December 1855 to discuss how local Blacks could be active in the abolition movement. Some local Black anti-slavery activists included members of the Shadd family, Osborne Anderson, Martin Delany, and Dr. Anderson Ruffin Abbott.[78]

They also battled racial discrimination in its usual forms. African-Canadian children were excluded from public schools in Chatham. In 1832 there was such strong opposition to their attendance from White parents that Black parents were forced to keep their children home. A segregated educational system lasted for about sixty years in Chatham and was even upheld by the courts until the practice was legally struck down in 1890.[79] Even with this, it would still be a few years, until 1904, when integration began to occur. During this time Blacks in Chatham fought against separate schools through numerous petitions, the first one in 1851, followed by a court challenge in 1861.

Residents of African descent could not purchase cabin-class tickets for a Chatham steamer and Blacks from out of town were denied hotel accommodations in local hotels. When a local White politician let his views be known that he did not want Blacks to settle anywhere near Chatham, the African-Canadian community used the power of their vote to remove him from office. Politician Edwin Larwill had expressed his racist views publicly many times. His intolerant position was representative of positions held by some of Chatham Whites who were showing increasing hostility towards Blacks as the number of fugitives and the number of European immigrants coming to the town increased. Some felt that Blacks had too many rights.

Beginning in the 1830s, the annual Emancipation Day commemorations in Chatham were celebrated against this backdrop of overt discrimination. In 1841, Emancipation Day was observed on July 20th. Over one hundred people gathered at the hospital building on the military base, the grounds surrounding the present-day Chatham Armoury on William Street North, beside Tecumseh Park. From there, the parade followed a band through some of the main streets. The procession was succeeded by a dinner and speeches, with William Lampton as chairperson. One speaker was Lindsay Taylor of Chatham who provided a detailed account of the beginning of the slave trade in Africa and its effects on the families and communities on the continent. Celebrations in Chatham in 1842 began at sunrise at the local military parade grounds with twenty-one rounds of ammunition being fired from a cannon by Chatham's Black militiamen. Along with civilian participants, one hundred Black soldiers marched through the town and prepared the meal for a military-sponsored dinner, speeches, and a dance. Josiah Jones, a local Black farmer and service member, gave one of the addresses. He expressed how wonderful it was to be able to gather and celebrate this victorious day and how much admiration Black settlers possessed for Britain for releasing its slaves. Jones announced that when the groundswell of abolition sentiments reached the enslaved African Americans in the southern states from Britain, they would all rise up and destroy the opponents of "liberty and humanity." Entertainment for the evening included musical performances and a dance in the officer's building.[80]

By the 1850s the size and scope of the August First festivals had grown dramatically. An editorial in the *Chatham Planet* described the order of events planned for August 1, 1856. Various associations, societies, and lodges were invited to join the parade that assembled on King Street in front of the Second Baptist Church. They marched to the Grand Truck Railway depot on Queen Street, led by musical bands, to welcome hundreds of guests coming from Elgin and other locales, then proceeded to march to McGregor's Grove at the south end of present-day Tecumseh Park to enjoy an extravagant meal. Reverend Mr. William King[81] and Mr. John Scoble of Dawn were two of the many renowned speakers. The evening activities included a bazaar in the town hall on King Street near Market Square, hosted by the Victorian Reform Society.[82]

August 1, 1860, was observed with reverence and seriousness by the almost five thousand in attendance. People came from Detroit, Windsor, and other nearby towns for the event organized by C.W. Prince and Reverend W.H. Jones.[83] A church service was held with the sermon featuring Genesis 28:17, which stated: "And he was afraid, and said, How dreadful is this place! This is none other but the house of God, and this is the gate of heaven."[84]

However, the commemoration of Emancipation Day was not only about enjoyment or an acknowledgement of the past. By the late 1860s the themes of Emancipation Day began to shift from celebrating liberation from slavery to advocating for the full rights and privileges as British citizens to ensure a better life for their children. With the increased persistence of anti-Black attitudes throughout parts of the province, as well as other areas of the country with sizeable African-Canadian populations, the gathering of hundreds of Black Canadians in one place provided an opportunity to boost public awareness of their mistreatment.

Observances in 1871 started off with a kilometre-long parade, replete with music, banners, and decorations from the BME Church Victoria Chapel. The crowd marched down Wellington Street to William Street then to the train station to receive guests from Windsor and other centres. The train from the west had thirteen full coaches; others arrived by carriage and by steamer. Guests joined the procession and approximately four thousand people, including the many visitors from Detroit and other American cities, walked to McGregor's Grove. Black parents, greatly concerned about what the future held for their children, often had their offspring participate in the parade, such as the thirty little girls dressed in white dresses with wreaths of flowers around their heads that were featured that year.

Isaac Holden[85] shared the history of Blacks in Ontario since the 1850s wave of fugitives. After a two-hour dinner accompanied by music by the Jones' Brass Band and a band from Detroit, the lineup of speakers continued. R.L. Holden, a lawyer from Cleveland, Ohio, and brother of Isaac Holden (R.L. later moved to Chatham) gave the next address characterizing the progress of Blacks in Canada as being behind the United States even though British territories obtained freedom first. He particularly noted the increase of racial prejudice in Ontario and in British Columbia.

Reverend William Hawkins, bishop of the BME in Canada West, who had spoken earlier to praise emancipation, addressed the listeners again. He reinforced R.L. Holden's point, stating that at least Blacks in the United States helped to fight prejudice through the use of force. The next speaker, from Detroit, said that he, too, agreed with Holden because there were no more segregated schools for Blacks in Detroit, but this segregation still remained in Canada. The civil rights of African Canadians were not improving over time, but were being severely eroded, a trend that needed to be changed. Otherwise, what kind a life would the future hold for young African Canadians who had been born and raised here, for Canadian-born citizens, and for established immigrants?

When the meeting closed, participants reorganized the procession and escorted guests to the train station and the harbour. St. John's Lodge No. 9 held an evening program at the Drill Shed and the funds raised from ticket and food sales were donated to their widow and orphan charity. Just as in other city centres like London, Hamilton, and Toronto, fraternal orders in Chatham were very involved in Emancipation Day functions, an event that helped them build support for various causes benefiting the Black community.[86]

At times Emancipation Day was used to fulfill a more political agenda based on issues that Ontario's African-Canadian citizens were experiencing at that particular time. In 1874 Chatham cancelled most of the traditional festive activities. Instead they held a political rally to protest the racial discrimination faced by Chatham Blacks and the twenty-year failure of the Conservative Party to meet the needs of its African-Canadian constituents. Over two thousand people marched in a street procession led by the Union Brass Band. The protest began at Princess and Wellington Streets and included a cavalcade of about 150 carriages and wagons carrying the chairperson Grandison Boyd — the Black businessman who owned Boyd's Block a section of commercial real estate on King Street West — invited speakers, and Masonic lodge members along with their wives and daughters. Participants marched to Mr. Tobin's farm for the day's program. E.C. Cooper outlined how the ruling Reform Party had secured political and civil rights for Blacks in Chatham in the past three years.

The following speaker, J.M. Jones, criticized the Conservatives for attempting to gain Black votes by bribing them with a free boat trip to Detroit during election time and likened it to the ride given to Africans in the horrendous Middle Passage. Exercising the power of their vote would be critical to obtaining the full rights and privileges held by other Canadian citizens. He stressed that their votes should be strategically placed for the Reform Party. Jones then went on to discuss two similar but separate cases of racism. The first case was that of a daughter of a former militiaman of the 1837 Rebellion. In the second case, two men were denied soda water at a Chatham restaurant, and the men were subsequently charged with disorderly conduct. Although the counter clerk admitted that he refused service to the men because they were Black, the court case resulted in the male defendants being sentenced to keep the peace for one year. Jones also brought up another matter, which was the political scandal labelled the Elgin Association Fraud. In an apparent political ploy to attract Black votes, Reverend William King (former managing director of the Elgin Settlement) and incumbent provincial member Archibald McKellar were accused by the Conservatives of misusing settlement money for personal expenses. At the conclusion of the meeting a motion was passed: "Therefore resolved that we as electors of the counties of Kent and Bothwell, do exonerate the gentlemen above-named from all charges brought against them which we have found so basely untrue; charges made, in our opinion, to injure the colored people as well as those they were brought against; and hereby express our fullest confidence in them, and in the Government of Ontario, of which Mr. McKellar is a member; and pledge to them our united support, so long as they pursue the course they have done in the past."[87]

After a picnic lunch, MP Archibald McKellar was the next person to address the audience. McKellar, like King, had a long relationship with the Black community in Kent County. An attorney, he was one of two White men in Chatham to support William King's settlement project. Blacks in Kent County helped to vote him back in during the 1856 election, which he won over Edwin Larwill. (Larwill had beaten McKellar in the 1854 election.) The efforts of local activists such as Martin Delany to mobilize Black voters in support of McKellar resulted in almost three hundred African-Canadian votes, enough to create the winning margin. In his speech, MP McKellar outlined how he and his political party, the Clear Grits (Reform Party), treated Blacks fairly by pointing out that they had appointed Isaac Holden as councillor, designated Dr. Anderson Abbott as county coroner, and selected some Black men, like Charles Watt of Raleigh Township, as justices of the peace. African Canadians, as part of their British citizenship and rights as property owners, took advantage of their right to vote, a privilege at that time denied to the majority of African Americans. They understood the importance and the impact of voting and used their votes to remove racist politicians like Colonel John Prince and Edwin Larwill. They also utilized their votes to defeat politicians who did nothing for Blacks in parliament such as challenging the Common Schools Act. All of the Black voters in Kent County were able to sign their names in the voting register, but many of their White counterparts could only "make their mark."

The next speaker was George William Ross, the MP for West Middlesex. He emphasized how Emancipation Day and reform were closely linked: those who agitated for liberation were themselves reformers of their day and Reformers now worked to free people from failed governance.[88]

When no commemorations were held in 1877, an editorial was written in the *Tri-Weekly Planet* on August 2nd, asserting that Blacks had become ungrateful and indifferent towards Britain who freed them. E.C. Cooper, president of the Chatham Literary and Debating Society, wrote a letter to the editor criticizing the opinion piece. He strongly disagreed with the editorial, pointing out that the land that was described as "free and just" refused to pay the former slaves (who were now labourers) the full value of their work and then left them to fend for themselves after being forced to work without pay. Cooper argued Emancipation Day should not be celebrated by Blacks any more than by the Irish. He asked whether the Irish were ungrateful, too because they didn't recognize the Irish Emancipation Act of 1829. Cooper then suggested that the Irish be forced to celebrate for generations. Why didn't the *Planet* tell Irish settlers they owe their liberty to Britain?

The absence of the annual celebration of freedom reveals the extent of discrimination against Blacks in Chatham and in varying levels of society across Canada. Because of their colour, Cooper argued, they could only stay in one hotel in Chatham, the Garner House, but in Windsor and across the border in Detroit Blacks could frequent any first-class hotel or restaurant without prejudice. Cooper pointed out that if one thousand Black visitors came for an Emancipation Day celebration tomorrow they would face blatant discrimination because there would be only one place they could go get a soda or an ice-cream cone. He asserted these were the reasons why Blacks in Chatham did not celebrate Emancipation Day. The sentiment among local Black residents was that limited rights for African Canadians should not be celebrated and that perhaps this move would force Whites in Ontario to acknowledge and end their racist practices.[89]

Consequently, the 1870s saw growing opposition to Emancipation Day celebrations in Chatham. Why celebrate freedom when basic rights and privileges were being denied? Anderson Ruffin Abbott echoed similar sentiments in an editorial piece he wrote for the *Missionary Messenger* in 1873, while living and working in Chatham. The change in opinion towards August First during this decade appears to exemplify the tumultuous state of civil rights and race relations in Ontario and the fact that Blacks seemed quite discouraged by their worsening social conditions.

Several identified factors were contributing to this situation. First, the Black population began to diminish, with hundreds of African Americans who had been living in Ontario now returning to the United States after the abolition of American slavery in 1865, a shift that affected the dynamics of the Black community. Simultaneously, there was a surge in European immigrants arriving in the area that led to a decline in opportunities for Blacks. White involvement in issues relating to the rights of Blacks steadily lessened. Further, when some Whites realized that a segment of the fugitive population planned on permanent settlement, anti-Black attitudes and White opposition swelled because of the imminent threat of close social interaction and intermarriage.

Interestingly, Emancipation Day commemorations in Chatham did resume shortly afterwards, as in 1882 a large number of people were described as gathering together for August First despite the stormy weather conditions in the morning. Celebrants, comprised of numerous lodge and cultural association members as well as people of the general public, travelled by train from other Ontario towns and many American states. In the afternoon, Isaac Holden gave a moving speech following the procession. He stressed the importance of recognizing those who actively fought for the freedom of Africans enslaved in British colonies and touched on the falling of the horrific institution of slavery in the United States seventeen years before. In closing, he reminded listeners to take advantages of the opportunities to improve themselves and strengthen their communities, to show themselves worthy of the rights and privileges granted to them in British North America. Later, the mayor, town council members, and Black and White gatherers attended a picnic in Tecumseh Park.[90]

However, those unresolved social inequality issues from several decades before resurfaced at Emancipation Day observances during the remainder of the century, such as the one held in 1891. The gathering at Tecumseh Park did not follow the regular program of church service, parade, and merriment in a relaxed atmosphere. James C. Richards, the chairperson of the day (he later became a BME minister) and leader of the new Kent County Civil Rights League (KCCRL), instructed speakers not to give the usual thanks and praises, but to speak about the goals of the League and why it was formed. After the hundreds in attendance, both Black and White, enjoyed a social luncheon at the Drill Shed and listened to music played by a band from Dover (just west of Chatham), the speeches began. This time the focus was on educating listeners on the organization's aims and encouraging the community to address several grievances.

An Emancipation Day street procession at King and Fifth Streets in Chatham in August of 1885.

The lineup of speakers for the day was announced by the chair. Racial discrimination was the topic addressed — African Canadians in Chatham were not being allowed to exercise their full democratic rights. The Civic Rights League stemmed from the Chatham Literary Association, which had been formed to improve the lives and conditions of local Blacks. The main goal of the KCCRL was to unify Chatham Blacks in seeking redress for the many injustices they experienced: the lack of public schooling for African-Canadian children; Black men being barred from serving on a jury, especially in the trial of another Black person; and the denial of hotel accommodations and service at local food establishments. One argument presented was that if Blacks were accepted at bars, which were public places, they should be allowed to frequent all public places. The League sought removal of these barriers, to be followed by access to full citizenship rights. The first objective on the agenda was to launch a campaign against segregated schools. The monies raised from this Emancipation Day were to help pay for the initiative.

The underlying question was why did Whites view Blacks differently, even though they had demonstrated themselves to be just like any other Canadians? R.L. Holden argued sarcastically that there was no distinction when viewing Blacks as criminals. Reverend Josephus O'Banyoun, in sharing a personal example, commented on how he was ostracized at school in Brantford where he was born and raised, and on how he was singled out because of his racial background. Holden and Garrison Shadd reiterated the fact that Black citizens were just as loyal as White citizens were, "just as patriotic, just as willing to die for his country, as a white man and his citizenship should be as fully recognized."[91] As O'Banyoun stated, African Canadians only wanted fair treatment, not favours.

The constant struggle for equality in a racially hostile environment gave rise to different perspectives on the relevance of Emancipation Day, which Colin McFarquhar examines in depth.[92] Many questioned whether Africans' liberation from slavery should continue to be celebrated or if it should now serve another purpose. O'Banyoun suggested that Emancipation Day should be a time to celebrate what African Canadians should be and aspired to be, goals that were achievable through education. Garrison Shadd boldly voiced his opinion that these annual Emancipation Day celebrations "gave thanks for nothing" and that in order to overcome inequality and racism people of African descent should educate themselves and take an aggressive stance against injustice. He further stated that Blacks must always set high standards and not be satisfied with their present level of attainment and that struggle is inevitable to achieve greatness. He stressed the importance of self-determination and future success through education and economic initiatives and the redefining of freedom based on political involvement and economic opportunities.

The 1893 observance of Emancipation Day marked a significant milestone in the civil rights fight in Chatham because it was the year that public schools were legally integrated. Participants marched to the Grand Trunk Railroad Station on Queen Street to receive guests from Detroit. The Detroit City Band led the procession followed by uniformed lodge members of the Knights Templar and Eureka Commandery No. 1. All marched to Tecumseh Park where Mayor S.T. Martin, Colonel Webster of the United States, Reverend Josephus O'Banyoun, and Consul George R. Nevells of Detroit gave speeches. Although Black residents could now claim a partial victory in their battle against discrimination, they still had concerns, which were voiced at the event. O'Banyoun and another African-American speaker from Detroit challenged Whites, many of whom were in attendance, to end the prejudiced treatment practised against African Canadians. Did Whites really understand the Black point of view? Colin McFarquhar argues that they did not, because Whites saw Blacks as receiving equal treatment.[93] The police magistrate, M. Houston, delivered an address telling Blacks to do whatever they must in order to "gain acceptance in Canadian society" and to conduct themselves well in the face of discrimination. This line of thinking put the onus of social improvement on Blacks by merely taking advantage of the opportunities available to them in Ontario and across Canada. Mayor Martin commented how delighted he was that a large number of White residents were taking part in the recognition of Emancipation Day. The afternoon program consisted of sport activities such as a baseball match between Chatham and Detroit and tugs of war. A banquet was held in the evening, beginning with a concert by several bands and followed by a lavish dinner and dancing.

White politicians such as city councillors, police chiefs, mayors, members of the provincial parliament, and federal members of parliament normally made appearances and spoke at Emancipation Day observances. So when the sixty-third anniversary of the passage of the 1833 British Emancipation Act was recognized at Tecumseh Park in 1897, and neither Liberal MP Thomas Letson Pardo nor former MP Archibald Campbell were in attendance, and no letters of apology were sent, it solicited some negative reaction from Black guests. In his study, Mitchell Kachun points out that during this time period the "decline in interest among White government officials is particularly striking."[94] While there was a decline in the number of attendees, some public officials did continue. One White politician present that year was MP James Clancy of Bothwell, Ontario. He spoke on freedom and was well received by the crowd because it was evident that the sentiments he expressed were close to him.

Another White politician to address the gatherers was Dr. W.R. Hall, provincial Conservative candidate for West Kent. He stated that emancipation from slavery was just and moral and that Blacks had proven to be as worthy and loyal as their White counterparts. He spoke about the progress Blacks had made and how they filled all kinds of trades, professions, and callings with "dignity, profit, and grace and honour to their race,"[95] mentioning the educational and political achievements of attorney Delos Davis and former Chatham Alderman Henry Weaver. Hall then stressed the importance of education in improving their lives and in eradicating prejudice and discrimination that acted against them. He reinforced the sentiment held by African Canadians that the right to vote was a powerful mechanism that comes with responsibility. Finally, Hall closed by expressing his hope for the quick destruction of all things that divided the races as it was important that everyone work together for the common good. And, as usual, a grand banquet and ball at the Drill Shed in Tecumseh Park ended the evening.[96]

White politicians continued to deliver speeches at Emancipation Day. In 1899, Mayor T.A. Smith welcomed observers to Tecumseh Park and highlighted some of the local examples of the advancement of Blacks since the Emancipation Act of 1833. He cited the accomplishments of Anderson Abbott, appointed to the Chatham Board of Health, and Isaac Holden, a city councillor. Most Whites did not speak to the anti-Black prejudice that persisted, choosing instead to note African-Canadian achievement as if to unintentionally imply that discrimination was not an impediment.

African-Canadian speakers, on the other hand, knew that Emancipation Day afforded the ideal platform to talk about racism and the infringements of their liberties. On the same occasion, Reverend A.W. Hackley of St. Paul's AME Church in Hamilton noted that:

> We are here today to celebrate our freedom. But are we free
> to go everywhere and do we enjoy all the privileges of other
> taxpayers? What has the Negro of Kent County done that
> he is unable to go into the ice cream parlour? What has he
> done that he should be ostracized from restaurants?[97]

In spite of the differing points of view on the social conditions of citizens of African descent in Chatham and the simmering racial strife, Blacks and Whites came together on Emancipation Day to be intellectually stimulated and to have some leisure time. For well into the 1920s Tecumseh Park was the place to be on August First for a program of speeches, picnics, sports, and contests, along with dancing and concerts at the Drill Shed.

Dawn and Dresden

Dawn was established in 1842 by Josiah Henson,[98] a former slave from Maryland who escaped to Canada in 1830. It was an eighty-hectare Black settlement in the Dresden area, almost thirty kilometres north of Chatham. Created to provide newly arrived escaped slaves with land, employment, education, training, and sense of security, it contained homes, a church, a sawmill, and a school called the British American Institute. Within about a decade of its beginning, approximately five hundred Blacks lived in the colony. Before the development of the Dawn Project, people of African descent had lived in the vicinity (then called Fairport) from as early as the 1820s. It was to be expected that Emancipation Day celebrations would blossom in the 1850s in areas like Dawn that had attracted a considerable number of newly escaped African-American freedom seekers. They took this time to recognize the liberty, rights, safety, and opportunities they had on British soil, while publicly advocating the end of American slavery.

Occasionally, matters of contention in relation to the Black community would arise at August First observances, as was the case at Dawn in 1854. The large gathering began with a procession that formed at the schoolhouse (the British American Institute) at midday. Celebrants marched to Green Lawn where the opening ceremony was held with Reverend Josiah Henson

Josiah Henson's work as an abolitionist included assisting slaves in their escape to Canada on the Underground Railroad and playing a key role in the establishment of the Dawn Settlement. His life story was the inspiration for Harriet Beecher Stowe's novel, *Uncle Tom's Cabin*. In 1983, Henson was the first Black person to be featured on a Canadian postage stamp.

Courtesy of the Uncle Tom's Cabin Historic Site, Dresden, Ontario.

presiding over the day's events. The appointed chair briefly addressed the crowd and then introduced a special guest speaker, Frederick Douglass,[99] the African-American abolitionist, who, according to the *Provincial Freeman*, apparently received a cold reception from the majority of the audience due to recent events.

Douglass had been on a lecture tour in Upper Canada since May of 1854, including a stop at the St. Lawrence Hall located at Jarvis and King Streets in Toronto, where he had spoken to a mixed-race audience. While there, Douglass received an invitation from John Scoble (the secretary of the British and Foreign Anti-Slavery Society in England who had been asked to come to Dawn to implement a new management system) asking Douglass to join him in attending Dawn's twentieth anniversary of Emancipation Day. At the time, Douglass was receiving public criticism from some members of the African-Canadian community in Canada West, including from Mary Ann Shadd Cary's editorials in the *Provincial Freeman*. Douglass was being attacked for being an integrationist who did not support African-American immigration to Upper Canada or separate Black communities.

To add fuel to the fire, when matters of the mismanagement of the Dawn Settlement[100] were raised during this otherwise festive occasion, Douglass was met with further opposition from those assembled when he rose to speak a second time. Many felt he sided with Whites, in particular with John Scoble, and not his Black brothers and sisters even though he was unaware of the recent conflict at Dawn. When Reverend William King rose to speak to the gathering, he refused to give his address from the same spot as Douglass or Scoble. No one from Dawn would transport Douglass to Chatham for two days after Emancipation Day, causing his speaking engagement there to be delayed. Upon his return to his home in Rochester, New York, Douglass later wrote a commentary on the controversy in his newspaper, *Frederick Douglass' Paper*, which offers a slightly different perspective than the coverage by the *Provincial Freeman*. In it he commented that the Black guests enjoyed Scoble's speech and described his address as "fluent, exact, rhetorical, and sometimes truly eloquent."[101]

The planning committee for the 1857 Emancipation Day observance in Dresden included H. Damrell; William Crosby; David Smith; James Hollinsworth,[102] the secretary; and Aaron Highgate,[103] the chair of the event. These were Black men who lived and worked in the town. In preparation for the annual affair, the committee extended a written invitation to African-American anti-slavery activist William Whipper,[104] who operated a few businesses in Dresden but lived in Columbia, Pennsylvania. Whipper sent his regrets but offered some words of encouragement and enlightenment, perhaps to share with those who would attend. He acknowledged the importance of the day:

> "That historic occasion; especially on British…, where the … you have assembled to commemorate, has not only become sacred to the affections and feelings of the people, but has created an *event*, that has become interwoven with her national policy, and embodied in her history as one of the proudest and noblest achievements that marked the records of time."[105]

Whipper noted that fugitive slaves from the United States who found refuge in Canada had much to celebrate:

> Now my dear friends, you who have proved to be such a national blessing to a people who have robbed and plundered you, and wrested from you all the blessings due to our common humanity, how much more grateful ought you to be the country of your adoption; where you have the exalted privilege of possessing and enjoying all Divine and civil attributes pertaining to life, liberty, and the pursuit of happiness …[106]

He encouraged them to "stand forth redeemed, regenerated and disenthralled by the irresistible genius of British emancipation" and closed by stating that "I remain yours in the cause of Justice and Freedom."[107] No doubt this message, heard by hundreds at the gathering or read in the *Provincial Freeman*, would have engendered support for the abolition movement against American slavery.

Information about Emancipation Day celebrations in Canada comes not only from newspaper articles, but also from letters and personal records such as the diary of Reverend Thomas Hughes, minister of the Christ's

Church Anglican in Dresden, who mentions the event in a diary entry
dated the first of August 1861:

> This day the anniversary of the Emancipation of Slavery
> in the British W. Indies is quite the "red letter day" with
> the colored population of Canada. There was quite a
> large gathering at Windsor to which a considerable
> number have gone from this neighbourhood. The people
> here have had a sort of "pic nic" in the bush, which has
> been well attended.[108]

Hughes arrived in Dresden in 1859 to answer his calling to work
with fugitives. He was the supervisor for the mission school for ex-slaves
operated by the Colonial Church and School Society, the mission arm of
the Anglican Church. The mission school was of particular importance to
the community as Black children were not admitted to the local common
schools. Reverend Hughes was described as "an untiring advocate of the
equality of man, and knows not complexional distinctions."[109] As such,
Hughes participated and even organized Emancipation Day observances.

Parker Smith, a local correspondent for the Philadelphia newspaper
the *Christian Recorder*, reported on a gathering that took place at the
mission school in Dresden. It appears to be a school-organized assembly
in recognition of Emancipation Day although it occurred on the sixth
of August after students exams. In the afternoon at the end of class, the
pupils and some adults stood around the British flag in front of the school
and sang "God save the Queen," then took the flag down and marched
with it to a field on Reverend Hughes' property. The adults and children
in attendance ate a picnic lunch, enjoyed a concert by the students, and
listened to speeches from church ministries, one White minister and two
Black ministers. William P. Newman and Reverend Davis, both Baptist
preachers, publically denounced the discrimination that existed in Canada
against people of African descent, and praised the efforts of Hughes "to
destroy a prejudice which exists here on account of colour,"[110] and expressed
gratitude for the safety afforded to them on British soil. Newman pointed
to the flag that stretched across the stage and remarked that "No where on
earth could any man be so secure as under the British flag, (loud applause

and Hear, hear.)"[111] The third speaker, Reverend Gunn, delivered an address to the largely fugitive group. He stated that "It would be wrong to kill your masters in attempting to escape, for the word of God teaches me, Servants obey your masters."[112] Needless to say, these words did not sit well with the audience and stirred up anger. This comment reinforced the belief that Blacks were inferior, natural slaves, while Whites were superior and born masters, a sentiment which was reflective of the mindset of some Whites in the Dresden area.[113]

During the 1850s White residents who opposed the Dawn Settlement called Dresden "Nigger Hole." According to Robin Winks, blatant discrimination and prejudice were part of daily life for Black residents that continued well into the next century. School segregation was a major issue for African Canadians living in Dresden, with Whites vehemently rejecting the idea of integrated education. In 1852, a local Black man named Dennis Hill wrote a letter to Eggerton Ryerson to complain that the common school would not let his son, and later two children, attend classes there, even though he was a taxpayer. His complaint went before the courts and Chief Justice John Beverley Robinson ruled that once a separate school had been established for Blacks, it was legal to force them to attend it and ban them from the all-White common schools.[114]

Emancipation Day gatherings in Dawn, and later Dresden, continued to be used to attack the racial discrimination faced by the village's African-Canadian settlers. There was a huge celebration in Dresden in 1890 in commemoration of the fifty-seventh anniversary of the abolition of slavery. Approximately eight thousand people converged on the village. The lineup of speakers included the Honourable David Mills, MP for Bothwell, Ontario; the Honourable Robert Ferguson, MPP for Kent West; Reverend O'Banyoun of Hamilton; Reverend Morris from Toledo; and Mr. Coats of Tilbury, among others. Live music was furnished by the Maple Leaf Band and the North Star Band, both out of Chatham. Mr. Mills eloquently connected the theme of liberation to the ongoing international dispute between the United States and Great Britain and Canada over control of the northern Bering Sea. He questioned how the United States could be so concerned about ensuring the right of seals when they have denied these same basic rights to its own citizens. Mills declared that: "The preservation of seals is of far less consequence than the preservation of our rights as a free people...." and warned that "we ought not to yield, under pretence of preserving the seals, that which the United States refused in order to save the men and women from chains and slavery."[115]

The dwindling of the Black population due to lack of opportunities and racism saw the end of Emancipation Day in Dresden. The African Canadians who continued to live there in the early twentieth century observed August First with their neighbours in Chatham.

Fittingly, in 2005 Uncle Tom's Cabin Historic Site became the location for the revival of Emancipation Day in Dresden. The event appropriately encapsulates the struggle of freedom and civil rights, while paying tribute to Josiah Henson a passionate activist who worked tirelessly to better the lives of his fellow citizens. This site that once served as both a haven and a battleground now has an interpretive centre, three historic buildings from the original colony, and two cemeteries where some of the first settlers, including Josiah Henson, are buried.

The hosting of the August First commemoration at an African-Canadian heritage site such as Uncle Tom's provides a rich learning experience for all who attend and provides participants the opportunity to learn about the individual stories, collective struggles, and exceptional perseverance of Blacks in Dresden and the surrounding area. Further, it illuminates a part of Canada's national heritage that's been systematically marginalized. To continue the legacy of remembrance through Emancipation Day, the organization has drawn on a number of notable figures.

The Honourable Lincoln Alexander has not only been involved in the organization of Emancipation Day at Uncle Tom's, but is also a monument to African-Canadian history himself. Born in Hamilton, Alexander achieved recognition as a lawyer and politician. He is the first Black lieutenant-governor in Ontario, Canada's first Black member of parliament, and the first Black cabinet minister. For the first two years of the new commemorations, Lincoln Alexander was the keynote speaker. He discussed the racism he had experienced, how he overcame it, and how Canadians, both Black and White, have fought for equality in Ontario and in Canada. He encouraged "people to stand up and be counted and never let this sort of thing [slavery] happen."[116] Alexander also pointed out that "there's always needs to be vigilant about racism," noting "that's why legislation such as the Canadian Race Relations Act is in place."[117]

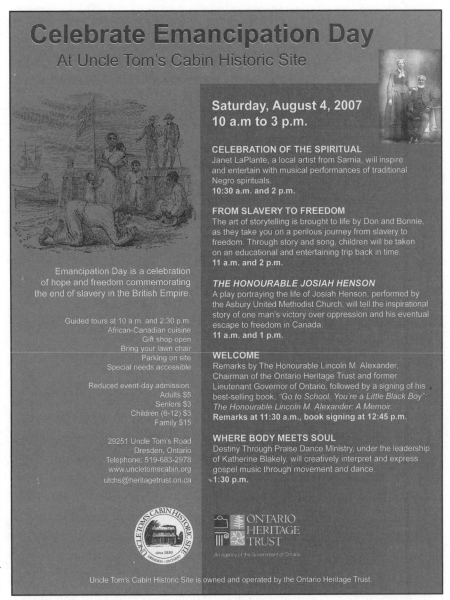

Celebrate Emancipation Day

At Uncle Tom's Cabin Historic Site

Saturday, August 4, 2007
10 a.m to 3 p.m.

Emancipation Day is a celebration of hope and freedom commemorating the end of slavery in the British Empire.

Guided tours at 10 a.m. and 2:30 p.m.
African-Canadian cuisine
Gift shop open
Bring your lawn chair
Parking on site
Special needs accessible

Reduced event-day admission:
Adults $5
Seniors $3
Children (6-12) $3
Family $15

29251 Uncle Tom's Road
Dresden, Ontario
Telephone: 519-683-2978
www.uncletomscabin.org
utchs@heritagetrust.on.ca

CELEBRATION OF THE SPIRITUAL
Janet LaPlante, a local artist from Sarnia, will inspire and entertain with musical performances of traditional Negro spirituals.
10:30 a.m. and 2 p.m.

FROM SLAVERY TO FREEDOM
The art of storytelling is brought to life by Don and Bonnie, as they take you on a perilous journey from slavery to freedom. Through story and song, children will be taken on an educational and entertaining trip back in time.
11 a.m. and 2 p.m.

THE HONOURABLE JOSIAH HENSON
A play portraying the life of Josiah Henson, performed by the Asbury United Methodist Church, will tell the inspirational story of one man's victory over oppression and his eventual escape to freedom in Canada.
11 a.m. and 1 p.m.

WELCOME
Remarks by The Honourable Lincoln M. Alexander, Chairman of the Ontario Heritage Trust and former Lieutenant Governor of Ontario, followed by a signing of his best-selling book, *"Go to School, You're a Little Black Boy": The Honourable Lincoln M. Alexander: A Memoir*.
Remarks at 11:30 a.m., book signing at 12:45 p.m.

WHERE BODY MEETS SOUL
Destiny Through Praise Dance Ministry, under the leadership of Katherine Blakely, will creatively interpret and express gospel music through movement and dance.
1:30 p.m.

ONTARIO HERITAGE TRUST
An agency of the Government of Ontario

Uncle Tom's Cabin Historic Site is owned and operated by the Ontario Heritage Trust.

A poster advertising the Emancipation Day commemoration in 2007 in Dresden.

Earlier, equity laws had been strongly advocated by people in Dresden. In the 1940s and 1950s, the town was a centre of the Canadian civil-rights movement. Blacks there established an affiliate of the Canadian League for the Advancement of Coloured People based out of London, Ontario. The 1954 Fair Accommodation Practices Act, which declared that "no one can deny to any person or class of persons the accommodations, services, or facilities usually available to members of the public," was tested by local civil rights activists like Hugh Burnette, a second generation African-Canadian,[118] and others who travelled from all over the province to bring attention to anti-Black discrimination.[119]

Over the past four years the versatile programming has included other notable speakers, such as Adrienne Shadd, an historian and descendant of Mary Ann Shadd Cary; Dr. Bryan Walls, great-grandson of the ex-slave John Freeman Walls who settled near Puce, close to Windsor; and historian Afua Cooper. Musical performances, book readings, storytelling, art, re-enactments, and activities for children have also been incorporated. In 2008, about five hundred people attended, many coming from places across Ontario, the United States, and Europe and several hundred participated in the various activities at the Emancipation Day commemoration at Uncle Tom's Cabin on August 1, 2009.

Middlesex County: London

The Wilberforce Settlement developed in the area of the current town of Lucan in Biddulph Township, Middlesex County, in the 1830s as a place where newly arrived immigrants established themselves. In 1832, about twenty-five families lived on the eighty-hectare colony, where they grew wheat and other crops. To ensure the success and survival of settlers, schools and churches were put in place. Two schools, S.S. #18 and Summerville School, were established to educate the children. One of these schools was attended by a small number of White children. BME, Baptist, and AME church congregations were started as soon as people arrived, but initially members met in homes until the church was erected.

These settlers possessed a range of skills and varied backgrounds. Among them were coopers, former War of 1812 soldiers, carpenters, shoemakers, and gunsmiths. Some became entrepreneurs, owning businesses such as sawmills, while others found construction jobs, built plank roads, laid railway tracks, or cleared land. Wilberforce, however, only lasted to the mid-1830s, and settlers dispersed to other parts of the province, including London.

In the early 1830s, there were approximately thirty Blacks in the town of London, and that number had increased to just over five hundred by the 1850s. The majority were refugees from the United States who fled enslavement via the Underground Railroad through Ohio. Many crossed Lake Erie on cargo vessels with the assistance of abolitionist captains. They settled in all-Black sections on Thames Street near Horton and the area bounded by Thames Street on the west, Ridout Street North on the east, York Street on the north, and the train tracks on the south (the present site of Copps Lumber). It received the derogatory label of "Nigger Hollow." Blacks also lived on Grey Street east of Wellington Street, and near the Wellington Street Bridge at Grand Avenue. They worked as waiters, painters, plasterers, and woodcutters for the railway. African Canadians in London also ran businesses like barbershops, cobble shops, grocery and supply stores, and pharmacies.

London became another centre of anti-slavery activity during the 1850s through the activities of African-American fugitives and White abolitionists. In April 1853, a large party of escapees from London and the surrounding vicinity convened in London, where they more than likely would have discussed how to help new arrivals and how to counter the racial discrimination they faced. Elijah Leonard, the mayor of London in 1858, was firmly against the practice of slavery and that year devised a scheme to prevent a young Black boy named Sylvanus Demarest from unknowingly being sold into slavery in the South. While waiting for a train, he asked a Black porter at the Great Western Train Station on York Street (present-day site of the VIA Rail Train Station) to send a telegraph to Chatham to rally a group that would help to free the boy. At the Chatham stop one hundred armed Black men and women of the Chatam Vigilance Committee were waiting and forced the release of Demarest, who would live briefly with the Shadd family in Chatham before moving to Windsor.[120]

There were a number of White anti-slavery activists in London who participated and lent their support to initiatives in the Black community, including Emancipation Day observances. Two such people were Reverend William McClure, minister of the Irish New Connexion Methodist Chapel on Clarence Street, and Reverend William F. Clarke, a Congregationalist minister. McClure's church hosted Samuel Ringgold Ward in 1852 when Ward was on a provincial speaking tour on behalf of the recently formed

Anti-Slavery Society of Canada to agitate public abolitionist feelings. In this meeting they voted to open a branch of the organization in London with McClure, William F. Clarke, and Aby Beckford Jones (brother of pharmacist Alfred Jones) as executive members. Five years later, Clarke accepted a post in Victoria in the colony of Vancouver Island where he continued take a stance against anti-Black racism. In 1858 he was one of a small number of ministers who welcomed the African-American settlers from San Francisco in his church without restrictions despite demands from White churchgoers for a separate seating section for Blacks. He returned to Canada West and settled in Guelph.[121] Both men delivered addresses at the 1852 Emancipation Day commemoration that began with a procession through the main streets led by the Royal Artillery band. The participants marched to the property of J.B. Askin Esquire for lunch and to hear other speakers such as Reverend Mr. Basfield and Reverend Lewis.

Blacks in London faced much of the same racism as Blacks in other parts in Canada West, including segregated education and worship. From as early as the 1840s, African-Canadian children in London were not allowed to attend local common schools, although their parents paid taxes like White residents. People like Alfred Jones, a former slave who became a wealthy pharmacist,[122] led the opposition to segregated schools, declaring that his eight London-born children were British citizens like other White children and therefore entitled to the same rights and privileges. He further stated that if African-Canadian children continued to be mistreated in this manner, they would grow up hating their own country. In local White churches, restricted seating or complete exclusion delivered the message that they were not welcome. The exception was St. Paul's Anglican Church, where Reverend Marmaduke Martin Dillon offered integrated church services and encouraged Black members to participate in all aspects the church had to offer.

To ward off the effects of prejudice, London's African-Canadian community, both adults and children, attended and supported private schools for Blacks operated by White missionaries like Dillon.[123] They also founded their own churches such as the Second Baptist Church[124] started by Reverend Daniel A. Turner in 1847 and the Beth Emanuel BME Church (also called Fugitive Slave Chapel), which was first established in 1848 on River Street then moved to its present-day location on Grey Street in

1856. These churches and other organizations offered refuge and support to fugitive slaves.

Military service was another way for African-Canadian men in London to ensure security and prosperity for themselves, their families, and their community. Shadrach "Shack" Quarles Martin[125] was one of many Black men to settle in London and enlist to fight in the American Civil War. He first came to London in 1854 and stayed for five years before returning to the United States to work for a short period. During this time the Civil War broke out. He was one of the first Black men to sign up for duty in the Union navy. He relocated to London in 1863 where he operated a successful barbershop on King Street and remained very active in the Black community, including assisting with the organization of Emancipation Day commemorations.

As noted, August First observances, which grew dramatically with the influx of escaped slaves, was a significant cultural institution supporting community development and became an important platform in the drive for change and the achievement of complete democratic freedom. The first recorded commemoration in London took place in 1838. The occasion was an opportunity for all present to contemplate the impact of abolition and to discern what freedom and human rights meant to them. Reverend McClure reflected on magnitude and meaning of Emancipation Day in his diary on August 1, 1854:

> This day slavery in all the British Colonies has come to end. Eight hundred thousand have dropped their shackles and gone forth freemen. Thus one of the foulest stains that ever sullied the glory of Britain has come to an end, and the voice of Mercy that has long been crying, "let the oppressed go free," has at length been attended to, and justice has been forced on the bloody cruel slave-holder. Many a dark cloud has burst on England because of the cry of the slave. May her judgment now be averted.[126]

Observances by London's Black community in 1855 included a church service conducted at St. Paul's Church on Richmond Street by Reverend Dillon from England, a missionary to fugitive slaves in London at that time. His message came from John 13:34–36. The first verse read, "A new commandment I give unto you, that ye love one another; as I have loved you, that ye also love one another." Possibly Dillon preached that the fugitives should love their White neighbours who mistreated them while the White residents in London should demonstrate Godly love towards their new African-American neighbours. A parade of six hundred to seven hundred people marching with banners followed. Led by a military band, they proceeded to an afternoon meal attended by the mayor of the city along with many citizens of the city, both Black and White.

During the 1862 celebration in London, a parade from Court House Square on Ridout Street North to St. Paul's Episcopal Church [127] kicked off the day, proceeded by a sermon delivered by Reverend John McLean. One invited speaker outlined the obligations that came with freedom and another speaker urged the crowd to maintain the recognition of August First because of its many benefits to the community, including maintaining historical recollection and community building.

In the 1880s there was an increased involvement of fraternal orders in London's Emancipation Day events. The 1885 gathering of over four hundred people saw the participation of the all-Black bands and lodges such as the Excelsior Band and Peter Ogden Lodge from Toronto, the Union Cornet Band and Mount Brydges Lodge from Hamilton, and the Brantford Independent Band. Local Blacks met incoming visitors at the train station where they began the parade, marching up Richmond Street to the Exhibition Grounds near today's Victoria Park then on to the Crystal Palace, an eight-sided white building on Richmond Street. At the Palace they were treated to a bountiful dinner, fine musical entertainment, and informative speeches. One address was delivered by lodge Elder Masterson, who compelled listeners to unite for the uplifting of the race and to obtain an education. The day ended with a ball at city hall, also on Richmond Street.[128]

American guests came from Cleveland and Detroit, and regional attendees came from surrounding villages and towns such as St. Thomas and Lucan (former Wilberforce settlement) as well as other nearby rural and urban centres like Guelph, Toronto, St. Catharines, Woodstock, and Ingersoll. In 1895, as with the other celebrations of the time, these visitors arrived by steamer, train, and carriage. The street procession, observed by many onlookers, started at Market Square by Talbot and King Streets and continued to Queen's Park (the present-day site of the Western Fair at Dundas and Ontario Streets). The participation of fraternal orders like the Grand United Order of Oddfellows (GUOOF), Knights of Pythias, and the Prince Hall Order of the Eastern Star brought about the annual presence of their lady auxiliaries, especially in the parades. The female societies, like the Daughters of Samaria, sponsored carriages in the cavalcades led by the Detroit City Band. The bands' director was John W. Johnson, a former Londoner. Highlighted speakers were Reverend R.L. Holden of Chatham and Mr. Wind of Toronto. Sporting competitions were hosted at Queen's Park and in the evening a gospel concert was held with performances by several Detroit church choirs. There was a notice placed in the Victoria, British Columbia, *Daily Colonist* on the day of the emancipation anniversary, demonstrative of the national scope and recognition of August First.[129]

Lady lodge auxiliaries had another strong showing in the 1896 street procession. Of the approximately twenty carriages in the parade, about seventeen of them carried Black women, along with two White women. Participating female benevolent societies included the Queen Victoria Benevolent Society (started by Ellen Toyer Abbott in 1840, the mother of Dr. Anderson Ruffin Abbott), Star Calanthe of the Knights of Pythias order, and the Household of Ruth, which belonged to the GUOOF with branches in London, Chatham, Toronto, Windsor, and Hamilton. It was noted that there was a huge turnout of Black women "with and without their escorts," beautifully dressed in gowns and hats. The procession took the familiar procession route from Market Square to Queen's Park with hundreds of spectators looking on. At Queen's Park those assembled listened to stimulating speeches delivered from the bandstand and danced along to the enjoyable music played by the Detroit City Band. To cover operating costs, admission was charged and a fee applied to participation in the sporting events.[130]

The strong presence of women's organizations is indicative of their extensive efforts in the Black community across Canada "to ensure academic, social, and economic endurance."[131] Not only did they provide socializing opportunities in their locales, they initially offered support to incoming fugitives and later to the general community, including such services as health care, shelter, insurance benefits, educational opportunities, literacy training, and programs aimed at empowering African-Canadian youth and adults. They also organized charities for various causes, and were "outlets for community and political activism" that addressed a wide range of issues. Other women's groups, such as the Women of the Eastern Star, offered similar supports in different Ontario towns. Both the male fraternal orders and the female-driven societies enabled Blacks to draw strength from each other and participate in the larger community as well.[132]

Black lodges were very involved in the sixty-third anniversary of the abolition of slavery in London. The August Lodge helped orchestrate the event in partnership with a Mr. Thomas Taylor, the acting chairperson for the day. Shack Martin was one of the committee members. Mayor John William Little, first called upon to give an address, extended a welcome to the visitors and a special greeting to the GUOOF who also held a general meeting that day. A few senior Oddfellow members who were part of the speaking lineup discussed the beginnings of Black fraternal orders. Because of the racism they experienced from the Independent Order of Oddfellows, which refused admission and charter status to Black lodges to even putting the term "White" in its constitution, they started their own organizations in the 1840s. They cited that in 1896 there were over twelve hundred lodges in Canada and the United States with over two hundred thousand memberships. A brief synopsis of their broad-based community work was described; from the assistance to widows, orphans, and the sick to the provision of burial assistance, along with a description of the initiatives undertaken by the women's groups.

One of the last orators of the day, Reverend R.R. Ball from Toronto, took the occasion to focus on the employment discrimination Black men and women in Ontario faced, asserting that they "had not an equal chance with the white men in obtaining work or position."[133] He stated that such events shouldn't focus on politicians and fun pastimes, but instead the primary goal should be to declare appreciation and to nurture patriotism, while at the same time demanding full Canadian citizenship with "Equal rights for all, special privileges for none." The event was capped off with a ball at the Richmond Street city hall, which was decorated with red, blue, and white streamers, the Union Jack, and the American flag. The music was provided by the Detroit Orchestra.

The early 1900s saw changes in the venue and the way Emancipation Day was observed in London. In 1926, the celebrations consisted of a

From the *London Free Press*, August 4, 1896.

THE PROCESSION ON RICHMOND STREET.

Early newspaper coverage of Emancipation Day events occasionally included images. This is a sketch of the Emancipation Day street parade in London, 1896.

picnic held in Springbank Park at Riverside Drive and Hyde Park Road, a site that would become the new location for the next sixty years. During the Depression era, the Canadian League for the Advancement of Colored People (CAACP) hosted the annual outing at Springbank Park.[134] As Blacks in London continued to experience racial discrimination in subtle and sometimes even blatant forms, James Jenkins spearheaded the development of this organization to bring attention to the inequality faced by Blacks in areas such as employment, education, and housing. Celebrations marking the passage of the Emancipation Act in 1833 remained important because they signified the fight for freedom and justice yet to be won. *The Dawn of Tomorrow*, the newspaper founded by James Jenkins, posted notices and provided coverage of August First events.[135]

The organizing of Emancipation Day in London was largely a family affair and remained thus as part of the approach to identifying the needs of the community. Christine Howson, the widow of James Jenkins, was part of a group that established the Community Family Club in 1948 and took over the running of the annual event as a component of its mandate. Like the now defunct CAACP, the Community Family Club targeted discrimination against Blacks in employment and housing as well as offering numerous programs designed to strengthen the community.[136] On Monday, August 2,

Courtesy of the London Free Press Collection of Photographic Negatives, The University of Western Ontario Archives, August 5, 1968.

Family-oriented August First picnics have been held at Springbank Park in London since 1926. This photograph was taken at the Emancipation day observance on August 5, 1968.

1948, a union picnic was held at Springbank Park. The Community Family Club hosted it and included activities such as ball games, races, and dancing.

The 1949 August First commemoration at Springbank Park demonstrated the multigenerational aspect of the occasion. The descendants of self-emancipated slaves who had settled in London were now the community elders, retelling the history of their ancestors to the children in attendance. Two such men were John Malot of Brantford and Roy Anderson of London. Both felt it was very important to pass down the experiences of some of Ontario's early Black pioneers, especially the personal accounts of their grandparents who escaped to Canada. Over four hundred people were in attendance at the park that day, including Mayor Ray A. Dennis and a former mayor of the city.[137]

Paul "Dad" Lewis[138] had been part of Emancipation Day celebrations in London for fifty-four years, serving in various capacities, including as a member of the executive committee, a participant, and an observer. He too said that it was about the children — teaching them about their past and providing a place to have fun.

After one hundred years, Emancipation Day commemorations across Ontario reflected the mixed marriages between Blacks and Whites. The line of racial definition was blurring, a reality for the descendants of the province's first Black settlers. The 1968 event was an example of a different interracial makeup of the annual holiday across the province. Once again the occasion became a demonstration of Black identity in Canada, but now of a racially blended identity. This reality contributed to the move away from the initial focus of the day as a celebration of freedom to become a more leisurely family event. In the 1960s and 1970s the Community Family Club still organized August First, but now under the leadership of Evelyn Johnson, daughter of Christine Howson who had died earlier that year. Evelyn stayed at the helm for fourteen years and the event remained at Springbank Park, where it was mainly a social affair instead of the acknowledgement of the attainment of freedom by enslaved Africans throughout British territories: "Nobody talks about emancipation and nobody knows when it happened."[139] Celebratory picnics lasted into the 1980s and the Community Family Club organized Emancipation Day until Mrs. Johnson's death in 1982 when her son William Turner took over.[140]

Oxford County: Norwich[141]

Waves of African-American migration in the 1830s, 1850s, and after the Civil War brought hundreds of settlers to various parts of Oxford County, just north of Lake Erie. Free Blacks from the northern United States like Ohio and New York were also part of the incoming colonists. They settled in or around places like Otterville, Norwich, Woodstock, Blenheim, Dereham, Summerville, and Ingersoll, all located in Norfolk and Oxford counties to the east of London and north of Lake Erie. Some escapees were driven inland by stagecoach from Lake Erie ports such as Port Burwell by local supporters. One such man was Harvey C. Jackson who drove and advised John Brown when he came to Ingersoll in April 1858 to solicit funds and enlist recruits for his abolition cause.

When the first influx of Blacks arrived, Quakers helped the fugitives to settle as did church missionaries such as Reverend William Clarke who worked with the newcomers in Norwich before going to London.

Clarke ministered to them and taught children in a small school there until 1848. A man named Peter Van Patter, a fellow runaway, provided temporary shelter for fugitives at his place of employment. He managed the Daly House Stables, which was owned by Absalom Daly. Other White sympathizers included Max and Leonard Bixel, both brewers; Thomas Brown, a tannery owner who hired Blacks; and Mr. Edwin Doty, the owner and operator of a stagecoach company at the corner of King and Thames Streets in Norwich.

In 1851, one hundred Blacks were recorded in the Township of Norwich census and in 1861, 165 were counted mainly in South Norwich. Over three hundred lived in Oxford County at around the same time. People from other parts of the province moved to this area, too, such as Susan LeBurtis from Collingwood, who relocated to Woodstock in 1895 with her husband after they married. These Black pioneers worked tirelessly under difficult conditions to make a good life for themselves and were determined to succeed. In spite of the hardships of opening up a frontier, Blacks in the hamlets and towns of this region of Upper Canada (Ontario) celebrated their self-emancipation from slavery and freedom from the racially restrictive Ohio Black Codes by participating in Emancipation Day commemorations.

In her study of the Black history of the surrounding vicinity, Joyce Pettigrew notes there were no local papers before the 1860s to provide information from the popular media of that time into the experiences of the residents of African descent. However, the few clippings that have been found give a glimpse into the August First observances of the Norfolk area and some insight into their social lives.

It can be assumed that regular celebratory events happened prior to the 1890s because the conditions were the same as in other parts of the province and the country that did observe Emancipation Day. Pettigrew describes three instances of African-Canadians celebrating the event. In 1897, Blacks from Woodstock travelled to Brantford to participate in commemorations there after the local gathering scheduled to take place at the Athletic Park did not happen. Apparently, in June a man from Toledo, Ohio, named Professor White claimed he was dispatched by the Independent Order of Cooks of Cleveland, Ohio, to select an ideal location in central Ontario and to coordinate a celebration. He chose Woodstock over Berlin (Kitchener).

An advertisement for Emancipation Day in Woodstock, printed in the *Daily Sentinel Review*, July 22, 1898.

But when the first three days of August passed and no assembly was called, no American guests arrived, and White did not show up, eager celebrants decided to take the train to Brantford. The true motives of White are not known, but his actions were not totally inconceivable. It was general knowledge there were a fair number of immigrants from Ohio living in the Norwich area, so some cross-border connection was plausible. This would explain why the local committee followed through on arrangements such as booking Athletic Park.

Woodstock hosted their own observance in 1898. An all-Black band from Dresden and the 37th Battalion Indian band from Brantford led the procession through Woodstock's streets. Participants marched to Athletic Park and as the day progressed more people trickled onto the grounds. The evening began with a theatrical performance of the tragedy, "The Lime Kiln Club." It was followed by a cakewalk (a popular African-American dance[142]) at the Opera House and a dance at a hall in MacIntyre's Block. The organizers, managed by a Professor Campbell, had hoped to raise a substantial amount of money to cover the operating expenses and to donate to the less fortunate. However, questionable weather in the morning and a modest turn out of just over one hundred people hampered the fundraising efforts.

An Emancipation Day observance to recognize the seventy-fourth anniversary of the passage of the legislation that abolished slavery took place in Ingersoll. Pettigrew also refers to a recollection by James Sinclair, a local historian:

> ... unusual services were held, and the name of Wilberforce and his influence on behalf of their race was made the theme of their oration. On one occasion a large gathering held a monster picnic in the grove behind the present Dufferin Street, then a suitable woods. The feature of the occasion was an elaborate barbecue when an ox was rotated whole, together with other animals. In the evening, a grand ball was held in the old Jarvis Hall [where Campbell Block now stands] for which elaborated preparations were made.[143]

He then describes the women wearing "fine hooped skirts" and the men dressed formally in "white vests, full dress coat, peg-top trousers, and white neck-tie with elaborate stand-up collars."[144]

The general population, including the number of people of African descent, began to decrease by the 1880s because by then the forests had been depleted, which in turn affected the main local industries and their ability to sustain themselves. Individuals who moved to larger, thriving centres likely took part in Emancipation Day celebrations in those places.

4

Central Ontario

Black men and Black men alone, hold the key to the gateway leading to their freedom.

— Marcus Garvey, *The Philosophy and Opinions of Marcus Garvey*, 1923.

Brantford

Brant's Ford, now Brantford, Ontario, was home to a diverse group of Blacks since the late eighteenth century. They included slaves such as Sophia Pooley[1] and at least two other male African captives of the over thirty mixed slaves owned by the Mohawk leader Joseph Brant (Thayendinaga) in the 1790s and the two Black slaves owned by John Thomas, a local merchant, as late as 1809, some fifteen years after the passage of lieutenant-governor John Graves Simcoe's Act to Limit Slavery.

A number of fugitive Blacks were seen in Brantford in the 1830s, some having arrived as hidden cargo in boats, just like their counterparts in Oakville and Collingwood. In 1830, a Black landowner named John Boylston was listed as a blacksmith. Three more African families bought land in 1832: Adam Akin, a labourer who lived on Darling Street; James Anderson, also a blacksmith, who bought property on Dalhousie Street; and Samuel Wright, a barber residing on Colborne Street. By 1846 fifteen

Black families had settled in or near Brantford. The town was a growing milling centre, providing adequate employment opportunities.

The families quickly established institutions to meet the needs of the growing community and to provide fellowship and support. The AME church opened in the mid-1830s and the BME Church, now called the Samuel R. Memorial Church, was formed first on Dalhousie Street then moved to Murray Street. Private schools were also established, as local common schools did not admit African-Canadian students. One Black school, opened in 1837, was said to have higher educational standards than the all-White school, which enticed some White parents to register their children there.[2] However, not only were the residents of African descent not welcome in the common schools, it was also made known that they were not wanted in the town. Some White settlers petitioned the provincial government to have Blacks relocated north to Queen's Bush, where a sizeable number of Blacks were clearing land for settlement.

As noted earlier, Reverend Josephus O'Banyoun, who was born and raised in Brantford, mentioned some of the racism

Reverend Josephus O'Banyoun was very active in Black communities across Ontario. His calling as a church minister and role as musical director for the O'Banyoun Jubilee Singers caused him to live in numerous centres in the province and to travel extensively around Ontario, in Canada, and internationally. His recurring participation in Emancipation Day commemorations in Ontario shows his involvement in addressing issues of concern to African-Canadians.

he experienced in a speech delivered at Emancipation Day in Chatham in 1891. He described how he was ostracized at school in Brantford and harassed because of his race. George Sunter, another Black Brantford resident, wrote a letter to the *Brantford Expositor* to express his disdain for the prejudiced sentiments towards fugitives displayed by some Whites in the town and in the province.[3]

Brantford's Black community gained public attention with the John Anderson case. A runaway accused of killing his master as he made his escape from slavery in Maryland initially made his way to Toronto and then to the Brantford area. He was the subject of a famous extradition case tried at Osgoode Hall in 1860. Anderson was freed after an appeal.[4] This precedent-setting case is an example of how extradition to the United States and Southern slavery was challenged in Canadian courts.

Although Brantford's Black population had decreased by 1860, there was still a sufficient number to publicly recognize Emancipation Day each year, with the event always receiving support from African Canadians from surrounding centres. The earliest known recorded account reported that a crowd gathered for a picnic on August 1, 1856, at a grove on the site of the Mohawk Institute on the Six Nations Reserve (the present-day location of the Woodland Cultural Centre). Both Blacks and Whites attended the evening reception that followed. Peter O'Banyoun,[5] the father of Josephus O'Banyoun, presided over the program of addresses that praised the British Crown and condemned slavery.[6]

Likewise, people from Brantford went to Emancipation Day celebrations in other nearby towns, as was the case in 1859 when a contingent travelled to Hamilton for the elaborate jubilee at the Auchmar Estates in recognition of the twenty-fifth anniversary of the passage of the British Emancipation Act. Again, in 1886, a group of about fifty people went from Brantford by train to attend the commemoration in Hamilton. The men, some of them members of the Coloured Citizen's band dressed in "black frock coats, light pants, white vests, and black plug hats,"[7] and marched together to the celebration site to participate in games, play baseball, and have dinner.

Heather Ibbotson, local historian and journalist for the *Brantford Expositor*, stated that Emancipation Day "events were held in different locations and boasted a variety of entertainment over the years."[8] When some locals stayed in town in 1859 and observed the freedom holiday, they enjoyed a picnic and speeches at Strawberry Hill in west Brantford. An evening ball took place at the town hall at Market and Colborne Streets. In 1865, visitors from Simcoe were part of the celebration that consisted of a dinner at the town hall and a soiree in the evening. A dance was held at the Day Hotel on Vinegar Hill, now Clarence Street on the eastern edge of Brantford, for the 1871 observance. On August 1, 1875, the festivities commenced with a procession through the main streets of the town proceeded by a picnic at the Fair Grounds, now Cockshutt Park at Ballantyne and Sherwood drives. Entertainment at the yearly events included music provided by local residents of the Coloured Citizen's Band, formed in 1880, and the O'Banyoun Jubilee Singer from the BME church. This popular choral group performed at many of the annual events including those in other towns like Amherstburg, Hamilton, and Guelph. Members included J. Lucas,[9] Thomas Snowden (no relation to Charles Snowden), Sarah Galley, and Beluah Curtis. In 1875, The Grand River Band, composed of local Native men, entertained

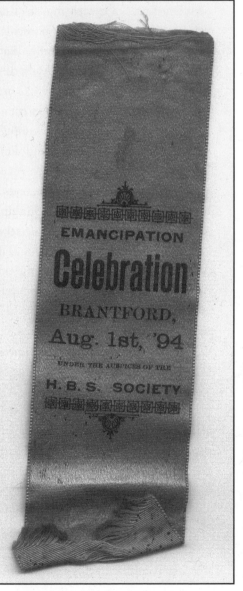

A souvenir ribbon from the Emancipation Day celebration held in Brantford in 1894, from the private papers and personal belongings of Charles W.F. Snowden (1868–1964) of Brantford, Ontario, inherited by his daughter Julia L. Snowden.

the gatherers. Visiting bands from other major centres like Buffalo and Toronto also played at these events. Other forms of amusement included canoe rides, baseball games, and a myriad of contests.[10]

Emancipation Day in Brantford continued into the early twentieth century. By this time the event was organized and attended by many first- and second-generation African Canadians from the region. In 1894, a number of Woodstock's Black citizens came to Brantford to celebrate. One of them, Solomon Lucas, a church minister and a member of the large Lucas clan living in Brantford, came to participate in the festivities and would have taken this time to visit his family. That same year, Jonathan "John" Tanner and his dance partner Miss Marshall won the cakewalk contest. Tanner was one of the founders of the Coloured Citizen's Band. That year people joined together for an afternoon parade from Market Square through the core of the town to the Agriculture Park (present-day Cockshutt Park) to participate in sports, games, and dancing. The evening program moved to Wycliffe Hall located on Colborne Street by the Market Square for a musical concert with performances by the Reed Coloured Band from Buffalo, musical solos, drama, and drum and baton skill demonstrations. Afterwards, the several hundred celebrants assembled at Brantford's town hall for the cakewalk followed by a dance, musical performances, and a night of dancing. Whites continued to recognize the end of slavery with their Black neighbours. Some who were present that day — Ab Grant, Mr. Stoleman, William G. Kilmaster, and Alderman Charles Whitney — were nominated by the crowd to judge the cakewalk.[11]

In 1903, an estimated one thousand guests from Toronto, Hamilton, Woodstock, Guelph, and other surrounding towns flocked to Brantford for Emancipation Day. After a street procession, all parties descended on Mohawk Park located on Lynwood by Mohawk Lake, where they spent the afternoon engaged in sport activities, boating on the lake, picnicking, and dancing in the pavilion. A baseball game was played between the Brantford team and a visitor's team with players from Toronto and Hamilton. A lively ball took place that evening at the Drill Hall at Alexandra Park on Colborne Street with a cakewalk and character dances featuring costumes that "added greatly to the entire effect."[12]

The organizing committee of the 1912 anniversary of the Emancipation Act was comprised of John McCurtis, Jasper Smith, Jesse Brown, Jerry

Okley, and Charles Snowden,[13] most of whom were descendants of fugitives that had settled in Brantford. Their plans accommodated the over seven hundred guests at Agriculture Park and included the usual activities. That year the baseball game was played between African-Canadian professional teams from Brantford and London,[14] which the London team won. Music for the event was provided by the 37th Haldimand Rifles Band, primarily made up of Six Nations volunteer militiamen. The night closed out with an evening concert at the Armouries on Brant Avenue, followed by a dance. This occasion appears to be one of the last Emancipation Day commemorations in Brantford, where, in spite of social inequalities, an interracial group with citizens of African, European, and Native background were able to come together to celebrate the idea of freedom.[15]

Hamilton

Hamilton's extensive Black history and sizeable Black population made it another key location for Emancipation Day commemorations. Black settlement in this large urban centre began with the slaves of Loyalists, followed by men of African descent who had fought for the British during the American Revolution and received land grants in British North America as compensation. From the 1820s through to the 1850s, dozens of African-American fugitives immigrated to Hamilton using the Underground Railroad. By 1861 there were 476 persons listed as "Coloured" or "Mulatto" in the Hamilton census.[16] There were two main areas of Black settlement in Hamilton — "Little Africa" on Hamilton Mountain bordered by Upper Wentworth Street, Concession Street, Sherman Avenue, and Fennell Avenue, and the other along Main Street from Dundurn Castle to Wentworth Street North on the north side.

Residents of these areas were employed as cabmen, cooks, waiters, teachers, washerwomen, domestic servants, and teachers. Others were flourishing business owners of inns, grocery stores, tobacco shops, restaurants, fruit stands, barbershops, and even an ice company. Many of these new colonists enrolled in local Black military units to defend provincial and British interests during the Mackenzie Rebellion. They volunteered their service in the coloured company of the Fifth Gore Militia to ensure the security of their new lives on free soil. Black men from Hamilton, like former slave Nelson Steven[17], also contributed to the fight to abolish slavery in the United States by going south to fight for the Union Army during the American Civil War.

Although Hamilton's Black men demonstrated their loyalty to the British Crown and proved themselves to be hard-working, industrious citizens, they and their families experienced racial discrimination in various spheres of public life. As in many other locations, African-Canadian children either could not attend the same common schools as White children or were limited to restricted seating in schools in Hamilton. Black parents, many of them fugitives, petitioned Governor General Lord Elgin for admission to segregated public schools. Although officially they were integrated in the 1840s, Blacks developed their own separate schools, which were also attended by adults who had been denied an education as enslaved children. Schools like the Christian school on Concession Street in "Little Africa" sprang up because of continued prejudice throughout the 1850s. The level of persistent discrimination caused the Honourable Isaac Buchanan, MPP for Canada West and champion of the Black community, to express his views on the matter: "I think we see the effects of slavery here very plainly. The children of the colored people go to the public schools but a great many of the white parents object to it, though their children do not that I know of."[18]

Black settlers in Hamilton also engaged in other anti-racism struggles. The Hamilton Black Abolitionist Society advocated for the end of African-American slavery and tackled particularly blatant forms of racial discrimination in the village of Hamilton, such as the time when Blacks were excluded from marching in "the parade that marked the laying of the cornerstone for the Crystal Palace."[19] Their protest, which also gained support from White residents, was victorious and citizens of African-Canadian ancestry participated in another major civic parade the following year. When Jesse Happy, a fugitive from Kentucky, escaped to Hamilton in 1837, a vocal Black community leader Paola Brown, the city bellman and town crier, successfully organized citizens to protest his arrest and imprisonment.[20] Brown was also selected to speak on behalf of the Black community against segregated schools.[21]

In an effort to meet the social, economic, and political needs of the community and to create a united front against anti-Black prejudice, African Canadians formed solid cultural institutions including voluntary associations, schools, and churches. An African Methodist Episcopal Church, St. Paul's, was established in 1835 on Cathart Street, then moved to Rebecca Street in 1856. The Coloured Baptist Church was organized in 1847 on McNab Street, and a British Methodist Episcopal Church was formed in the 1850s. Members of these sizeable congregations and other African-Canadian residents participated in the annual tradition of celebrating Emancipation Day, an event that also served their social and community development purposes. These August First observances extended their social network with support coming from African Canadians of the surrounding vicinity including Ancaster, Otterville, Toronto, Niagara, and Brantford.

In 1846, a musical band led an Emancipation Day parade through the main streets of Hamilton to the Anglican Christ's Church Cathedral where Reverend Mr. John Gamble Geddes, a supporter of Hamilton's Blacks, delivered a sermon, followed by dinner at city hall. The 1853 commemoration began with a street procession of about one thousand people where flags and emblems of various fraternal orders were displayed by marchers dressed in different uniforms. Gatherers sat together to share in a communal dinner at the Mechanics' Institute Hall and to hear speeches. A party in the evening concluded the day.

In 1857, a marshal led the August First parade on horseback. Participants marched down to the wharf to welcome visitors from Toronto, who upon their arrival "gave three cheers for the Queen, three cheers for the captain and officers of the boat, and three cheers for British emancipation."[22] The entire party continued on to Christ's Church for a service given by Reverend Geddes who preached about the similarities between the jubilation of the Jews when they were set free from Egypt and the day's affair, which celebrated the release of people of African descent from bondage. The celebrants then joined together at the Mechanics' Hall for a meal and for speeches that touched on the grace of freedom, the rights they now held like other human beings, and their appreciation to Britain for liberating African slaves in their territories.

For a number of years during the 1850s, the MPP for Canada West, the Honourable Isaac Buchanan, lent the grounds of his Clairmont Park estate as a host site for the Emancipation Day celebrations. Buchanan was a

Scottish immigrant and successful businessman who gave of his money and time in support of various local causes, including initiatives that promoted rights and opportunities for Hamilton's Black constituents. Buchanan and his family were described as, "big hearted folk [who] honoured the liberties of their fellowmen whether they were black or white."[23] Clairmont Park was an eighty-six acre (thirty-five hectare) estate that included a large, beautiful house named "Auchmar." It was situated on Hamilton Mountain, the part of the Niagara Escarpment that that surrounds the city of Hamilton to the south and is locally referred to as the "Mountain."

On one such occasion on August 2, 1859, over five hundred guests from the general public arrived at Auchmar at 1:30 p.m. after participating in a parade through the main streets and listening to Reverend Geddes's sermon at the Christ's Church Cathedral. The well-dressed guests, Black and White, were seated at tables covered by white linen and placed under the shade of apple trees. The sumptuous dinner, compliments of Mr. Buchanan, was comprised of, "roast beef, fowls, pies, pastry, oranges, fruits, nuts, and barrels of lemonade."[24] Afterwards, Buchanan addressed his company on the front lawn speaking about his hope for the extension and influence of British emancipation on the world. Other White community leaders such as John Scoble from Dawn addressed the visitors. Speakers of African descent included a Mr. Atkinson who articulated the history and atrocities of enslavement.

The 1864 celebrations began on McNab Street with a street procession formed by sixty men. They were led by the Storror's Brass Band and marched along Main Street, down Wellington, then onto St. Thomas Church where Reverend Charles Henry Drinkwater delivered a sermon. He preached from Galatians 5:1, the verse that says, "Stand fast therefore in the liberty wherewith Christ hath made us free, and be hot entangled again with the yoke of bondage." The theme of his message was that redemption is at the centre of deliverance because "Christ has made us free." He then went on to discuss the literal and figurative meanings of this Biblical text, the former referring to spiritual slavery through the captivity of sin. The latter and secondary meaning of this scripture, which was most relevant to the day, pertained to the yoke of slavery and the sufferings, which the enslaved had to endure. When they were deprived of all the rights of humanity, their deliverance came from the promised saviour who freed them from the

A SHORT ACCOUNT

OF THE MANNER IN WHICH

EMANCIPATION DAY,

FIRST OF AUGUST. 1864,

WAS SPENT IN THE

CITY OF HAMILTON,

TOGETHER WITH

THE SERMON

WHICH WAS PREACHED BEFORE THE MEMBERS OF THE

BROTHERLY UNION SOCIETY,

IN THE

CHURCH OF ST. THOMAS. HAMILTON,

BY THE REV. C. H. DRINKWATER, B. A., RECTOR.

PSALMS 68, 31.—" Ethiopia shall soon stretch out her hands unto God."

HAMILTON. C. W.

PRINTED AND PUBLISHED BY A. LAWSON & CO., AND TO BE HAD AT THE PRINCIPAL BOOKSTORES IN THE CITY AND PROVINCE.

Price—Five cents.

Early Emancipation Day commemorations had strong religious characteristics. The day began with church services giving thanks for the blessings of liberation. This is the cover of the published sermon delivered by Reverend Charles H. Drinkwater in 1864.

bondage of corruption and admitted them into the glorious liberty of the children of God. Such sermons were deeply meaningful to their African-Canadian audience as they tapped into and reinforced the religious beliefs held by Blacks, and solidified the conviction that they were chosen by God and emphasized the role God played in the freeing of Black slaves.

After that, the reverend highlighted some of the benefits of emancipation such as Black men in Jamaica and other islands becoming planters and owning land, and pointed out that Africans were living productive, independent lives all across British possessions. Drinkwater then spoke on the pending end of slavery in the United States stating that "man shall enslave his brother no longer" and "Christ is the Great Emancipator." He criticized people, including ministries, who wrongly used the word of God to justify slavery, and compared the deliverance from African physical slavery to deliverance from sin with Jesus' crucifixion. In closing, his advice was not to be a slave to sin, to do well, to silence ignorant critiques of emancipation, and to "First, be Christians, educate yourselves and your children succour and exhort the weaker brethren."[25] After the service the parade re-formed and advanced to the decorated Albion Hall in Miller's Block on McNab Street for a savoury dinner.

Approximately three hundred people, some from Toronto and London, assembled to partake in the meal and to listen to more speeches. Dr. Jenkins was the chair for the evening and he offered several toasts, first a salute to Queen Victoria, then a cheer for John Bull, and more. He encouraged Blacks to make use of the time to influence public opinion and to convince the world they were ready to fight and die for freedom. Reverend Thomas Kinnaird from Toronto gave the next address. He toasted Lord Lyons, the mayor of Hamilton, and Isaac Buchanan. Alexander Somerville, a White Hamilton resident and founder of the *Canadian Illustrated News*, spoke next providing a brief history of abolition and emancipation. A gala followed in the same building at which the Brotherly Union Society[26] was presented with a banner from the Black ladies of Hamilton as a token of appreciation for its service to the community. Several other lecturers spoke and, when that segment of the night concluded and the church ministers had left the venue, the dancing began until the early morning.

One month after the Dominion of Canada was formed with the union of Canada West, Canada East, Nova Scotia, and New Brunswick, the thirty-ninth anniversary of Emancipation Day was commemorated at the St. Paul's AME Church on Rebecca Street, just east of John Street North (now Stewart Memorial Church). An evening meeting, chaired by the minister Pastor S.C. Chambers, opened with a prayer and was followed by a night of thought-provoking speeches and discussions about the relevance of the day's observation. Reverend Jones felt that the first of August should not be celebrated with grand public affairs like the parades and other forms of entertainment, but rather by quiet social meetings. Jones believed that other issues were of greater concern to the community such as the establishment and support of community institutions, the promotion of morals and values, and encouragement of independence, all of which should take precedence over partying.

Reverend Abes disagreed with Jones for the reason that Britain's efforts and God's intervention needed to be recognized. He also expressed his appreciation of the Union Jack and the Stars and Stripes together, a display that symbolized a new, meaningful partnership between two powerful nations. Complete emancipation in North America had been achieved with the abolition of slavery in the United States and Canada was a new country on the world stage, poised to experience growth and change. Perhaps Mr. Jones thought that the province's African-Canadian community should focus on the future and keep their development in line with the forging of a new nation.

The annual recognition of freedom from slavery also provided the opportunity to witness the accomplishments achieved just one generation after abolition and in spite of racial barriers. At the 1878 August First celebration in Hamilton, Reverend O'Banyoun spoke of how honoured he was to be in the company of a Black lawyer, Mr. Orra L.C. Hughes from Harrisburg, Pennsylvania. Another example of Black success was the 1884 main speaker, E.H. Morris, the former president of the Chicago Bar Association and member of the Prince Hall Grand Lodge of Chicago. At events across the province and the country audiences sometimes also received reports on how well some Blacks in the West Indies were doing.

In 1878, about eighteen hundred delegates from Toronto, Brantford, St. Catharines, Bronte, Oakville, and other districts joined Reverend O'Banyoun[27] for a parade that marched up James and King Streets. They walked to the Crystal Palace grounds on King Street (present site of Victoria Park) for refreshments and speeches. Orators included the reverend himself; Orra Hughes, the principal speaker; A. Johnston of Nova Scotia; Mr. Collins from Drummondville; and Reverend William Butler[28] from Bronte, now a village in west Oakville. Hughes delivered a lengthy, eloquent speech that embodied the common theme, likening the slave history of Africans to the Israelites in Egypt and their deliverance from bondage, which "He regarded as the keystone to the achievement of the grand strides made in the direction of liberty of all kinds ever since," and also offered three toasts "one for humanity, one for temperance, and one for education."[29]

Education was another component of Hughes' address. He stated that any man who had an impact on the world acquired knowledge by some means and that education would be an important tool for Blacks in dispelling myths of African inferiority, while reclaiming their position as disciplined learners. He went on to provide the examples of the teachings Pythagoras received from an African, the advanced development of the Egyptians, along with modern-day examples of the success of peoples of African descent. Attendees were then treated to some entertainment, and the annual evening ball was held at Pronguey's Hall on James Street.

This commemoration also illustrated the divergent interests developing between the older and younger parties at these festivities. While the adults were keen on the educational aspect of the gathering, many of the youth did not listen to the speeches. In fact, they "frequently interrupted … talking very loud in the galleries and alongside the platform, so much so that the chairman was constrained to interfere and call for order three or four times."[30] Youth attendance was decreasing and in 1884 the guest speaker said, "There was something he wanted to say particularly to the young people, and he was sorry there were not more of them present to hear him."[31]

The Mount Brydges Lodge No. 1865 of Hamilton hosted the fifty-first anniversary of the abolition of slavery in 1884. Member Masons dressed in the regalia of their fraternal order accompanied fellow Masons from Toronto, Amherstburg, London, Chatham, Niagara Falls, St. Catharines, Guelph, Berlin (Kitchener), and Dresden lodges to local hotels and to their lodge hall. Guests from Boston, Massachusetts, Chicago, Illinois, and Rochester and Buffalo, New York, were also present. The street procession, led by a marshal on horseback, began at the Gore (the Town Square) and one thousand participants paraded down the principal streets to Crystal Palace for a luncheon and speeches. George Morton[32] presided over the speeches including the guest speaker of the day, E.H. Morris of Chicago. Alderman George Elias Tuckett and Mayor John James Mason both gave addresses.

The special mention of the day was the inclusion of the Hamilton and Toronto branches of the Household of Ruth, "which is composed of the wives and daughters of Oddfellows, who followed in carriages, and looked gorgeous in their regalia of gold braid and black velvet, with tiaras and crowns of glittering tinsel."[33] The group "attracted a great deal of attention" and their drill exhibition, with assistance by the Mount Brydges Lodge, was the highlight of the evening: "The uniformed ones were put through a number of difficult and intricate evolutions."[34]

While celebrations carried on throughout the 1890s, by then the attendance of Emancipation Day commemorations started to decline. The way in which the occasion was recognized was evolving. In 1902, a huge crowd of at least one thousand from across southwestern Ontario was expected, but disappointingly, the turnout was less than two hundred. One correspondent observed: "The days of the big demonstration on Emancipation day have evidently departed."[35] Consequently, many of the day's events were cancelled including the cakewalk, the games, contests, and concerts. Instead of large public demonstrations, smaller events were organized such as the picnic held in 1890 under the auspices of St. Paul's AME Church. About three hundred children and adults took a boat over to Bayview Park and in the evening the gatherers enjoyed a program by the children at the church, followed by refreshments.[36] In 1893, a modest group comprised of people from Hamilton, Bronte, Oakville, Brantford, Guelph, Buffalo, and other centres paraded through some of the main streets of the city led by a mounted marshal and the Oshweken Indian Cornet Band. They then assembled at Dundurn Park on York Boulevard for games, a musical performance by Josephus O'Banyoun's Canadian Jubilee Singers, and a dress parade at the palace rink. "The attendance was not so large as was expected."[37]

The seventy-third anniversary of Emancipation Day was celebrated with a presentation of a cantata, a type of musical play, at Treble's Hall on John Street North, just north of King Street East, sponsored by St. Paul's AME Church. The production of "Jephtha and His Daughter" was managed by F.R. Overstreet of Philadelphia, and was enjoyed by visitors from Buffalo, Oakville, and Toronto.[38]

August 1, 1909, passed without much fanfare, likely only some small-scale meetings at local Black churches or in private homes, but no public events. By this time very few former slaves were alive in Hamilton, a reality that was depreciating the meaning and importance of the freedom festival. Other large cities and smaller towns that once hosted elaborate Emancipation Day observances were experiencing a similar decline.[39]

In the new millennium, the uncovering of some of Ontario's deep, rich African-Canadian history in places like the Dundas Valley is leading to the restoration of August First as a day of commemoration of the end of slavery. Emancipation Day was first recognized at the Griffin House in Ancaster in 2002 after the history of the property, purchased by the Hamilton Conservation Authority, was unearthed. Just ten kilometres outside of Hamilton, Griffin House, was the original home and eighteen-hectare property of Enerals Griffin,[40] a fugitive slave who arrived in Ancaster in 1830. Anne Jarvis, who initiated the observances, has organized programs that have included the reading of an account from the *Hamilton Spectator* of Emancipation Day celebrations at Auchmar Estates and inviting speakers such as locals who were interested in Black history to speak on the occasion as well as members of the Central Ontario Network for Black History.

Oakville

Oakville received a sizeable number of fugitive settlers who entered Canada on the Underground Railroad with the assistance of White and Black residents of Oakville who engaged in anti-slavery activity. Captain Robert Wilson was a White abolitionist who transported escaping slaves to freedom by stowing them away in grain shipments aboard his fleet of small vessels or his main ship from American ports in New York. Two other captains, George Hardy Morden and James Fitzgerald, were also known to have carried refugees across Lake Ontario and Lake Erie. Former slave James Wesley Hill became an agent on the Underground Railroad once he secured his own freedom in Upper Canada in the late 1840s. He had rescued so many fugitives over several trips back to the United States and bringing them to safety in Canada that he earned the name "Canada Jim." Hill would then employ the refugees on his strawberry farm.[41] Some moved on to other Black settlements in the province, while others took up permanent residence in Oakville finding work as domestics, dockside workers, and farmers. One gentleman, John Cosley, published a local newspaper called *The Bee*.

In 1891, these refugee settlers and free Blacks also established an AME church with William Butler as the minister. It is now known as the Turner AME Church, named after Bishop Henry Turner, a church minister and community activist. President Abraham Lincoln designated him chaplain to the United Stated Armed Forces, the first African American to achieve this position. The church congregation included residents from Oakville and Bronte, with a mix of AME and BME followers. The religious institution also served as a community centre. Many social activities such as musical concerts, parties, banquets, and other celebrations took place there or were organized by the congregation.[42]

Celebrating citizenship as a British subject and the opportunity for an improved quality of life motivated African Canadians in Oakville to observe Emancipation Day. Beginning in the 1850s with the influx of self-emancipated African-American slaves, regular celebratory picnics were held in George's Square, a park located at Trafalgar Road and Sumner Avenue. Local African Canadians and many who previously lived there returned to commemorate the end of slavery. It was an annual tradition to march about one kilometre northwest of George's Square in a street procession up to "Mariner's Home," the house of Captain Wilson, to pay homage to the man who had helped them or their ancestors. August First commemorations gradually declined by the early twentieth century, which was reflective of the decreasing Black population. "As the years passed, the number of visitors dwindled until one year only one man climbed up the steps to Captain Wilson's door. The following year none came."[43]

However, events did take place intermittently as noted in a 1929 newspaper article that stated: "For the first time in many years, Emancipation Day was celebrated by the colored race here."[44] The assembly was organized by the AME church who hosted a garden party at Victoria Park. Guests came from Toronto, London, Hamilton, and St. Catharines to mark the occasion. The activities included a girl's softball game, speeches, and musical performances by the Oakville Male Quartet, the town band, and duets by Al and Bob Harvey of Toronto. Mayor Thomas Blakelock, chairperson of the day, gave opening remarks before turning the podium over to the keynote speaker, Bertrand Joseph Spencer Pitt, the attorney from Toronto who at that time spearheaded the "Big Picnic" in St. Catharines. Pitts's address focused on Britain's decision to make slavery illegal and congratulated the country for its efforts in abolition.[45]

Alvin Duncan, a descendant of fugitive slaves and a Second World War Royal Canadian Air Force veteran, recalls "marking Emancipation Day in August with a picnic in George Street Park," when he was young. [46] Today, the tradition has been revived by the Canadian Caribbean Association of Halton (CCAH) in partnership with the Oakville Museum at Erchless Estate. Since 2007 people gather at St. George's Square for a family-oriented picnic, while recreating history in celebrating the historic role Oakville played in securing the freedom of many people.

Toronto

The diverse population of early Toronto (called York until 1834) consisted of Africans of varying backgrounds. Some of the city's first Black inhabitants were enslaved Africans, the chattel property of British colonists and Loyalists settlers. Slave owners included Peter Russell, the administrator of Upper Canada, and William Jarvis, the first sheriff of York. There were about four hundred people of African descent living in Toronto. As a bustling city centre and a terminus of the Underground Railroad during the middle of the nineteenth century, Toronto also attracted many African-American fugitives. By the early 1860s, over two thousand refugees lived in Toronto. Free Blacks, who were locally born, immigrants from the United States, and a few from the Caribbean also resided in the city, especially after 1850 with the passage of the Fugitive Slave Act.

These Black pioneers possessed a variety of skills and abilities. Some were educated professionals, owned real estate, and operated numerous businesses such as barbershops, grocery stores, restaurants, a salon, a cab company, a livery-stable, an ice company, a carpentry business, a cobble shop, a ladies dress and accessory shop, and a hardware store/sawmill. Others found work constructing roads, and others as porters, farmers, bricklayers, sawyers, plasterers, blacksmiths, carters, waiters, washerwomen, domestics, and dock workers. Some widows made a living by operating boarding houses. The opportunities afforded enabled them to fare well economically.

They founded significant community institutions including businesses, churches, social reform societies, and political organizations. The churches established included the longstanding First Baptist, which was established in 1825 by Elder Washington Christian, initially located at Victoria and Queen Streets (site of St. Michael's Hospital today) before moving to D'Arcy Street in 1955. An African Methodist Episcopal Church formed at Richmond Street east of York Street first moved to Elizabeth Street, then to Sayer (now Chestnut Street) and Elm Streets, and is now on Soho Street. A Baptist Church on Teraulay Street and a British Methodist Episcopal church on Chestnut Street were established, and the Coloured Wesleyan Methodist Church was organized in the 1830s on Richmond Street, with the assistance of Wilson Ruffin Abbott, originally from Alabama and by then a wealthy businessman.

The Provincial Union started a Toronto chapter in 1854, led by Thomas F. Cary, the husband of Mary Ann Shadd Cary, and Wilson Abbott, father of Dr. Anderson Ruffin Abbott. The chapter offered services and programs to refugees. Black women established groups like the Queen Victoria Benevolent Society, founded by Ellen Toyer Abbott (mother of Anderson Ruffin Abbott), the Ladies Freedman's Aid Society, and the Society for the Protection of Refugees. These associations primarily helped fugitives coming into the urban centre.

One notable example of a fugitive was Joshua Glover.[47] On April 19, 1854, a travel-worn Black man trudged into Montgomery's Inn on Dundas Street in Etobicoke. He was hungry and homeless. Two years before Joshua had escaped slavery in Missouri and settled in the free state of Wisconsin. However, his former owner tracked him down and had him imprisoned in Milwaukee, pending his return to Missouri. Enraged Wisconsin citizens stormed the jail, and on March 11, 1854, Joshua Glover disappeared on the Underground Railroad. For four weeks he was concealed in barns, attics, and cellars around the Wisconsin countryside. Finally, he was smuggled aboard a ship in Racine, Wisconsin, and sailed for the security of Canada West. On that wonderful spring day in 1854, Thomas and William Montgomery (usually the most cautious of businessmen) lent this stranger fifteen shillings, and recorded the loan in their account book. They offered him work and shelter, and Joshua Glover lived the rest of his life in Lambton Mills on the Humber River, in a house rented from the Montgomery family.

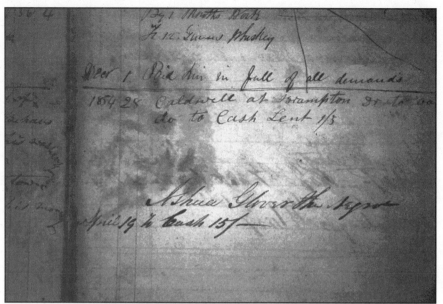

This telegram was sent from the superintendant of the Industrial House in Newmarket (the Poor House of York County) to William Montgomery, a businessman in Islington. Due to complicated circumstances, Montgomery was never able to locate Glover's body.

The presence of a sizeable fugitive population coupled a large number of Whites with strong anti-slavery feelings facilitated a wide array of activities in support of the cause. St. Lawrence Hall at Jarvis and King Streets was the venue used to host abolitionist speakers like Frederick Douglass, was the site of the meeting that formed the Anti-Slavery Society of Canada, and, on September 10, 1851, hosted the North American Convention of Coloured People.[48]

Several legal challenges to American slavery took place in the courts of Osgoode Hall located at Queen Street and University Avenue such as the 1861 John Anderson extradition case that was tried by Chief Justice John Beverly Robinson. Anderson was subsequently set free after an appeal to the British courts. In reverence to the "Great Emancipator" Abraham Lincoln — the man they perceived as having legislated freedom for African Americans with the Emancipation Proclamation of 1865 — Black Torontonians closed their businesses during Lincoln's funeral, held memorial services at several churches, and wore a Black armband for eighty days as a symbol of mourning.

A few newspapers using their pages to fight slavery were based in Toronto. The first office of the Black newspaper, the *Provincial Freeman*, was located at King and Jarvis Streets from 1854 to June 1855, and the *Toronto Globe*, published and edited by George Brown, also operated in Toronto. Brown was a staunch abolitionist and opposed racism. He, like the editors of the *Provincial Freeman,* used his paper to dispel stereotypes of Blacks, promote anti-slavery ideals, publicly denounce American slavery, share editorials on the atrocities of slavery, discuss the problems of runaways in the province, and provide reports on Emancipation Day celebrations in Toronto. Of anti-slavery in the city, Samuel Ringgold Ward, Black abolitionist and founder of the *Provincial Freeman*, said, "Toronto is somewhat peculiar in many ways, anti-slavery here is more popular there than any other city I know save Syrcuse [*sic*] …."[49]

Blacks in the Toronto of that period experienced fewer incidences of blatant racism and seem to have been more accepted by their White neighbours. William P. Newman, one-time editor of the *Provincial Freeman* stated: "Here there is no difference made in public houses, steamboats, railroad cars, schools, colleges, churches, ministerial platforms, and government offices. There is no doubt some prejudice here, but those who have it are ashamed to show it. This is at least true of Toronto."[50] A White traveller from the United States observed that Blacks and Whites worshipped together without distinction in several churches that had White and Black clergy. However, that does not mean that there was an absence of serious racial problems. Dr. Daniel Hill speculates that because the Black population remained fairly stable and did not increase drastically in a short time frame as in some towns in southern Ontario, there was less prejudice.

Still, Black Torontonians experienced discrimination and challenged occurrences of racism collectively and individually when they arose. For example, members of Toronto's African-Canadian community protested against minstrel shows that travelled to the city. White actors would paint their faces with Black makeup and perform songs, skits, and plays that disparaged Africans. In 1840 they successfully petitioned the city council to not allow companies that exhibited these acts to perform in the city. Visiting Blacks were denied hotel accommodations such as in two cases documented in 1888 and 1929. Black voters in Toronto protested two racist politicians, once against Colonel John Prince's racist comments in 1857 and the other in 1864 against a city councillor who persisted on "calling them niggers." A Black passenger on a boat sailing from Toronto to Kingston was not permitted to enter the captain's dining room. One exception to racial discrimination in Toronto, different to many other towns in Ontario, was that their children attended integrated public schools, colleges, and universities in Toronto. Graduates of Toronto's integrated schools included Emaline Shadd, Peter Gallego, Dr. Anderson Ruffin Abbott, Dr. Alexander Augusta, and William Peyton Hubbard.

Emancipation Day commemorations were also intertwined with the cultural, social, religious, and political lives of African Canadians in Toronto. Community leaders and business owners organized the celebrations and festive events convened in many of the Black establishments. J.R. Kerr-Ritchie discusses that from the 1830s through to the 1850s, the Black elite who assumed leadership on behalf of all African Canadians planned August First events in Toronto.[51] He further identifies two different kinds of Black Emancipation Day organizers and celebrants. The first group was made up of early Black Loyalists who established the older Black communities in the larger centres of Brantford, St. Catharines, Niagara, Hamilton, and Toronto. They instituted celebrations from 1834. The second group was comprised of the population of new fugitives who arrived in the 1840s and 1850s and settled in the southwestern Ontario towns of Chatham, Raleigh, Harwich, Camden, Amherstburg, Colchester, Sandwich, and Windsor. These Blacks in Kent and Essex counties commenced freedom festivals upon their arrival. Kerr-Ritchie's comparison of how these two groups recognized Emancipation Day reveals the diversity of ideas and political views among Black Ontarians.

An examination of Emancipation Day in the identified southeastern Ontario cities during the first half of the nineteenth century reveal elements of an Anglo-Canadian identity such as volunteering for military service, strong political support of the Conservative party, the adoption of British cultural customs such as drinking tea, close ties to the Anglican church, and public displays of patriotism, especially on August First. The recent fugitives in southwestern Ontario in the mid-century used Emancipation Day celebrations initially to show loyalty to Britain then later as a tool to engage people in the movement to end American slavery. This shift in the use and meaning of Emancipation Day brought about by the fugitives shows strong anti-slavery beliefs that created, changed, and influenced elements of African-Canadian culture through the incorporation of African-American customs, militancy, and the formation of new institutions such as a Black press, AME churches, and self-help societies.

The legislation that ended African slavery in British possessions was celebrated publicly in Toronto as early as 1838 and has carried on regularly since then. Black Torontonians found cause for celebration on August 1, 1838, when Jamaica ended the apprenticeships of former slaves two years earlier than expected. They celebrated again that year to mark the final emancipation of slaves in the British Empire. Community members attended a special church service at St. James' Cathedral Anglican, at Church and King, and Archdeacon John Strachan delivered a fitting sermon. Those assembled then ate a celebratory dinner.[52]

The Toronto Abolition Society, an association formed in 1833 that sponsored Emancipation Day commemorations in the 1830s and 1840s, organized the city's 1839 celebration. A church service was performed at the AME Church at Richmond and York Streets, where a Reverend William Miller from Philadelphia delivered the sermon. After that, the crowd formed a parade and marched to city hall, which then was located in the south building of the St. Lawrence Market at Front and Jarvis Streets. Various speakers, such as Mayor John Powell, a Conservative politician, addressed the celebrants. Reverend Henry James Grasett,[53] minister of the St. James Cathedral, also delivered a speech on British West Indian emancipation. Marchers then went on to the Commercial Hotel

Reverend Henry James Grasett, rector of St. James' Cathedral (1847–1882). Prior to this post, he was the assistant to John Strachan, Archdeacon of St. James' Cathedral, from 1835 to 1847.

at Front and Jarvis Streets for an elaborately decorated feast. A British flag was hung in honour of the day. Jehu Jones of Philadelphia, the first ordained Black Lutheran minister in the United States, was invited by William H. Edward of the Toronto Abolition Society to join the celebration the day he immigrated to the metropolitan. In a letter to Charles B. Ray, editor of the *Colored American*, he describes how inspired he was by the seemingly prejudice-free environment he observed in Toronto:

> The kingdom of Great Britain is open to all men where life, liberty, and the pursuits of happiness, without dissimulation, is distributed with an equal hand, to all men, regardless of the country or condition of any. This province especially, seems to invite colored men to settle down among the people, and enjoy equal laws. Here you need not separate into disgusting sect of caste. But once your elastic feet presses the provincial soil of her Britannic Majesty, Queen Victoria, God bless her, you become a man, every American disability falls at your feet — society — the prospects of society, holds out many inducements to men of capital; here we can mingle in the mass of society, without feeling of inferiority; here every social and domestic comforts can be enjoyed irrespective of complexion.[54]

The Black women of the city hosted a tea party in the evening at one of their homes on Elizabeth Street, to which Jones was invited. This is a demonstration of the adoption of British habits by African-Canadians in Toronto. He would remain in the city and live in Toronto for three years before returning to the States.

For the tenth anniversary of the abolition of slavery, St. James' Cathedral was again the central meeting place. The day was recognized with a street procession to the church for a religious service delivered by Reverend Grasett and was followed by a party in the evening.[55]

As part of the 1854 recognition of Emancipation Day, a thanksgiving service was held at the Second Wesleyan Chapel at five in the morning. It was followed by a parade marshalled by W.H. Harris, C.P. Lucas, and

W. Thompson, which began at the Government House on King Street West. This was the official residence of the governor general of Canada West (Ontario), which at that time was the Right Honourable James Bruce. Participants marched to Brown's Wharf (the Yonge Street Wharf) to meet arriving guests sailing from Hamilton on the *Arabian*. Here Thomas Smallwood Sr.,[56] one of the organizers and elected president of the day, addressed the arriving crowd.

> Fellow subjects of this noble province, and citizens of Hamilton, It is my pleasing duty, in behalf of a portion of my fellow citizens of Toronto, to welcome you, who have honoured us this day with your presence, to partake of a festival in commemoration of one among the greatest events in British history, when that magnanimous nation swept the bonds from 800,000 bondsmen, and made them free. Though some narrow-minded individuals object, saying, because we did not achieve it ourselves, it is disgraceful for us to celebrate this day; I am assured by your presence here to-day, that I speak your sentiments, when I say that I envy not the narrowness of the mind that can entertain such disloyal sentiments; so you are therefore heartily welcome to our hospitality.[57]

Afterwards the group continued on to St. James Cathedral to hear the special sermon delivered by Reverend Grasett, the regular speaker at Emancipation Day observances. Celebrants continued to march through the city to the Government Grounds on Front Street, between John and Simcoe Streets, for a grand banquet. After dinner, a program of speeches and entertainment began. The organizing committee asked George Dupont Wells, a local White lawyer, to read a speech they had written and dedicated to Queen Victoria expressed the gratitude of Toronto Blacks for Britain's abolition efforts. (See Appendix A.)

Mary Ann Shadd of the *Provincial Freeman* returned to Toronto from a southwestern Ontario tour in time to briefly address the crowd. It's not known what she said, but since Shadd had recently come back from soliciting newspaper subscribers, it is likely that she approached the gatherers with the same request. The evening was capped off with a fireworks display that was accompanied by a musical band. White residents of Toronto were involved as participants and observers in August First holidays. Some, like Reverend Grasett and Wells, lent support by being part of the activities, while other locals watched the parades along the main streets or attended some of the various events.[58]

Dr. Anderson Ruffin Abbott, the first Black, Canadian-born doctor, describes one of Toronto's Emancipation Day commemorations in the 1850s:

> On one occasion within my memory they provided a banquet which was held under a pavilion erected on a vacant lot running from Elizabeth Street to Sayre Street opposite Osgoode Hall, which was then a barracks for the 92nd West India Regiment. The procession was headed by the band of the Regiment. The tallest man in this Regiment was a Black man, a drummer, known as Black Charlie. The procession carried a Union Jack and a blue silk banner on which was inscribed in glit letters "The Abolition Society, Organized 1844." The mayor of the city, Mr. Metcalfe, made a speech ... followed by several other speeches of prominent citizens. These celebrations were carried on yearly amid much enthusiasm, because it gave the refugee colonists an opportunity to express their gratitude and appreciation of the privileges they enjoyed under British rule.[59]

Kerr-Ritchie argues that observances in Toronto and other major centres were more of a display of colonial patriotism by Black Loyalists who were freed by a benevolent state versus celebrations in southwestern Ontario towns that were freedom festivals in the true sense of the term by self-emancipated African peoples. The public display of allegiance and appreciation to Britain by both kinds of celebrants usually took the form of a street procession.

On August 1, 1856, African Canadians in Toronto took to the streets. The procession formed on College Avenue and marched down to the Great Western Railway Station on Front Street (now Union Station)

From the Toronto Globe, August 2, 1892. Adapted from the original and designed by Kaimera Media Inc.

ON EMANCIPATION DAY.

The Colored Population Hold a Celebration

AN OLD TIME CAKE WALK

Prizes for the Genteelest Couple on the Floor.

PICNIC AND GAMES AT EXHIBITION PARK -- IN THE EVENING AT VIC- TORIA HALL.

A replica of the advertisement for a dance held for the 1892 Emancipation Day celebration in Toronto. The cakewalk, developed by enslaved Africans on southern plantations, was a mix of traditional African circle dances and European dances, initially created to mock their White masters and mistresses. It became a popular dance across North America and internationally.

to receive visitors from Hamilton. The parade resumed with everyone marching east along Front, north on Yonge, east on Wellington, then north on Church to St. James' Cathedral. Reverend Grasett delivered a suitable sermon for the day after which the procession rejoined, led by an all-Black brass band, and continued to parade along various streets back to College Avenue for a tent lunch.[60]

There were no celebrations in Toronto in 1859, quite likely because many Black Torontonians attended the huge festival in Hamilton. It was practice for African-Canadians in Canada West to support Emancipation

Day observances in other parts of the province as a show of solidarity and community strength. But there was an August First demonstration in Toronto in 1860 that began with a church service at St. James Cathedral where Reverend Grasett once again delivered a sermon for the occasion. Celebrants then attended the leisure activities at Exhibition Park and a dinner and dance in the evening.[61]

On August 1, 1883, the forty-ninth anniversary of the Abolition Act of 1833 was put together by the Toronto branch of the Peter Ogden Lodge of the Grand United Order of Oddfellows, one of the few Black lodges established in Canada. The customary procession formed on Temperance Street headed by the Peter Ogden Lodge members and was followed by the Mount Brydges Lodge of Hamilton and the Victoria Lodge of Toronto. In front was the Excelsior band of Toronto, under the direction of Captain Jack Richards, who, like "Black Charlie" thirty years before, wore a blue and gold suit. Richards was also the drum major. Participants marched north on Yonge to Queen, then south on York Street to the wharf where they boarded a Turner ferryboat for Exhibition Park. Sporting activities and games in the afternoon included a half-mile race, a hopping race, a three-legged race, a half-hour race, and a hop, step, and jump competition. The amusement activities were followed by addresses by several Toronto and out-of-town notables.[62]

An interesting inclusion to the evening proceedings of Toronto's 1892 celebration held in Victoria Hall was the cakewalk. A prize, two large cakes, was awarded to the lady and gentleman displaying the most grace and charm while circulating the hall — the "genteelist" man and woman on the dance floor.[63]

The Peter Ogden Lodge played a major role in organizing the celebrations in 1892 as well. Members always marched in the parades alongside other lodges, associations, and societies. Part of the reason for their consistent involvement with Emancipation Day is found in the basic principles of the Order: "to obtain an honest livelihood, to be faithful to our Queen and country, to avoid turbulent measures, and to submit with reverence to the decisions of a Legislative Authority."[64] These shared objectives were part of the purpose of Emancipation Day observances.

Toronto did not host large Emancipation Day festivities every year. As was custom, the towns and cities that recognized August First took turns in holding large-scale events, and the various African-Canadian communities planned and coordinated with one another to make travel and accommodation arrangements. In 1895, for example, a newspaper article read:

> This is Emancipation Day, but local colored people are not indulging in any celebration. A number of the younger men of the Peter Ogden Lodge of colored Oddfellows, which organization has usually had considerable to do with the celebration of Emancipation have left the city and the old members who are left have not the … to have a big time like the young brethren. There is a big gathering of colored people to-day in London.[65]

And in 1902 several hundred Blacks from across the province, including Toronto, converged on Hamilton to commemorate Emancipation Day. By the 1920s, St. Catharines was the primary celebration site and people from Toronto attended regularly, taking one of two steamers across Lake Ontario to Port Dalhousie. The end of that eventful era saw public Emancipation Day gatherings return to Toronto and take on a new face.

During the 1940s, 1950s, and 1960s, Toronto was a site of civil rights activism. The demographics of the city's Black community had changed to include immigrants of African descent from the Caribbean, some as university students and some as female domestics. The newcomers encountered

Courtesy of the author.

The Civil Rights Movement was alive and well in Canadian cities and towns. African-Canadians and other minority groups fought for equal opportunities and equal access. Shown is a replica of a placard carried by marchers on Emancipation Day in Toronto on July 27, 1964.

prejudice and racism in their daily lives, in obtaining employment, in finding a place to live, and in many other aspects of life. August First provided citizens of the city who fought for equality for all to publicize the injustices taking place and to mobilize like-minded people to advocate for change. Local Black churches, as they had in the early observances of the 1800s, were active in mobilizing the community for the day. Dr. W. Constantine Perry of the city's AME Church used the occasion and radio waves to speak out against the discrimination levied towards Black nurses. In a radio interview on CKEY, Perry discussed the issue of the barring of women of African descent from working as nurses in hospitals in Toronto and other cities like Windsor:

> At the present time there exists an alarming situation in the shortage of nurses in our hospitals, a shortage which would not have been so great except for discriminatory indulgences," said Dr. Perry. His address was in connection with the celebration of emancipation of Negro slaves in British colonies ...[66]

Reverend Perry also made radio addresses in 1947 and 1951 that pointed to the discrimination against people of African ancestry in Canada.[67] In Windsor, "Mr. Emancipation" Walter Perry used the *Progress* magazine to bring awareness to and congratulate the Black women who were still pursuing a career in the nursing profession despite the employment discrimination. The first issue of the publication in 1948 featured two women from Windsor and Dresden, the first African-Canadian students to gain admission to the nursing program at Windsor's Hotel Dieu Hospital. The 1950 edition recognized the first Black graduate from that program, Cecile Wright.

Beginning in 1953, freedom events were held under the auspices of the Toronto Emancipation Committee (TEC). The revival of Emancipation Day observances in Toronto were spearheaded by Donald Moore, who pulled together numerous local Black community groups, churches, fraternal orders, and leaders under the umbrella of the TEC. Moore asserted that:

TORONTO EMANCIPATION COMMITTEE

2nd Annual Parade

Eighth Annual Service

The parade will move south from College & Spadina

at 2.15 p.m. Saturday, July 29, 1961

The presentation of Trophies

at 7.30 p.m 33 CECIL ST.

DANCING

FOR YOUR PLEASURE

at 8.15 p.m.

GRAND DRAW

at 10.30 p.m.

~*REFRESHMENTS*~

Bar-B-Q Ribs and Chicken Plates

Dance Admission $1.00

The Toronto Emancipation Committee organized Emancipation Day commemorations during the Civil Rights era.

> Every facet of the community became involved: the churches — African Methodist Episcopal, British Methodist Episcopal, First Baptist; the lodges — Peter Ogden Lodge No. 812, Grand United Order of Oddfellows, Victoria Household of Ruth N. 5354, Eureka Lodge No. 20 Free and Accepted Masons, Naomi Chapter

No. 8 Order of Eastern Star, John Henry valentine Lodge
No. 740 Improved Beneficial and Protective Order of
Elks, Queen City Temple No. 1003, IBPOE; associations
– Universal Negro Improvement Association, The Home
Comfort Club, the Brotherhood of Sleeping Car Porters,
the Ladies Auxiliary Pullman Division, and the Toronto
Negro Women's Club. Also involved were the Toronto
Negro Veterans under President Jim Marson and Treasurer
Edward Clarke, and the Toronto Veterans Colour Guard
under Commander Sergeant Aubrey Sharpe, E.MC.D.[68]

They used the August First holiday to commemorate the abolition of
slavery and to pay tribute to the Black men who served in the Canadian
military, from the Coloured Corps who fought in the War of 1812 to the
men who served in the Second World War. The intent of the memorial
service was:

- To offer thanks for emancipation from slavery.
- To pay due respect to those who laboured unselfishly to bring
  it about.
- To place a wreath on the cenotaph to our glorious dead who gave
  their lives in defence of Canada.
- To look forward with love and determination to remove those scars
  which slavery has left.
- To gather strength for the road ahead.[69]

In his memoir, Moore detailed the typical format of an August First
program at Victoria Memorial Park at the end of a street procession, which
consisted of opening prayers by church ministers followed by speeches by
local community members, Black and White. These speakers included the
likes of Stanley Grizzle, citizenship court judge and one-time president of
the Toronto chapter of the Brotherhood of Sleeping Car Porters; Black
community activist Esther Hayes; John Collingwood Reade, CFRB radio
host; and a wide array of Toronto-based, and national lecturers. Speakers
discussed the ongoing struggle for freedom and equality, the importance
of education, and the vigilance that was needed to maintain and extend

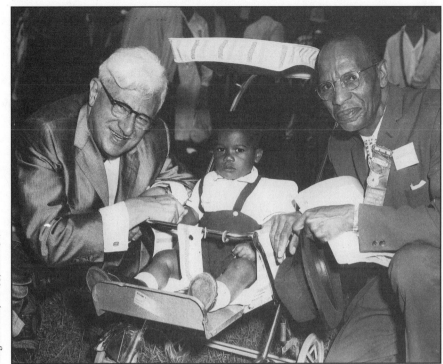

Community activist and Director of the Negro Citizenship Association, Donald Moore (right), with Mayor Nathan Phillips (left) and seventeen-month old Eugene Hood at Victoria Memorial Park on August 1, 1960.

universal freedoms. Another characteristic feature was the receiving of greetings from politicians at the municipal, provincial, and federal levels like the Honourable Lester B. Pearson and John Wintermeyer, national leader of the Liberal party and the Ontario Liberal leader, respectively. The TEC also used the opportunity to publicize the racial inequality African Canadians continued to experience through the selection of appropriate speakers.

When Donald Moore addressed the audience himself in 1954, he talked about the entrenched racism faced by people of African descent from the period of enslavement to the current discriminatory immigration practices against Blacks from British territories. He stressed the importance of remembering the past — where Blacks have come from and the journey to get here — in order to know future direction. Moore then reminded the crowd to call upon the endurance and resilience of their ancestors at the

Sergeant Aubrey Sharpe of the Toronto Negro Colour Guard War Veterans and the young Beatty brothers at the Victoria Square cenotaph on August 1, 1957. As part of Emancipation Day commemorations sponsored by the Toronto Emancipation Committee, wreaths were laid at the war memorial park in memory of the many African-Canadian soldiers who died defending Canada in the Coloured Corps (War of 1812), the First World War, and the Second World War.

Silver Cross mother, Edith Holloway, places a wreath at the cenotaph at Victoria Memorial Park on August 1, 1960. She lost her son in France during the Second World War. Beside her is Jim Marson, Warrant Officer II of the Toronto Negro Veteran Association Drill Team.

time of battle, such as the challenging of Canada's immigration policies. In closing, he asserted, "Today we cannot be content with being wards of society. We must share in the responsibilities of citizens and see that no one prevents us from sharing in its glories."[70] His speech encapsulated themes that have persisted since the inception of Emancipation Day

The Emancipation Day parade in Toronto, July 29, 1961, led by the Toronto Negro Band. The procession is arriving at Victoria Memorial Park at Niagara and Portland Streets.

commemorations, indicative of the racial inequality that every generation encountered, even 120 years of the passage of the Emancipation Act.

In 1958, the invited guest speaker was attorney Violet King,[71] the first African-Canadian woman admitted to the bar in Canada, who told the crowd of over one hundred "that you cannot legislate against prejudice, but you can legislate against discriminatory acts which further prejudice."[72] This was a powerful message coming from a Black attorney. Just as in the United States, African Canadians were seeking to bring about social change through the implementation of human rights legislation, including an overhaul of the immigration laws, equal admission to nursing programs, and access to employment opportunities.

Seven years later, in 1964, over six hundred paraders and observers participated in the eleventh annual commemoration with a procession from Lansdowne Public School, down Spadina Avenue, to the Victoria Memorial Park on Wellington Street West.[73] Many of the marchers held signs that called for racial equality in Canada, and were accompanied by several bands including fife and drum bands of the Orange Order and several army and veteran bands. The crowd listened to a speech delivered by Rabbi Abraham Feinburg that promoted racial harmony and special honour was paid to the Black servicemen who fought and died in the War of 1812 with a memorial service in the park.

The West Indian immigrants who settled in Toronto in the mid-1900s introduced the carnival feature to the celebration of Emancipation Day with the establishment of Caribana in 1967. Rooted in the carnival in Trinidad, the forty-two year old event includes a huge parade with the colourful representation of many Caribbean islands, including Guyana, Jamaica, Barbados, the Bahamas, and Brazil. It is a mainstay cultural festival that draws thousands of local and international spectators annually over the long weekend to downtown Toronto to enjoy the costumes, dance, music, art, and food of the West Indies. While the roots of the festival are a distant memory and not known to many of the revellers, some aspects of the Caribbean style of celebrating Emancipation Day remain present.

In 1996, the Ontario Black Historical Society (OBHS) revived the annual celebration and it has continued yearly. Events have been held on August 1st at the Parliament Building, Queen's Park, and at Nathan Phillip Square.[74] Since then, Rosemary Sadlier, president of the OBHS, has been advocating for legislation at the municipal, provincial, and federal levels to proclaim August First as Emancipation Day. To date there has been some measure of success. In 2008, official recognition came from the provincial government making the first of August Emancipation Day in Ontario.

5

The Niagara Region

Freedom is a precarious thing, a sometime thing, a completely
unpredictable quantity.
— Saunders Redding, *They Came in Chains*, 1950.

The earliest residents of African ancestry in the Niagara region in the 1780s
were slaves who came into the area with their Loyalist masters or Black
Loyalists, freed for their military service to Britain. They worked side by
side with their owners, clearing land, building homes, and farming the
land. By 1791, over three hundred Blacks lived in the Niagara area. That
number grew drastically as an influx of escaping slaves entered the region.
Many came north with assistance from the Underground Railroad in the
1850s or on their own, crossing the Lower Niagara River or entering from
Buffalo into Fort Erie. The most notable "conductor" stationed in this area
was Harriet Tubman.

Black communities were established quickly in Niagara-on-the-
Lake (Newark), Port Robinson, Fort Erie, Drummondville (became part
of Niagara Falls in 1882), Chippawa, Niagara Falls, and St. Catharines.
For some, these districts were stopovers for fugitives who had run out
of money on their arduous journey to freedom. Like Josiah Henson,
they would work, save some money, and then move on further into the
interior. Hundreds took up residency in close-knit neighbourhoods such
as an area located along William Street between King and Butler Streets in

Niagara-on-the-Lake, and some lived on Mississauga Street, in Bertie Hill and Snake Hill in that same town. "Little Africa" in Fort Erie extended from Ridgemount Road to where the Niagara Parks' Commission marina is now. In Drummondville, a small Black community called Pollytown was formed, while in St. Catharines Blacks settled around Welland Avenue and Geneva, Queenston, William, St. Paul, Niagara, and North Streets.

Blacks found ample employment cutting trees, clearing land, working as carpenters in local shipyards, in construction, in the spa industry, as hotel waiters, tourist guides for trips behind Niagara Falls, as stewards on steamships that travelled from Niagara across Lake Ontario, and on farms. Many others were self-employed as tavern-keepers, farmers, livery owners, grocers, and barbers.

In a demonstration of allegiance to Britain for liberation from enslavement and of having citizenship on free land, dozens of Black men served in all-Black militias in the Niagara region. One group was Captain Runchey's Company of Coloured Men, formed in 1812 to defend against American attacks. While some soldiers received land grants in various towns in Upper Canada, some did not receive the six-month severance pay that was promised to all militiamen. Another company, organized in 1838, was comprised of one hundred African-Canadian men of various ranks whose duty it was to protect Upper Canada from attacks by the American supporters of William Lyon Mackenzie's Rebellion. Another Black militia formed in 1840 and stayed active for over ten years. This unit cleared forests to build the Cayuga Road between the village of Drummondville and Simcoe, after which they were assigned to the site of the Welland Canal to quell tensions and fighting among the Irish construction workers.[1]

Churches were erected across Niagara to meet the spiritual and social needs of African Canadians residing in the towns. An AME church was built in Niagara at Murray and Allan Streets in 1836, and a BME congregation built a larger church at Grey and Peer Streets in the 1850s.[2] A Baptist church was formed in Niagara-on-the-Lake in 1831. In St. Catharines, the BME church, Salem Chapel, and the Zion Baptist Church were both constructed on Geneva Street.[3] African Canadians along the Niagara Peninsula developed their own educational institutions as Black children, as in many other parts of Upper Canada, were either not permitted to attend local common schools, were limited to restricted seating, or forced to attend inadequate separate schools. The segregated school established in the 1850s had over 130 students by the mid-1860s.

The Niagara region is historically significant in the movement to end slavery as the first piece of anti-slavery legislation, the 1793 Act to Limit Slavery, was introduced by Lieutenant-Governor John Graves Simcoe at Upper Canada's first legislative assembly at Newark (Niagara-on-the-Lake).[4] This law that gradually abolished the enslavement of Africans in Upper Canada, but instantly freed incoming fugitives, attracted American bondsmen and bondswomen. Once arriving on free soil, most refugees rejoiced in their new-found freedom and the possibilities at hand as British subjects. And when Britain followed Simcoe's lead in 1833 with the complete abolition of slavery, Emancipation Day provided the ideal public stage for native-born and immigrant Black Canadians to express overwhelming gratitude for liberty, embrace their citizenship, and to chart the course for the future.

St. Catharines was the site of one of the first recorded Emancipation Day celebrations in Ontario. On August 20, 1835, a parade was held along the two main streets of the town and ended at the new church, Salem Chapel, where a bountiful dinner was served. People from Black communities in the surrounding Niagara Region joined the momentous occasion. This time provided an opportunity for the expression of thankfulness and gratitude to Britain and their adoptive country for the freedoms afforded to them under British law and to remind the beneficiaries that these privileges should not be taken for granted. A pamphlet distributed to the visitors said, "… to show that your conduct may be worthy of the trust that has been so liberally placed in your hands, may you continue to be good citizens, and never offend the law the Government, by any outrageous acts, to incur their censure or displeasure."[5]

The first of August 1838 was summarized in the *St. Catharines Journal* as a "Great celebration." A musical band, followed by the marshal of the day riding on a white charger, led the morning parade. After a service at the African church, the almost two hundred celebrants continued to march through the village to Henry Gray's[6] for a plentiful dinner where these twelve toasts were given:

- The Queen;
- The Earl of Durham — the Lieutenant-Governor and their families;
- The Army and Navy — defenders of our rights and privileges;
- May peace and prosperity reign throughout the Canadas and never again be disturbed by internal commotions or foreign policy;
- Our coloured Brethren and Sisters all over the world;
- May those who are now cruelly detained in slavery soon enjoy the same freedom as ourselves;
- Honour, honesty, humanity, humility, health, and happiness;
- Prosperity to the plough and axe;
- May unity, concord, and friendship always exist amongst us;
- When the devil comes into our ranks, may we all help to kick him out;
- Prosperity to civilization in African and the free settlements of Liberia; and
- Success to Great Britain and all other countries interested in the cause of freedom.[7]

Such salutations were commonplace in the nineteenth century and were often reprinted in detail in local newspapers. It is likely that the media of the time wanted to provide insight into the social life and collective consciousness of the people of African background living among them. Perhaps, as well, some newspapers hoped to foster more understanding and tolerance from Whites in the revelation that Blacks shared many of the same sentiments they did.

While St. Catharines grew to be one of the principal locales to host these annual events during the 1800s and 1900s, the village of Drummondville was also a host location of Emancipation Day observances. An advertisement posted in the *Niagara Chronicle* in 1844 reads:

> Anniversary of African Emancipation. The friends of African Emancipation are requested to attend a Public Dinner on the 1st day of August, on the Battle Ground on Drummond Hill, for the purpose of celebrating that glorious event. Tickets $1.00 for a Lady and gentlemen. Committee: Isaac Thomas, Henry Brooks, Samuel Scott, Henry Garrett,[8] President.[9]

The site chosen for the gathering was symbolic of the battle to end slavery and the victory over inhumanity. It was also a gesture of respect to the Black men who fought to protect the freedom they enjoyed. Likewise, the selection of Lundy's Lane was demonstrative of the struggles yet to be won in the pursuit of equality.

Drummondville was the principal celebration site in Canada West in 1861, attended by a large number of refugees. The main speaker, William J. Watkins, a Black abolitionist from Rochester, New York, spoke about the inevitability of the end of slavery in the United States and how the efforts of particular abolitionists had not been in vain. This event was taking place at the same time that anti-emancipation arguments had been circulating internationally. Watkins refuted the ideas of the liberation of slaves as a failure. He gave advice to fugitive slaves in the crowd to do everything they could to elevate themselves in their new, free life: "Be intelligent, industrious, economical. Aspire daily to something higher. Show your appreciation of the blessings of liberty. Be self-reliant. God helps those who help themselves."[10]

The celebration of August First in St. Catharines remained a fixture in the emerging city and a unifying tradition in the lives of African Canadians. A variety of activities were held over the course of the years in venues such as Fowler's Hall, the town hall, George Adams' meadow, the fair grounds, and the Crystal Palace. However, the holiday was not always just about creating a diversion from everyday life. In fact, the occasion lent itself to confronting issues that affected their daily living. Perhaps this is why the annual gathering was cancelled several times in Ontario when members of the province's Black communities had complaints about the racial discrimination that they faced. In 1871, the festivities in St. Catharines were cancelled because of opposition to the refusal of local common schools to admit African-Canadian children. That year August First changed temporarily from a big party to an instrument for political protest against the unjust treatment of taxpaying citizens of colour.[11]

In the early part of the twentieth century, Emancipation Day celebrations moved to Port Dalhousie, a waterfront town in the St. Catharines area located along the shores of Lake Ontario. Bertrand Joseph Spencer Pitt,[12] a Toronto lawyer born in Grenada, organized the event known as the "Big Picnic" at its new location from 1924 to 1951. The

Courtesy of St. Catharines Museum, St. Catharines Standard Collection of Photographic Negatives, S1940.19.5.1.

Lakeside Park, Port Dalhousie, Emancipation Day, 1940. The "Big Picnic" attracted a racially mixed crowd from across the province.

annual event was held on the first Thursday of every August and included a church service held at the local British Methodist Episcopal Church, Salem Chapel. Families would then gather together at the beach resort of Lakeside Park that featured a dance pavilion and skating rink, a restaurant, a bake shop, vending stands, bathhouses, locker-rooms, assorted amusement rides, and swimming at the beach.

The Universal Negro Improvement Association (UNIA) Toronto chapter (Spencer Pitt was the president and legal counsel), used the August First observances in St. Catharines to raise the racial consciousness and pride of its celebrants. He has been credited with operating the famous, well-organized event for over twenty-seven years. Spencer Pitt and the UNIA worked in partnership with park management and local officials to ensure the event ran smoothly each year. As its popularity grew, more and more Toronto residents of African ancestry took the one-hour steamer ride across Lake Ontario on the *S.S. Dalhousie City* or the *Northumberland* to attend, joining in with busloads of visitors from Rochester, Buffalo, and

Niagara Falls, New York. Lots of White people also joined in the festivities. At its peak, as many as eight thousand people would congregate at Lakeside Park to celebrate the day.

Local African Canadians, young and old, looked forward to the August holiday. Everyone brought picnic baskets filled with sandwiches, fried chicken, salads, cakes, pies, breads, and drinks, all well-prepared for a fun-filled day. Marjorie Dawson and Harry Harper, descendants of fugitives who settled in St. Catharines, remember how people dressed up to come to the Big Picnic during the Depression era: "They bought new clothes. We used to look forward to that — new laces, butterfly skirts, and sailor suits. Everybody wanted to look their best.... And zoot suits. Everybody was trying to look like Cab Calloway."[13]

By the mid-1950s activities at Port Dalhousie had dwindled for several reasons. Both boats that transported revellers across Lake Ontario were lost in a fire in 1950. Spencer Pitt retired from law and stepped down as the event coordinator in 1954 due to serious illness. A 1971 newspaper article notes that there were only about twenty people at Lakeside Park on August 1st. From that point on, descendants of original Black settlers have organized yearly picnics with more of a family reunion theme. One person recalled that "If you hadn't seen anyone for awhile, the Big Picnic was certainly the place to go. You would wander around, and eventually you would run into them."[14]

The Big Picnic at Lakeside Park, Port Dalhousie, was one of the grandest Emancipation Day affairs in the country. During its peak, it was the premier African-Canadian social event in Ontario cultural and a prime example of the cultural life of the Black community.

6

Around the Northern Terminus

To be free means the ability to deal with the realities of one's
situation so as not to be overcome by them.
— Howard Thurman, *Meditations of the Heart*, 1953.

Grey County: Owen Sound

Owen Sound, located on the southern shores of Georgian Bay, was the
northern most "station" of the Underground Railroad. Blacks who arrived in
this part of Grey County (often by steamer or wagon) settled in the nearby
communities of Negro Creek, Priceville, Virginia (now Ceylon), Holland
Centre, and Nenagh. Some African Americans who had settled first in Queen's
Bush relocated to the Owen Sound area in the 1850s. It is believed that some
of them settled along the Old Durham Road, which runs just south of the
former Highway 4 running in a westerly direction from Flesherton through
Priceville towards Durham. Ongoing research in the area has determined
that a number of the lots along this road were initially cleared by Blacks
seeking to set up homesteads. The Old Durham Pioneer Cemetery, located
at the intersection of the Old Durham Road and Grey County Road 14, is
where many of these people were buried. Several stories are told of the rise
in prejudice and discriminatory practices that escalated as the English, Irish,
and Scottish immigrants moved into the region; there were even rumours of

Father Thomas Henry Miller, lay preacher, Little Zion Church (BME) in
Owen Sound.

Ku Klux Klan activities. As result, many of the Black pioneers moved out,
some heading further north to the Owen Sound or Collingwood areas.

More recently, some members of the local Old Durham Road Pioneer
Cemetery Committe[1] undertook a restoration project involving extensive

These women were members of the BME Church in Owen Sound around the early 1900s, back row (l to r): Pearl Green, Myrtle Green, Viola Johnson, and Ethel Earll; front row seated (l to r): Josephine Scott, Georgina Douglas, and Elizabeth Harrison.

research on the Black history of the area and archeological explorations of the site. As a result, the few old cemetery gravestones that could be located were returned to the cemetery, and in 1990 the Old Durham Road Pioneer Cemetery was restored and rededicated by Lincoln Alexander, then the lieutenant-governor of Ontario. Today it is marked as an historic site.[2]

These freedom seekers worked to clear land in Grey County, establishing homesteads and securing as positive a life for themselves and their developing community as was possible. To do so they established their own institutions to assist one another and to strengthen their community.

The "Little Zion" BME Church, at the present-day site of Market Square in Owen Sound, was started in the early 1850s by Reverend Thomas Miller, son of a slave. Later, Josephus O'Banyoun came to take over the responsibilities of the church in 1856. Blacks in Owen Sound established close social ties with those living in Collingwood, almost sixty kilometres to the east, as a way of extending their support system in a new, free land. It was a tradition for Black residents of Owen Sound and of Collingwood to support each others' Emancipation Day celebrations. Many would walk from Owen Sound to attend the festivities at Georgian Bay Park in Collingwood.

Thomas Henry Miller, the preacher of the BME church, spearheaded celebrations in 1856. James "Old Man" Henson, an escaped slave from Maryland who settled in Owen Sound in the late 1840s, regularly provided a detailed depiction of his recollection of slavery and his escape from bondage in the United States to John Frost Jr., enabling Frost to write *Broken Shackles* in 1889 under the pseudonym of "Glenelg."[3] John "Daddy" Hall,[4] one of the first Black settlers in Owen Sound, announced Emancipation Day celebrations and other town happenings in his capacity as town-crier, a role he had for fifty years.

Prior to obtaining Harrison Park as the permanent location for the occasion in 1912, members of Owen Sound's Black community travelled by steamer to the waterside village of Leith on the northeast shore of Georgian Bay and to Presque Isle north of Owen Sound in the former Sarawak Township to commemorate August First celebrations.

On one occasion, sometime between the 1870s and the 1890s, participants from Owen Sound took a steamer to Presque Isle to attend the observance held under the auspices of the BME Church. White Methodists ministers and some of their congregation from Owen Sound were part of the group of celebrants as well as local residents of Presque Isle. Superintendant of the Sabbath school, Mr. S. Graham, presided. James "Old Man" Henson was given a warm reception when he was called upon to speak to the gatherers. He shared a few insightful anecdotes on separation based on race, and pointed out how things were changing; an example being that particular day when both Black and White men and women were having a good time together. Reverend Miller addressed the assembly and provided some background on the abolition of enslaved Africans. He extended gratitude to members of the White community for joining them in the celebration and for helping the church's Sunday school. Speeches were also delivered by W.P. Telford, Reverend Kerr, and Reverend Holmes. Captain Ludgate performed a musical solo of the hymn, "I am satisfied with Jesus Now." The event closed with a brief concert by the choir before returning to the shores of Owen Sound.[5]

Annual activities at Harrison Park in the early 1900s were comprised of cookouts, games, races, musical performances, and readings alongside

Drew Ferguson (left), Mayor of Owen Sound Ruth Lovell, and Mario C. Browne (MPH, CHES) Project Director, Center for Minority Health, University of Pittsburgh Graduate School of Public Health, at the Emancipation Day festival at Harrison Park, Owen Sound, 2007.

the Sydenham River. The Eastern Star Lodge and Masonic Lodge of Owen Sound helped to organize, sponsor, and promote the events in both Owen Sound and Collingwood. Called "the longest continuous running Emancipation Day celebrations in North America," this annual tradition has continued through into the twenty-first century, changing and adapting to attract a large, diverse audience. Some gatherers visit to get together with family and friends, while others who are less familiar with the festivities attend to learn more about this part of Ontario's and Canada's Black history.

Owen Sound's Emancipation Day held its 147th event in 2009. Now a three-day festival organized by Dennis Scott, a native of Owen Sound, and his wife Lisa, along with an ensemble of volunteers, the event serves to educate and enlighten people through a range of programming including art exhibits that feature the works of African-Canadian artists at Grey Roots Museum and Archives, a lecture series, book launches, and readings, all supplemented by a variety of African-influenced music. In 2008, a cycling tour of bike riders from the United States honoured the escapees and agents of the Underground Railroad by travelling on some of the arteries taken en route to Canada. This tour may become a new tradition. The annual picnic held on a Saturday at Harrison Park, situated off Second Avenue, is filled with even more activities, music, storytelling, craft presentations, games, races, and award presentations, and is a cherished tradition in the life of Owen Sound.[6] Now an international event, the annual celebration attracts visitors from all over Ontario and parts of the United States.

Queen's Bush

Blacks settled in a portion of the Queen's Bush as early as 1833. This yet-to-be-surveyed territory was located southwest of Lake Huron and included parts of present-day Wellington County and Waterloo County, as well as today's Dufferin, Grey, and Bruce counties. The main area of the African-Canadian settlement known as the Queen's Bush Settlement was around the village of Conestoga, just north of and between Waterloo and Guelph, but also included areas around present-day Hawkesville, Elmira, Glen Allan, Wallenstein, and Galt (now Cambridge).[7] Some of the region's Black pioneers were militiamen who defended the Crown in the Rebellion of 1837, but many were either fugitives from the southern American states or free Blacks. Sophia Pooley — once owned by Joseph Brant in Brantford and Englishman Samuel Hatt in Ancaster — relocated to the Queen's Bush when she was freed as a result of the Emancipation Act.

At its peak, as many as two thousand people of African descent resided within the Queen's Bush. They had settled on unsurveyed Clergy Reserves, which meant that they could not purchase the land they squatted on, even though they cleared lots, started farms, put up fencing, built homes, and laid roads, along with other improvements. Several petitions were made to the Earl of Elgin, governor general of Upper Canada, who in 1850 eventually offered a deal for Black and White squatters to purchase the land they settled on, but the Black settlers could not afford the payment terms. By the late 1850s, the displaced settlers began the mass migration out of the Queen's Bush and relocated to other African-Canadian communities. Although they were in the Queen's Bush Settlement for a short period of time, Blacks were able to establish a strong, supportive community despite the harsh physical conditions and unfair and expensive land deals.

With the assistance of church missionaries and support from each other and Blacks in different centres, they worked hard to build a life on free soil. Several social institutions were established to meet their needs. By the mid-1840s, almost 250 students attended the two mission schools set up for African-Canadian children because they were excluded from the White common schools. Black churches of the AME, BME, Baptist, and Wesleyan denominations were also established in these villages, which were "not only religious centres for the widely dispersed populace, but also places for public meetings, social occasions, and the creation of self-help and moral improvement societies such as temperance associations."[8] In spite of many obstacles, a fair numbers of the pioneers fared well and still had reason to celebrate freedom.

Members of Queen Bush's Black community celebrated Emancipation Day in the hamlets of Hawkesville, Elmira, and Wallenstein in Wellesley Township, Waterloo County. Some of these residents sponsored an Emancipation Day celebration in Hawkesville on Saturday, August 1, 1863, to commemorate the twenty-ninth anniversary of the abolition of slavery. Approximately twenty-five hundred visitors gathered. The Berlin Band led a street procession to the town hall where a Reverend Milner delivered a sermon. Celebrants then went on to Temperance Island in the Conestoga River near the mouths of Boomer's and Spring creeks. A number of cooks and waiters served an elaborate dinner over three lunch shifts. It is unlikely that any alcohol was served at the event as many of the fugitive settlers in the vicinity were part of the Temperance Society of Hawkesville who denounced the consumption of rum and other spirits and were known to have "cold water" picnics on the island. Speeches were given by Reverends Downey, Milner, Lawson, and Miller.[9] Presumably, the most talked about issue at this affair was the Civil War and the pending overthrow of the institution of slavery. Following the end of that war, many ex-fugitives living in Queen's Bush returned to the United States to reunite with family or moved to other established Black communities in Canada West because of the mounting racial prejudice and the increasingly difficult conditions. However, those who did remain in Queen's Bush continued to get together for the August holiday.

Elmira, located in Woolwich Township, was the main centre of activity for Blacks in the Queen's Bush. They would often come into town to shop and sell goods. Emancipation Day celebrations were also hosted on the

Elmira Exhibition Grounds and at the local Black church, located about six kilometres to the northwest. The last celebration in Elmira seems to have taken place in 1886. It was attended by about two hundred people who pitched tents, barbecued, and enjoyed musical entertainment provided by a band and a group singalong.[10]

Other nearby towns hosted Emancipation Day as well. On August 1, 1890, the fifty-seventh anniversary of the abolition of slavery was recognized in Berlin (now Kitchener), just twenty kilometres south of Elmira.

> A grand barbecue was held and various games were indulged in. The principal sporting attraction was the baseball match between Hamilton and Toronto. The visitors came from Toronto chiefly, but there was quite a representation from London, Brantford, and Hamilton. This evening a grand ball and cakewalk were held in the rink.[11]

Another Emancipation Day observance took place in Berlin on August 2, 1894. A Black fife and a drum band led the street procession to West Side Park (now Waterloo Park) where there were many sporting events. A dance, held at the town hall in the evening, included a cakewalk contest.[12]

At times the Emancipation Day celebrations were held under the auspices of the local church, providing an opportunity to raise money to support community initiatives. In 1935, the African Canadians of Wallenstein had a picnic in commemoration of Emancipation Day and to fundraise for the building that was used as both a school and a church. The Black community gradually dissipated as the elders passed on and the younger people relocated to larger cities in search of better opportunities.

Simcoe County: Collingwood and Oro

During the nineteenth century people of African descent settled in several villages and hamlets in Simcoe County including Oro and Collingwood. Oro-Medonte Township, located on the western shore of Lake Simcoe northwest of Barrie and southwest of Orillia, was home to around 150 Black residents at the peak of its population. They settled on Wilberforce

Road, one concession east of Penetanguishene Road, which they helped to extend northwards. These families also farmed on the plots of land they received from the government. Others went to Shanty Bay, another area in Oro Township. African-American refugees, who escaped using the Underground Railroad, comprised the majority of the citizens including those in Collingwood. Many fugitives arrived in Simcoe County by boat from such American ports as Chicago and Milwaukee, and Canadian Great Lakes ports like Sault Ste. Marie. Northern Railway operated a line of steamships in the Great Lakes and ships sailed on a regular route from Chicago and Milwaukee, up Lake Michigan, across Lake Huron, and into Georgian Bay to Collingwood and Owen Sound. It was not uncommon for fugitives to stow away on these ships.[13]

The town of Collingwood, founded in 1834, is located on the shore of Georgian Bay in the northwest section of Simcoe County. In the early 1900s there were an estimated 120 Blacks living mainly in the southwestern section of the town. One of the first Black settlers in Collingwood, in the 1850s, was a man named Harris who owned a tavern and hotel.[14] Others include Elizabeth Piecraft who also arrived in the 1850s. She was a cook and the first caretaker of Central High School, while her husband was a labourer, the town's bell ringer, and a fiddler on some of the passenger boats. "Dr." Susan LeBurtis was a successful herb doctor and lived in a nice home on Sunset Point. Mrs. Bolden owned a hat shop on Hurontario Street. Abraham Sheffield worked as a pearl-ash maker and Pleasant Duval owned a barber shop and an ice cream and soda shop on Huron Street while his wife ran a dress-making business out of their home. Others were employed as house servants, whitewashers, lime-burners, bakers, plasterers, day labourers, barbers, waiters, and chefs on boats like the *Armstrong* and in public facilities like the North American Hotel. Joseph Cooper, a free Black and Civil War veteran, came to Collingwood in 1866 at the age of twenty-four. He worked as a labourer then opened a cork factory in 1882 where he employed eleven people. In 1904, his sons opened a contracting business to pave and repair town roads and helped to construct the old Victoria Public School, some local factories, and other buildings.[15]

The Sheffield family played a prominent role in Collingwood's history. One descendant, Howard Sheffield, who passed away a few years ago, was an athlete of considerable talent and a powerful hockey player, but was barred from the major leagues because of his race. He and his niece, Carolyn Wilson, with the support of other members of the family established the Sheffield Park History and Cultural Museum, which commemorates the extensive Black history of the area.

With only a fairly small population in comparison to other places in Ontario, the Black community needed strong social supports to sustain their existence. Simcoe' Blacks interacted at church, such as the Edgar AME Church, established in 1848 under the leadership of Reverend Richard Sorrick, or the BME Church, which met in people's homes until a building was constructed on Seventh Street in 1871. In particular, they gathered at the home of Pleasant and Mariah Jane Duval on Sixth Street. Pleasant Duval is said (according to family oral history) to have walked from New Orleans to Collingwood. The Duval home was described as the social centre for Blacks in Collingwood, Owen Sound, and surrounding region. Parties, picnics, and other occasions were held there. The Blacks of the area also came together for the August First holiday.

Numerous celebrations were held in Simcoe County, usually spread over two days so that celebrants could support events and spend time with friends in Owen Sound. These affairs would have been attended by members of the Collingwood community and guests from surrounding centres.

Members of Oro's African-Canadian community also held many commemorations. A local White author wrote an account of the celebration from personal recollection:

> One of these great occasions is in the beginning of the long hot days in August when Darkey Hollow empties its brilliantly altered population into the Maple Grove above the Wanda Falls where they hold a monster picnic, commemorating their fathers' emancipation from slavery. Then, perhaps, for the first time in the year we feel in touch with our less fortunate neighbours. There is nothing like the mention of slavery to touch the heart of one who revels in the glorious freedom of the Land of Maple. Thoughts of their great day of darkness come back on this day of their great rejoicing, to give us sympathy and to keep our hearts warm from our downtrodden brethren

during the coming trials of winter. But the first of August
under the maples, with Joshua DeForest playing the fiddle
and Miss Lavinia Lodice Smith in all glory of a flaming
blue gown and white veil ...[16]

They conducted street processions on Wilberforce Road, marching
together, playing small instruments, and singing spirituals and plantation
songs.

While the tone of this description is very patronizing, it is useful
for three purposes. One, it gives details on how Blacks in Oro observed
Emancipation Day. Secondly, it reflects the attitude of some White
Canadians at that time, and third it speaks to the tenacity of the fugitive
settlers who continued celebrating and rejoicing their freedom, even
though they experienced hardships in their new home, struggling with
poor farmland and harsh winters.

According to another account, there was a regular soccer game between
Black and White players from local teams that attracted a large number of
spectators from near and far. "The negroes were skilled at hitting the ball
with their heads and sending it great distances. Their weak spots were their
shins, a fact that their opponents kept in mind."[17] In a poem written by
W.R Best, another White resident of Oro, he says: "Emancipation day they
had a glorious time...."[18] From these pieces of literature, the conclusion
can be drawn that August First commemorations were an important social
institution in the county.

When John Nettleton[19] arrived in Collingwood with his family in
1857, he recorded his observations on the early town:

> There was also quite an extensive colored settlement
> between 6th and 7th streets, near Walnut street. Being
> nearly all escaped slaves from the United States they
> celebrated the British Emancipation Day on the 1st of
> August by a picnic and dance, under the big elm trees on
> Third Street. Mayor McWatt, Adam Dudgeon and Peter
> Ferguson delivered orations to them about the glories and
> freedom of the British Empire and the citizens used to
> join them in the evening in dancing.[20]

Whites and Blacks celebrated together, as noted by Nettleton and by the following description in an article dated July 30, 1862, from a slightly torn copy of *The Spirit of the Age*, a local Barrie newspaper:

> being the twenty-eighth anniversary ... Emancipation by England of the ... slaves is to be kept by the ... people of this county with more.... [ordinary] signs of rejoicing and thankfulness. They are to meet at Barrie and among the proceedings of the day have arranged for a religious service, at the conclusion of which a sermon will be delivered by the Rev. Mr. Morgan. In the evening the party will dine together, and afterwards hold a soiree, when several able speakers will address the meeting. The rejoicings are not to be confined to the coloured people, but all who feel friendly towards them are desired to join their party. We trust the interesting proceedings will pass off successfully.[21]

By the 1860s interracial groups of Simcoe County residents were meeting at Sunset Point Park on Georgian Bay, having followed a parade through Collingwood to the waterside site. Joined by Blacks from Owen Sound, who walked about sixty kilometres to get there, they listened to speeches and picnicked for the afternoon. The evening program consisted of a lively dance or a festive banquet.[22]

Eventually, the number of African-Canadians living in Simcoe County gradually declined when some faithful Oro followers of Reverend Sorrick moved to Hamilton in the 1840s after he accepted a position there. In the 1850s and 1860s, some who were living in more rural areas relocated in Collingwood, and Emancipation Day festivities were kept alive well into the 1900s. Just at the turn of the century "Colored people from all parts of the county gathered at Nottawasaga River ... to celebrate Emancipation Day" where they enjoyed the day at the beach.[23]

In the mid-twentieth century, some people in Simcoe County got together at Sunset Point for a picnic, games, and social interaction. The older kids who were good swimmers would go up the road to swim at Black Rock and the younger ones played on the swings or played baseball. First of

August festivities were usually combined with the Sunday school picnic in the 1950s, then gradually faded out as the younger generation moved away.

After that celebrants went up to Owen Sound. The two BME churches, the Masonic and Eastern Stars, and Black fraternal orders, tended to join together for events then, just as they do today, to strengthen the numbers attending. This shared event approach was a natural evolution as everyone was related in one way or another, and Collingwood had a much smaller Black population. Those adults who really wanted to party usually went to a house party in the evening.[24] Alternatively some of the small number of local Blacks would travel to other celebrations like the colossal ones held in Windsor or St. Catharines.

Part III

Celebrations in Other Parts of Canada

7

Quebec: Montreal

All the great things are simple, and many can be expressed in a
single word: freedom; justice; honour; duty; mercy; hope.
    — Sir Winston Churchill, *Churchill by Himself,* 2008.

Enslaved Africans were imported to the early-established French settlements
of Quebec (New France then Lower Canada) almost as soon as they were
founded. The French initially enslaved Native people, which the French
referred to as Panis — primarily the Pawnee (Panis) people originally of
the Great Plains — until 1859 when they were forced to Oklahoma. Slaves
were needed to work in the developing industries of fishing, mining, and
forestry, but the Panis were sometimes difficult to control so colonists began
to use Africans as a source of free labour as early as 1628. Slaves worked
as field labourers, miners, or household servants. By 1759, some 1,132
African slaves and 2,472 Native slaves were counted.

Following the American Revolution, a number of enslaved African
Americans arrived in St. Armand, Quebec, with Loyalist Phillip Luke. Their
labour was directed towards making bricks and potash, which were shipped
to Europe. Many others were skilled tradespeople such as sailors, coopers,
wainwrights, blacksmiths, wheelwrights, and even executioners. Most of
the slaves lived in Montreal, one of the largest centres of the French colony.

When the Articles of Capitulation under the Treaty of Paris were
signed in Montreal in 1760, one of the conditions reinforced the right of

the slaveholders of New France to keep their slaves under British rule.[1]

Well-known Montreal residents owned slaves, among them James McGill, a wealthy fur-trading merchant and founder of McGill University; Mother Marie d'Youville who ran the Hôpital-Général; and the Reverend David Charbrand Delisle of Montreal's Church of England. Enslaved Africans in early Canada resisted their oppression and sought their freedom in many ways, sometimes simply taking flight just like their counterparts in other slaveholding territories. Advertisements for these runaways can be found in the early newspapers of New France and Upper Canada.

Montreal was the scene of a dramatic resistance to enslavement when, during the spring of 1734, Marie-Joseph Angélique allegedly set fire to her mistresses home to protest her pending sale. Forty-six buildings burned down. She was charged, tried, found guilty of this crime, and subsequently tortured and hanged.[2] It is not known how many slaves were freed in Quebec with the passage of the Emancipation Act in 1833, but in 1804 there was approximately one hundred and forty-two slaves on record in Montreal and three hundred and fifty throughout the rest of Quebec.[3]

With a long history of enslavement, resistance, and the fight for freedom, it is not surprising that one of the first Canadian Emancipation Day celebrations occurred in Montreal, Quebec, in 1834, the very date the act took effect. Members of the Black community converged in the public hall on the second floor above St. Anne's Market (Place d'Youville) on Commissioner Street between Peter and McGill Streets. The monumental celebration commenced with a scripture reading from the Bible and a prayer led by John Patton, a Black shoemaker. The keynote address, given by Anthony Grant[4] expressed utmost gratefulness for the freeing of eight hundred thousand of his brethren from bondage. Grant exclaimed:

> I am sure that you will join me heart and hand in giving our warmest acknowledgements to Great Britain for the noble act she has performed; and that you truly congratulate your brethren, that they were placed in a situation to partake of the blessings you enjoy. I am also sure that you will join me in hoping that, under the protection of the British flag, (that flag which has borne that battle and the breeze for a thousand years), our emancipated brethren

will so conduct themselves as peaceable and loyal subjects, as will prove to the world that they not only duly estimate their privileges, but are worthy of the glorious boon bestowed upon them.[5]

He scolded the United States in his speech stating "… America will then stand alone, the champion of those principles which will receive the curse, the contempt, and the detestation of the civilized world; for slavery and the trade in human blood are violations of the laws of God and the rights of man."[6] The crowd expressed loyalty to England with "three hearty cheers for Old England, the true land of the brave, and the home of the free." The banquet that followed took place at the St. George's Inn along the shore of the St. Lawrence River and included the giving of toasts and musical entertainment throughout the evening. The celebrants witnessed the ships in the port raising their flags in honour of the day. The editor of the *Montreal Gazette* remarked, "The day has at length come when England, and not America, is entitled to the undisputed honor of being 'the land of liberty'…."[7]

Free Blacks were also residents of the city. A Black man named Thomas Wily, former colonel of the British 83rd Regiment, was appointed the chief of police in Montreal in 1844, and held this position until 1849. Montreal became a hotbed of anti-slavery initiatives during the 1850s and 1860s, partially fuelled by the fugitive slave population there since the 1830s, one that had swollen dramatically with the passage of the Fugitive Slave Act in 1850. A large number of them lived either in the St. Antoine's Ward or on St. Urbain Street, the areas of the city with the highest concentration of Black settlers. Many, like Shadrach Minkins,[8] were active in the American abolition movement, helping to raise funds for freedom initiatives such as the liberation efforts of John Brown and the John Anderson extradition case when these men came to speak in the city. When John Brown was executed in December 1859 for leading the attack at Harper's Ferry, almost one thousand Black and White Montrealers attended a public gathering at Bonaventure Hall to pay respects to the martyr. Local White sympathizers included *Montreal Witness* editor John Dougall,[9] D.S. Janes,[10] a flour merchant, William Craig Baynes of McGill College, and John Redpath of Redpath Sugar. These men were active in the fight against slavery in different ways. Dougall and Janes were executive members of the national Anti-Slavery Society of Canada. All of these men also participated in Emancipation Day observances during this time period, where fugitive and native Blacks expressed gratitude for freedom on British soil, embraced their new African-Canadian identity, and demonstrated their allegiance to Britain and Canada.

Members of Montreal's Black community participated in an August First observance in 1861 against the backdrop of the American Civil War. It was held under the auspices of the Young Men's Christian Association (YMCA), the group that had hosted several Emancipation Day commemorations during the 1850s and 1860s. For some time the Montreal YMCA had been actively protesting against slavery in the United States.[11] People congregated in the morning and in the evening for one of two religious services at the five-storey Bonaventure Hall, located on the northwest corner of St. James Street (Rue St. Jacques) and Victoria Square (Rue du Square Victoria). Each session, the morning chaired by Reverend Dr. Henry Wilkes and the night's events by Reverend John McVicar, was opened with the singing of hymns and the offering of prayers, but speeches on the theme of the day were delivered only in the evening. This meeting was especially emotional, because the audience was commemorating the freedom, rights, and opportunities they were enjoying as British subjects while hoping that the Civil War would result in the liberation of their enslaved American brethren.

Reverend McVicar began his discourse with a synopsis of the arguments of the Northern and Southern states, currently engaged in battle against one another and argued that God would intervene and rectify the situation. The second speaker was John Dougall, who discredited the idea that American slave owners had any rights to compensation once slaves were freed because they had no rights to human beings and they had already benefitted from their free labour. He described how the relationship between the slave owner and the slave would change once emancipation arrived and rebutted some arguments against freeing enslaved Africans.

Then a Reverend John McKillican gave a detailed account of the political state of affairs in the Northern states, having just recently returned from New England, and spoke of the many men going off to fight on the Union side. Next, a former slave described his horrific experiences as a bondsman and extended sincere thanks to the British Crown for a new, free life. He also denounced the practice of slavery around the world. The final speaker was YMCA president Francis E. Grafton, who wrapped up the speeches with a discussion on emancipation, gave examples of the international fight to obtain freedom for those in bondage, and urged those in attendance to pray for the demise of slavery in the United States.[12] Some of the Black men in attendance that day would later head for the Northern states to fight in the Union Army in an effort to do their part in eradicating slavery. In 1863, when Blacks were allowed to serve in the northern forces, they joined approximately five hundred White French-Canadian men from Montreal who had enlisted by 1862. All fought and some sacrificed their lives in the name of justice.

The twenty-eighth anniversary celebration of the end of British enslavement of Africans took place under similar conditions — fugitives, Black and White anti-slavery activists, and White sympathizers all anxiously waited for the fall of American slavery. An interracial group enjoyed the day together. In the morning a church service was held at Bonaventure Hall, where Black and White community members prayed, sang hymns, and listened to a sermon. A picnic was held in the afternoon, and in the evening guests attended a public gathering to hear Reverend James Green, a man of African descent. He implored listeners "to show by their diligence, piety, contentment and thankfulness, in this land of freedom."[13] The next speaker from England provided a detailed history of the abolition movement in his homeland prior to the emancipation of slaves in British possessions as an example to show what's to come in the United States. The third speaker pointed out the expected liberation of enslaved Africans in the southern United States and paid homage to the ancestors by noting that "the innumerable prayers of generations of slaves, had not gone up in vain."[14]

Additional addresses were delivered by Reverend Alex F. Kemp, minister of the St. Gabriel Street Free Church; William Craig Baynes of McGill College; John Dougall, editor of the *Montreal Witness*; and two African-American fugitives — Mr. John Watkins and Mr. George Davis. Throughout the observance the focus was on celebrating the freedoms enjoyed in their new homeland and on "willing" the abolition of slavery in America.

When President Abraham Lincoln, the man who signed the Emancipation Proclamation, was assassinated in April of 1865, the city council officially declared a day of mourning and services were held across the city, one of them at the American Presbyterian Church where D.S. Janes worshipped. The Black citizens of Montreal also held their own memorial at Bonaventure Hall to "express their sympathy at the fate of John Brown."[15] Janes was appointed chairman of this meeting and several men — including L. Holton, John Dougall, Reverend Kemp, Mr. Musgrove, and Mr. Baynes[16] — were also in attendance. Montreal's association with their American neighbours (in relation to people of African descent) had evolved over time from the United States being a supplier of slaves to becoming a haven for a considerable number of slaves and even Confederate refugees. Montreal itself was a base for the continental anti-slavery movement.

One year after the end of the American Civil War and one year before Confederation, African Canadians in Montreal celebrated another Emancipation Day. Thomas Cook, Charles Wilson, George Davis, and John Watkins organized the demonstration. Although a sizeable portion of the self-emancipated slaves from the United States began returning south of the border, many were still in Montreal on August 1, 1866, to celebrate the liberation of enslaved African-Americans and the complete abolition of slavery in North America. The program was held at the YMCA building.[17] What these events illustrate is that Blacks and Whites worked and socialized closely together with the aim of improving race relations and of advocating for liberty and equality for all citizens. Although the Black community in Montreal remained relatively small during the mid-nineteenth century, Emancipation Day played an important, consistent role. The celebrations served to provide an outlet for Blacks and Whites to speak out against slavery and to bring awareness to democratic and human rights.

There has been an effort to revive the celebration of freedom in Montreal by the Universal Negro Improvement Association (UNIA). In August 2009, the ninety-year-old Black organization hosted an Emancipation Day commemoration at their building on Notre Dame. Through inviting guest lecturers and setting up other activities, the group endeavours to educate young and new Canadians about the contributions of Blacks to Canada's development as a Dominion.[18]

8

The Maritimes

The sweltering summer of the Negro's legitimate discontent will not pass until there is an invigorating autumn of freedom and equality.
— Dr. Martin Luther King Jr., "I Have a Dream," 1963.

Nova Scotia

The earliest Black pioneers of Nova Scotia (at that time part of Acadia) and other parts of the Maritimes were enslaved by French, and later by British, colonists. As the practice of slavery declined, Black pioneers (the free Blacks who worked for the British military during the American Revolution) relocated to Nova Scotia. They were followed by Black refugees, the escaped slaves who helped to defend Britain during the War of 1812. For their service, almost two thousand Black refugees migrated to Nova Scotia between and 1815 and 1834 to live on free soil in areas like Shelburne, Birchtown, Hammond's Plains, Preston, Digby, Yarmouth, and Halifax, including Africville.[1] These families linked themselves to their African kinsmen throughout Nova Scotia in celebrating their shared liberation from enslavement and their desire to build a new life and rejoiced through August First commemorations.

From 1846 to 1867 Emancipation Day celebrations in Halifax were organized by a benevolent society called the African Abolition Society

Reverend Richard Preston was an anti-slavery activist and community leader. He established eleven Baptist churches in Nova Scotia and organized the African Baptist Association of Nova Scotia.

(AAS). Started by Baptist minister Richard Preston[2] in 1846, the mixed group of former American slaves, descendants of Canadian slaves, and free Blacks "dedicated itself to the eradication of an institution that had been illegal in the British Empire since 1834...,"[3] but also aimed to improve the lives of Black residents through charity, education, religion, and community development. They provided help to fugitives during the peak period of their arrival between the 1840s and the 1850s, invited speakers to lecture on African history, slavery, and the impact of the 1850 Fugitive Slave Law. They also hosted other community events including celebrations of the anniversary of the abolition of British slavery.

Amani Whitfield in *Blacks on the Border* describes the AAS as being run almost exclusively by former slaves. In a move to solidify autonomy and minimize the influence of local Whites, the organization barred them from joining the society's executive committee so that they could not participate in any decision-making regarding internal policies or practices. However, the AAS did invite Whites to attend AAS public lectures and some meetings.[4]

Emancipation Day was a way for the new arrivals to establish a connection with other people of African origin across the British Empire and to see themselves as subjects of the Crown and free people. The festivities also served to focus the attention of Blacks living in Halifax on abolition in the southern United States as well as on the racial discrimination they faced in their daily lives. Most of them faced residential segregation as their communities were intentionally and completely secluded from white settlements, as determined by the way land grants were issued. The plots they received were on poor, rocky land, which limited their farming opportunities and adversely affected their quality of life.

Additionally, common schools were separate by law in their isolated communities and since Black schools did not receive sufficient funding, primarily White church missionaries and White abolitionists delivered the education. Another instance of letting Blacks know they were not necessarily welcome in Nova Scotia was the passing of "An Act to Prevent the Clandestine Landing of Liberated Slaves ... from Vessels arriving in the Province" in 1833, enacted by a local government apprehensive of a potential flood of fugitive slaves pouring into Nova Scotia once the Emancipation Act took effect. Enforcement focused on ships coming into the harbours that might be carrying refugees. Any Black refugees found on these ships were to be denied entry to Nova Scotia. The captain of the ship would be fined if escapees were found on his vessel or would have to give surety for the ones he knew of and would vouch for. This legislation was in effect for two years, after which the assembly attempted to renew the bill. However, the British Parliament prohibited any renewal and deemed the bill to be discriminatory, citing that it countered the intention of the Emancipation Act as people of African origin were now entitled to the same rights and privileges as any British subject.[5]

The refugees, the Loyalists, and their descendants generally accepted their conditional freedom and sometimes poor quality of life as better than being chattel property. As a female refugee pointed out, "I'll live on 'taters and salt and help fight myself till I die, before I'll be a slave again."[6] However, they actively pursued the ideal of equal citizenship and the full democratic rights entitled to them as British subjects and worked to improve the situation for themselves and future generations.

August First commemorations were representative of this dilemma. On the one hand, Blacks in Halifax expressed gratefulness for the liberty on British soil, however limited, yet they employed this public medium to rally for racial equality. Also the day was one of the few times each year for African Canadians who lived near and far to socialize. To ensure a sizable turnout and to make a public request for their brothers and sisters, the AAS placed ads in mainstream newspapers such as the *Novascotian* and the *British Colonist* to encourage White employers to give their workers of African descent the day off. The occasion usually consisted of a procession

CELEBRATION

THE Abolition Society intend to Celebrate the Anniversary of the Abolition of Slavery in the British Dominions, on the First of August next, by a PIC NIC, &c., To take place at Belmont. The Committee of Management therefore request the attendance of all the colored people of Halifax and the vicinity, and all the Friends of Liberty and Freedom. They would likewise appeal to the Ladies and Gentlemen of Halifax for permission to the colored Servants in their employ, to hold this one day of rejoicing as a Holiday.

A Procession will start at 9 o'clock from the African School House, and proceed to Church, where service will commence at 10 o'clock, after which they will proceed to Belmont, and pass the remainder of the day In healthful and innocent enjoyments. Tickets to be obtained at the Gate. Entrance 77. By order of the President.

THOMAS JOHNSON.
July 17.   Secretary.

Adapted from the original and designed by Kaimera Media Inc.

A reproduction of an advertisement that ran in the British Colonist (Halifax) on July 19, 1851, requesting that White employers give Black employees the day off to commemorate Emancipation Day.

through Halifax, followed by speeches from former slaves and government dignitaries, and concluding with picnics and other festivities in the evening.

In 1847, the African Abolition Society hosted their second annual Emancipation Day celebration. Led by a military band, those assembled paraded through the streets of Halifax carrying banners praising "freedom and British liberty." They marched to the Government House[7] at Barrington and Bishop Streets, just south of Spring Garden Road, to listen to a schedule of addresses. Members of "the Society departed to the festive grove at the North Farm where the remainder of the day was spent in the usual pleasures."[8] The North Farm property belonged to the governor and was situated at the north end of Gottingen Street where Devonshire Avenue crosses today.[9]

The 1850 celebration that recognized the sixteenth anniversary included a procession led by the band of the flagship *Wellesley*. They marched about one kilometre northwest from the African School House[10] at the corner of Gerrish and Maynard Streets to the African Baptist Chapel on Cornwallis Street. A moving sermon was most likely delivered by Reverend Preston, then the gatherers continued to Belmont House, south of Oakland Road and west of the southward extension of Robie Street. At that time it was owned by John Howe Jr., half brother of Joseph Howe. He commonly offered the grounds of Belmont for various public and private events. Here they were treated to more speeches, refreshments, and entertainment. The increasingly interracial crowd included Joseph Howe, provincial secretary, former editor of the *Novascotian*, and father of confederation, who evidently had a pleasurable time at Belmont:

> The Hon. Provincial Secretary was driven to the ground in a cab, seated on the knee of one of the coloured men … We have no disposition whatever to cast a slight upon the members of the Abolition Society, but we do not think it exactly becoming the dignity of the chief officer of the Province to embrace them or to sit upon their knees … Oh Joseph, thy career has indeed been glorious, and thy children will think upon their father with pride!"[11]

The thirteen toasts drunk at the event reflected the racial and global awareness of the established Black community in Halifax and their loyalty to Canada. The first salute memorialized "Africa, the land of our Forefathers," then the Queen, Prince Albert, local government officials, and church leaders. The ninth acknowledgement was to the AAS, "may she never fail in promoting the cause of her poor and oppressed people, from every nation beneath the Sun" and the following thanks was extended to "The Printers, who have been so kind and liberal towards the cause of Emancipation."[12] As the newspaper was the mass media of that time, it was important to maintain a relationship with the editors and the printers in order to have access to a large audience. Mainstream newspapers across Canada reported on Emancipation Day that took place in their cities and towns as well as in other jurisdictions.

In 1852, Emancipation Day was observed on August 3rd with a street procession to the African Baptist church to hear a service, most likely by Reverend Preston. The band of the 97th regiment led the large numbers of gatherers through the main streets of Halifax, and then continued onward to the Belmont estate for various festivities. On the way back to the city, the band played the tune of "Get Out the Way Old Dan Tucker," more than likely a popular Emancipation version of the song with anti-slavery lyrics (see Appendix B). The 1853 observances took place at Melville Island and were attended by lots of people. Melville Island[13] is located five kilometres west of Halifax, at the head of the northwest arm of Halifax Harbour.

The African Abolition Society hosted a private dinner in 1855 to recognize Emancipation Day where forty society members and guests attended to partake of a shared meal. At the events during the 1850s, at least fourteen toasts were raised each year. The salutations always covered the globe from Africa, to Britain, the West Indies, and North America. The proposals reveal the global perspective they held and the many components of their African-Canadian identity. Homage was always paid to the African's land of origin, gratitude to Britain for discontinuing an inhumane practice, for opportunities in Canada, strong opposition against American slavery, and the promise for a brighter future.[14]

One month after Confederation in 1867, another large group assembled and paraded through the main streets of Halifax out to the shores of the Bedford Basin to enjoy a bountiful picnic. Unfortunately, the day was marred by a racially motivated attack. The participants returning to the city core were assaulted by a crowd of White thugs that could only be quelled by police reinforcement. Consequently, the evening soiree at the Mason Hall on Barrington Street was cancelled.[15] This was not only a physical clash, it was also a conflict of ideals that simmered in all parts of Canada. While native-born and immigrant African Canadians felt that the union of the provinces of the nation would further secure their citizenship and that they would be finally be embraced as contributing members of society, a segment of the White Canadian population believed that there was no place for them in the new Dominion. The sentiment of people of African descent not being true "Canadians" lingers today in the trite question, "Where are you from?"[16]

Shortly after 1867 Emancipation Day was commemorated chiefly with small group picnics. Why did the grand public affairs end with the confederation of the Canadian provinces? It is likely some American residents repatriated to the United States, thus reducing the number of Blacks in the vicinity. As such, with the end of American slavery there was no longer the pressing issue of emancipation. Perhaps many assumed that the formation of the Dominion of Canada further guaranteed their rights and place in Canadian society, thus rendering the civic demonstrations unnecessary for the purpose of mobilizing for political and social causes.

African-Canadian settlements in Guysborough County have also held Emancipation Day commemorations. Through to the 1950s, New Road, a Black neighbourhood now known as North Preston, held their Emancipation Day celebrations in isolation from observances in other nearby Black communities in Cole Harbour and Halifax. In 1856 Richard Preston established the Second Baptist Church in the New Road vicinity.[17] As chief organizer of August First observances in Halifax and minister of eleven Black Baptist churches in Nova Scotia, it is likely that he coordinated events in other locations or planned joint commemorations.

Nova Scotia marked the 175th anniversary of the abolition of slavery by the British parliament with an emancipation celebration called Black Freedom 175. Organized by the Amistad Freedom Society of Nova Scotia, the main highlight of the week-long festival at the Maritime Museum of the Atlantic in Halifax was the visit of the schooner *Amistad*, a replica of the famed ship that was seized by the United States Navy for illegal slave trading. Since 1807 by British law and 1808 by American legislation, the slave trading across the Atlantic had been prohibited. One of the captives, named Cinque, led a revolt and all were charged with mutiny and murder. In a historic court decision by the United States Supreme Court in 1841, it was determined that the native Africans were kidnapped and not Cuban-born slaves and were recognized as never being legal property, but were human beings with human rights. They were subsequently returned to Africa through the assistance of abolitionists of the Amistad Committee. The decision also struck out against ongoing American slavery by marginally recognizing the human rights of Blacks.

The event also consisted of a welcome gala, performances by numerous local and international musicians, drumming, poetry, speeches, public tours of the replica tall ship, and activities for youth, including a sail and workshops to build leadership skills, explore diversity, and appreciate freedom. Natal Day, the official birthday of the communities of Halifax and Dartmouth is now the recognized August First holiday.

New Brunswick

Enslaved Africans first settled in the present day Maritime provinces of Nova Scotia, New Brunswick, and Prince Edward Island, historically known as Acadia. Up until the end of the eighteenth century when the practice of slavery dwindled, a few hundred enslaved Africans lived in numerous New Brunswick Loyalist settlements including Otnabog, Carleton, Gagetown, and Fredericton. The number of Blacks increased during the Revolutionary War when escaped slaves who were granted freedom by British soldiers settled in Loch Lomond. They were joined by Black pioneers; free Blacks employed by the British army during the American Revolution. A large number of these Black Loyalists created a settlement at Elm Hill. Another wave of African-American immigrants entered New Brunswick in 1815 when nearly four hundred Black refugees of the War of 1812 arrived. Some would receive eight- to twenty-hectare land grants in several towns, including an area just east of Loch Lomond where they established a Black community called Willow Grove, about ten kilometres northeast of Saint John (now part of East Saint John). Yet more would come to New Brunswick, most fleeing the United States from the reach of the 1850 Fugitive Slave Act.

The experiences of African-Canadians in New Brunswick were similar to those of their counterparts in other Maritime provinces. Although they were no longer enslaved on either side of the border, their freedom was restricted by local and provincial governments. Some were denied the land grants they were promised by Crown officials, while those who did receive land grants were often given property in isolated, poor, rocky, or marshland areas. The lots were often smaller than promised and smaller than the ones given to White Loyalists. Furthermore, most did not receive sufficient aid to assist in settling in to their new homes. When the City of Saint John incorporated on April 30, 1785,[18] its charter placed several restrictions specifically on the growing Black community. People of African origin could not become free men[19] and were prohibited from practising a trade or selling goods in the city, barred from fishing at Saint John Harbour, and could not reside within the city limits unless employed as a servant or a labourer. These stipulations, which remained city law until they were removed in 1870, severely restricted not only the development of the African-Canadian community in the area surrounding Saint John, but limited personal development as well; the separate schools that their children attended were inadequate and they also had to fight racial prejudice in its many forms. In 1830 a Black man and several Black women were victims of a racially motivated physical attack.

In spite of the obstacles brought about by racism from government authorities and some of their White neighbours, many Blacks remained in New Brunswick. These people included African Canadians of multi-generations and recent colonists who were determined to live in freedom, albeit restricted, and to contribute to their communities. Robert Whetsel, a fugitive from American slavery, settled in Saint John around 1852. He was originally from Virginia, but had escaped to Chicago and eventually made his way to Saint John. Whetsel was an entrepreneur: first establishing a barbershop, followed by an oyster saloon, then a successful ice business, the only one of its kind. Whetsel was very active in the Black community and highly respected by both Blacks and Whites. He was described in his obituary as one of Saint John's "representative colored citizens."[20] Therefore, it is likely that Whetsel played a role in or attended a celebration of the nineteenth anniversary of the end of British slavery. A tea was hosted at St. Stephen's Hall at the corner of King Square and Charlotte Street, followed by speeches "by some of our leading philanthropic and public men."[21]

Another fugitive slave who did well in New Brunswick was Cornelius Sparrow, who made the difficult journey from Virginia to Saint John in 1851. After working as a labourer for ten years, Sparrow opened the first of three successful business ventures, including two restaurants and a

Militiamen Dan Taylor and Alex Diggs attended the Loch Lomond Fair circa 1900.

unisex hair salon. Black men like Dan Taylor and Alex Diggs continued to volunteer in militias in Saint John and Fredericton to defend their country and demonstrate their loyalty to the Crown, even though they were forced to lead segregated lives. They enlisted in the all-Black company of the York County Militia until 1849, the African Staff Company that had been organized and attached to the Saint John Regiment in 1813, and in the all-Black Pioneer 104th Regiment, which had formed in 1814. Black men from New Brunswick served in the Construction Battalion Number Two in the First World War, and in regular integrated military forces.[22]

African Canadians in New Brunswick, as in other communities, established churches such as the St. Philip's AME Church in 1859 in Saint John and the Willow Grove Baptist Church for worship and fellowship. Blacks celebrated Emancipation Day together despite their limited citizenship rights and the racial discrimination they faced. They were still thankful for what they had, but were determined for themselves and their successors to live a freer life on British soil and for their brethren in America to be released from bondage. A brief article in the *Novascotian* on August 15, 1859, reported that:

> The colored population of Saint John, New Brunswick, celebrated the anniversary of the emancipation of the slaves of the British West Indies on the 1st inst. At a meeting held at the Mechanics' Institute in that city, capital speeches, interspersed with songs, glees, etc., are said to have been delivered.[23]

In 1863, as the Civil War swept across the United States, African Canadians in New Brunswick observed Emancipation Day. A local newspaper reported that about five hundred people congregated in Saint John at Mr. Smith's building in the evening. Robert Whetsel chaired the meeting and delivered an address, followed by an African-American guest from Boston named Francis. It was an interracial gathering with several members of the Irish community attending and speaking, such as Timothy Warren Anglin, founder of the *Saint John Weekly Freeman* newspaper, and a few other community leaders in attendance. The speakers extended gratitude to Britain, expressed the desire for victory over the South in the Civil War, and deliverance from bondage.

Entertainment included music by the City Band and a performance by Mr. Patterson, who "sung a song on Emancipation to the air of 'Old Dan

Tucker.'"[24] The tune "Get Off the Track!" appears to have been quite popular among African Canadians celebrating August First in the Maritimes. The author of the lyrics predicted the end of American slavery would come at the end of the Civil War: "Emancipation soon will bless our happy nation."[25] In the 1860s, the folk music by Black and White abolitionists carried a strong political message against the institution of slavery. It instructed enslaved Africans and all friends of liberty to jump aboard the freedom train: "Ho! The car Emancipation rides majestic thro' our nation."[26]

As discussed in the section about Nova Scotia, the number of African Canadians on the east coast lessened with the victory of the Union Army in the Civil War. Many of the refugees returned home to the United States and with the abolition of slavery Emancipation Day gatherings declined and eventually ceased. Today the first of August is a provincial holiday called New Brunswick Day.

9

British Columbia

Those who deny freedom to others deserve it not for themselves.
— Abraham Lincoln, Letter to Henry L. Pierce, 1859.

Although separated by a considerable distance from the African-Canadian communities of eastern Canada, Blacks in the British colony of Vancouver Island were very much a part of the international movement for freedom and equal rights. Emancipation enacted by Britain was equally as significant to the Black settlers in British Columbia as to their eastern Canadian counterparts. The act provided them with a homeland free from slavery, readily available soil, and more of a political voice. For most there were employment and educational opportunities, and rights and privileges they intended to exercise. They demonstrated their willingness to fight to defend these by volunteering for military duty, petitioning local and provincial government officials, and working together to confront racism.

The Emancipation Act was also relevant to Vancouver Island's Native community as slavery was a long-practised cultural institution among some of the Pacific Coast Native groups,[1] making that part of Canada a unique and difficult locale in which to bring about the abolition of slavery. To compound the situation, senior staff and employees of the Hudson's Bay Company (HBC), mainly European fur traders or explorers of Scottish and French descent, became involved in the enslavement of Natives either through their Native wives or by purchasing slaves themselves. An estimated five thousand

James Douglas appears in an official photograph, 1863.

Courtesy of the Royal British Columbia Museum, B.C. Archives, A-01232.

Natives were enslaved on HBC land west of the Rocky Mountains.[2] When the Emancipation Act came into effect, its stipulations had a significant impact on the western British colony's social, political, and economic landscape.

The HBC immediately issued instructions to all senior personnel, including the chief factor James Douglas[3] in Vancouver, to suppress slavery; a practice that the company had tolerated until then in order to avert a public relations calamity. Britain could not have a company, in which they had made a huge investment since 1670, failing to abide by its laws. In 1849, an author reviewing the workings of the Hudson's Bay Company questioned whether the profit seeking of HBC merchants was above British law and more important than the freedom of enslaved Natives or the interests of the country.[4] Douglas did what he could, short of using force, to enact the new law. He spoke about the importance of moral influence in the eradication of slavery of Native people and delivered a statement condemning the practice. He assured all that each person living on HBC land was free and possessed the legal protection and rights given by law, rights that would be upheld under his management. To his credit, he found ways to encourage the abolition of slavery in British Columbia. Douglas liberated a young enslaved Native boy and gave him a job with the HBC as a paid labourer, a practice the other senior officers repeated. This was a sincere gesture, and he had hoped that this example would encourage HBC officers and employees and Native leaders to do the same. However, in 1838 Douglas conceded that despite his efforts to curb slavery among the Native people very little had changed.

As an abolitionist and a man who detested intolerance, Douglas used his political power to become a more effective player in the quest for complete democracy and citizenship for African Canadians and Native people in Vancouver. In July 1860, Douglas sent three British warships from Esquimalt Harbour along the island's coast. On board was a team of naval officers sent to arrange talks with chiefs of different Native groups. The officers were instructed to attempt to establish an agreement among the chiefs to follow British law prohibiting human enslavement. Many Native leaders did pledge in agreement, but others held out. The navy also patrolled along the coastline, visiting islands and Native villages, making contact with Native leaders and continuing to negotiate an end to slavery, all done without the use of force.

Douglas had the support of abolitionists Admiral John Moresby and Admiral Joseph Denman, the naval officers who were conducting patrols under Douglas's command. They had been involved in the African slave patrols near the coasts of West Africa to enforce the ban on the Transatlantic Slave Trade and were now stationed in Vancouver. The eradication of slavery of Native people was a slow process partly because the practice was deeply entrenched in the social and political relationships along the Pacific Coast and partly because it was not given the same level of priority as that given to African slavery.

Likely in recognition of the agreements made with Native leaders to abolish slavery, Governor Douglas threw a ball in honour of Emancipation Day in 1855 for British and American navy officers at the naval base in the port town of Esquimalt.[5] The practice of enslavement gradually declined over the course of almost one hundred years following the Emancipation Act of 1833 as warfare with Natives lessened (thus fewer prisoners of war) and as the HBC continued to denounce slavery. Another factor was the growing presence of missionaries and other community activists of European background who assisted escaping slaves.

The meaning of freedom on Vancouver Island would change again in early April 1858. Victoria, the capital of Vancouver Island, was a small town of about eight hundred people (including Whites, Natives, and a few Blacks), serving primarily as a trading post for the HBC. But, the discovery of gold in the late 1850s resulted in a population surge, a growth that included a number of people of African descent. The British territory's Black community grew significantly when approximately eight hundred African Americans from San Francisco arrived in Victoria just weeks before thousands of Whites from the western United States, other Canadian provinces, and other nearby countries flocked there for the Fraser Gold Rush.

A small party of Black delegates landed in Victoria in 1858 to scout out Vancouver as a possible relocation area. They were fleeing increasingly repressive laws that prohibited Blacks from jury duty, restricted African-American immigration into California, enforced segregated schooling, and supported slaveholding although the practice had been officially banned in San Francisco. To their delight, the migrants found an ally in James Douglas of the Hudson's Bay Company, who in 1851 was appointed as the governor of the colony of Vancouver Island, a title he held until 1864. Governor James Douglas extended an invitation to the group to settle on the island.

Douglas himself was of African heritage, having been born in Demerara, British Guiana (now Guyana) to a part-Black mother who was free and a Scottish father plantation owner, an ancestry that surely influenced his actions even though he did not publicize his background. He and other officials ensured the settlers that they would be treated equally under the law and that all rights and privileges would be extended to them, including the right to purchase land immediately, to vote after nine months of residency, and to obtain British citizenship after seven years.

The Black Californians differed from other African Americans entering Canada West in that the majority of them were free Blacks with only a small number of fugitives among them. Some freedom seekers, however, had just been recently released. Examples include Archy Lee, a young boy escaping slavery who had stowed away on the *Commodore*, the boat they had taken from San Francisco; Howard Estes who bought his own manumission; and a number of previously enslaved men who hoped to strike gold in order to purchase their families out of slavery in the South.

In contrast to the Black Californians, the African Americans coming in to western Canada in the 1850s were primarily self-emancipated. Back in San Francisco they owned a substantial amount of property and businesses, a high percentage of them could read and write, and many came to British Columbia as skilled workers. On Vancouver Island many opened various kinds of businesses to meet the high demands of the growing colony, from barbershops, to taverns, to farms, to running canneries. A large number accumulated wealth through real estate, having entered the market prior to the development of the island. Black colonists also migrated there from British Caribbean countries, such as Jamaican-born John Giscome, Henry McDame from the Bahamas, and Henry Wilkinson Robinson from Bermuda. Like many of British Columbia's early immigrants, they came to participate in the Fraser and Cariboo gold rushes.[6] In search of gold and opportunity, some of the newly arrived settlers moved to other towns on Vancouver Island, such as Saanich, Nanaimo, Esquimalt, and Salt Spring Island.

They soon found out, however, that while they fared better in British Columbia than in California, they could not completely escape racism.

Blacks were not welcome as volunteers for the fire brigade. They were either refused entry to public institutions such as churches, theatres, and taverns or were assigned to segregated seats. They were also banned from serving jury duty, participating in public ceremonies, and even from attending the 1864 farewell banquet for their highest-ranking supporter, Governor Douglas.

The new Black families found allies in two church ministers, Reverends Edward Cridge and William F. Clarke, in the battle for equal rights. Cridge, an Anglican minister and chaplain to the HBC, was also a close friend of Douglas. He immediately opened his services to the African Americans and extended a warm hand to them, although some Whites declined to worship with them. Clarke, originally from London, Ontario, was commissioned by the Colonial Missionary Society of the English Congregationalist Union Church to begin a mission in Victoria for all settlers and refused to establish a "Negro corner" at the request of some White parishioners. His actions resulted in the circulation of a petition that asked "Shall white men or niggers rule this colony?"[7] In a show of protest, Clarke resigned and returned to Canada West.[8]

Mifflin Gibbs, one of the Black newcomers from California, spoke out on many issues concerning the Black community in Victoria, including the racial discrimination they were experiencing and the need for emancipation in America. His general store in Victoria became a meeting place for Blacks where these topics could be discussed and tackled. Gibbs had worked for anti-slavery groups in Pennsylvania, where he was born free, and he continued the fight to end American slavery in his new homeland.

A successful, sharp businessman, he opened a general store with the support of a business partner to service the incoming flood of prospectors. Gibbs was also instrumental in the organization of the Victoria Pioneer Rifle Company, an all-Black militia formed in 1860. He was elected to the Victoria city council, becoming one of the first Black politicians in Canada. For a brief time Gibbs was the acting mayor, and because of his business savvy was appointed as the chair of the city's finance committee. He also helped in the effort to encourage British Columbia to join Confederation.

In 1859 he wrote a passionate letter to the editor of the *British Colonist* in response to an article originally from the *London Times* that had been reprinted in the newspaper criticizing the emancipation of

African slaves. Gibbs asserted Emancipation was a moral and just act on the part of Britain and that Blacks were doing all the things a person with full citizenship would do. Former slaves were pursuing an education in large numbers, they were legally marrying and building strong families, achieving high level positions in a short period of time, and overall were showing themselves to be productive citizens who contributed to the communities they lived in.[9]

The wives of these Black men involved in the abolition movement — women such as Emily Allen, Sarah Pointer, Maria Gibbs, Sydna E.R. Francis, Julia Ann Booth, Amanda Scott, Nancy Lester, and Catherin Gant — "engaged in public efforts to 'uplift the race.'"[10] As the Committee of Coloured Women, they organized fundraisers and collected donations to assist freed slaves in South Carolina and Philadelphia. They sewed a silk Union Jack flag for the Rifle Corps and presented it to them just moments before the farewell banquet for Governor Douglas, which they could not attend. The women made the presentation because they knew the Corps':

> loyalty to this government is proverbial. The fostering care it has shown to the oppressed of our race, leaves us under many obligations to the sagacity and wisdom of her statesmen. Yet in this far-distant Colony of Her Majesty's Dominion we have many causes to complain. True, you have not as yet been called on to rally under this flag for protection; yet war of complexional distinction is upon us, it is more ravaging to us as a people than that of Mars. But men, as long as this flag shall wave over you, you may rest assured that no man, or set of men, or nations, can successfully grind you down under the iron heel of oppression.[11]

This excerpt is illustrative of some of the ways British Columbia's African-Canadian community supported the African liberation struggle. It also exposes the fact that these new colonists faced discrimination because of their skin colour, with not all of the White immigrants responding to them as favourably as did Governor Douglas, Reverend Edward Cridge, and Reverend William F. Clarke. In spite of, and even because of, the

The African Rifles' only White member was the bandmaster. Fortune Richard, a member of the original group of settlers from San Francisco, and two other men were elected officers at the time of formation in April 1861. The all-Black militia was the only armed corps on Vancouver Island for one year. They self-financed their military service, purchasing their own uniforms and building their own drill hall on Yates Street through enrolment fees, subscriptions, and community fundraisers.

racism they experienced here and back in the United States, Black men and women in Vancouver Island participated in the celebration of freedom in British colonies. The women of the community both prepared meals and participated in the annual Emancipation Day celebrations held at the African Rifles Pioneer Hall and Drill Hall on Yates Street in Victoria.

A variety of Emancipation Day gatherings occurred regularly during the 1860s, including the gala affair hosted by Governor Douglas prior to his retirement in 1864. This event exemplifies Douglas's anti-racism position. He actively challenged the racial discrimination experienced by his Black residents through various measures, including the hiring of Black men as police officers on Victoria's first police force. The all-Black militia, the Victoria Pioneer Rifle Company, was formed with the approval of Governor Douglas who gave them guns for training and defence.[12]

BRITISH COLUMBIA ALMANAC.								

Begins on Thursday.　　　AUGUST, 1895.　　　**31 Days.**

MOON'S PHASES.

	D.	H.	M.
Full Moon	5	5	38 A. M.
Last quarter	13	9	5 A. M.
New Moon....................	20	4	43 A. M.
First quarter	26	9	30 P. M.

Day of the Month.	Day of the Week.	Sun. R.	Sun. S.	Sun's Decl.	Sun Slow.	Moon. R.	Moon. S.	Moon South.	
		h. m.	h. m.	N° ′	m.	h. m.	h. m.	h. m.	
1	T	4 35	7 37	17 57	6	5 51	0 11	9 28	Emancipation Day.
2	F	4 36	7 36	17 41	6	6 36	1 6	10 21	Death Sir Jas. Douglas, 1871. B.
3	S	4 37	7 34	17 26	6	7 9	2 10	11 12	C. becomes Crown Colony, '58.

Emancipation Day was listed in the *British Columbia Almanac* in 1895.

On Thursday, August 2, 1861, just over two hundred African Canadians in Victoria attended a celebration in observance of the twenty-seventh anniversary of Emancipation Day. Participants gathered for a big picnic at Cadboro Bay, five kilometres northeast of the capital city. The event included speeches by Mr. Plummer, Mr. Soule, and Reverend Mr. Good (an Episcopal minister), as well as other entertainment and dancing, as was customary. The event at the bay ended with a group singing of "God Save the Queen." Later that night a gala was held at the African Rifles' Pioneer Hall. The following year a commemoration was held at Elk Lake on Vancouver Island, thirteen kilometres north of Victoria, and records indicate another event being held in 1863.[13]

These families of African-descent joyously celebrated the end of slavery in the southern United States on the December 31, 1866 as the New Year ushered in freedom for their kinsmen: "EMANCIPATION SALUTE — The colored citizens will fire a salute of 21 guns, at noon on Beacon Hill, in honor of the emancipation of the American slaves by President Lincoln."[14]

By the turn of the twentieth century, though, the frequency of large-scale Emancipation Day celebrations seems to have lessened considerably with the exodus of the majority of the African Americans in British Columbia returning to the United States. Prejudiced attitudes had been present since they had settled in the province in the mid-1800s and increased in intensity during the 1870s shortly after British Columbia joined Confederation.

Melinda Mollineaux's exhibit, "Cadboro Bay: Index to an Incomplete History," consists of present-day images of the location where Blacks in British Columbia once celebrated Emancipation Day.

Vancouver Island was no longer a viable place for African Canadians to live. August First is now only known as British Columbia Day, a provincial holiday since 1974. There is no public memory of the Black frontiersmen and women who braved unchartered territory and who saluted Britain for the freer, albeit somewhat restricted lives they led.

In an attempt to keep the narrative of the early Black settlers alive and honour their existence, artist Melinda Mollineaux created an art exhibit entitled, "Cadboro Bay: Index to an Incomplete History." The exhibit memorializes the public Emancipation Day celebrations the Blacks in British Columbia held in the mid-to-late 1800s. It includes photos of Cadboro Bay without any images of the people who may have celebrated there to illustrate the all too frequent exclusion of the Black narrative in Canadian history. Instead, she artistically incorporates text to rightfully place Blacks in that public space and to invoke their memory through listing the names of the "British-supporting" Black pioneers who more than likely attended to celebrate freedom:

Courtesy of Melinda Mollineaux.

One perspective of the present-day landscape of Cadboro Bay. The absence of the people who may have commemorated Emancipation Day in the 1860s was creatively used to symbolize the absence of the Black narrative from Canadian history.

> John Craven, J.J. Moore, Elizabeth Leonard, Rebbecca Gibbs, Sarah Jane Douglas Moses, Willis Bond, Samuel Booth, Emma Stark, Samuel Ramsay, Pricilla Stewart, Nancy Alexander, Samuel Ringo, Nathan Pointer, Fortune Richard, Sarah Lester, Mifflin Wistar Gibbs, Mary Lowe Barnswell, Stephen Whitley, and Cornelius Charity.[15]

There was a short-lived revival of Emancipation Day commemorations in British Columbia during the civil-rights era, organized by the British Columbia Association for the Advancement of Coloured People (BCAACP). Formed in 1858, the group sought to build a more positive public perception of people of African ancestry and to engage in social change. Racism against Blacks, Asians, and other minority groups remained commonplace in the 1950s. Blacks were barred from city swimming pools, and discrimination in employment, housing, and hotel accommodations were common occurrences. The community organization reinstituted the freedom festival in 1961[16] as a way to bring awareness to the civil rights struggle in Canada, to build solidarity among the province's diverse Black community, and to mobilize the masses for the cause of equality. It also served to appeal for liberation of a different kind.

Part IV

Other Elements of Emancipation Day

10

The Role of Women in Emancipation Day Celebrations

When I liberate others, I liberate myself.
— Fannie Lou Hamer, "The Special Plight and Role of Black
Women," from speech delivered in 1971.

African-Canadian women played key roles in Emancipation Day commemorations. During the nineteenth century women's involvement was primarily, but not limited to, behind the scenes. The restrictions of the Victorian period and certain standards of civic conduct and social order were placed on women. All women were excluded from many aspects of public venues, and for Black women this sometimes meant exclusion from parts of the August First programming. In St. Catharines in 1835, "after the removal of the cloth, and the withdrawal of the ladies, the following toast were drank...."[1] Women did not have full citizenship rights, they could not vote or own property (though they could inherit property and keep it in their name), and they could not obtain professional employment, unless in the capacity of a teacher. Employment opportunities were largely limited to working as a seamstress or running a boarding house. A number of Black women earned an income working as domestic servants and washerwomen. Generally women were expected to obey their husbands, bear children, and take care of the home. These social mores influenced the extent to which women could participate in early Emancipation Day celebrations.

It does not appear that any women were engaged as speakers at any time in the 1800s in Canada, with the possible exception of Mary Ann Shadd. She may have addressed the Toronto audience in 1854 when she returned from a tour to raise funds for the operation of the *Provincial Freeman* by selling subscriptions to the newspaper, but no record of her having done so has been located. However, Shadd did not get or search for the detailed coverage received by male speakers. It was not customary to heavily publicize female activities and male subscribers likely would have disapproved to the point of causing financial harm to the paper. Shadd used her initials in the *Provincial Freeman* until the fall of 1854, and when her identity was revealed the backlash charged that the newspaper had "Editors of the unfortunate sex."[2] The first Black female speaker to be publicly recorded was Mary McLeod Bethune, civil rights activist and advisor to President F.D. Roosevelt, in 1954 at Windsor's Emancipation Day, 120 years after the liberation of enslaved African men and women. Then, in 1958, lawyer Violet King delivered an address in Toronto. In keeping with the times, the chairperson for the August First celebratory events was always male — no woman would ever have been considered for that role.

However, the role that African-Canadian women played should in no way be minimized. Their work and labour was integral to the success of these annual civic and social events. As members of the planning committees, women helped to raise money for the various Emancipation Day festivities. They were responsible for creating a comfortable, welcoming atmosphere through the decoration of the many halls and venues they used, and for preparing literally tons of much-appreciated food. Their innovative community activism was harnessed on every August First holiday. Black women used Emancipation Day to fundraise in support of other social issues impacting Black citizens. When waves of fugitives arrived in Canadian centres, it was the women of the community who ensured that newcomers had food, clothing, and shelter.

By the end of the nineteenth century, women were playing a more visible role in August First events. Increasingly, women appeared in public street processions, marching with the benevolent societies they were members of, such as the Household of Ruth, Daughters of Samaria, and the Star of Calanthe in London in 1896. For example, the Household of Ruth, made an appearance in an event in Hamilton in 1884: "The Household of

Women played a major role in the Emancipation Day celebrations in Windsor in 1954. Pictured here (from the left) are three unidentified members of the Hour-A-Day Study Club; Genevieve Allen-Jones; First Lady Eleanor Roosevelt, wife of President F.D. Roosevelt; and Mary McLeod Bethune.

Ruth ... is an organization composed entirely of women, and the Toronto and Hamilton branches of it took part in the demonstration...."[3]

Women performed regularly at Emancipation Day, singing solos or as members of choirs or ensembles. These were roles that were considered respectable, as the music realm was not as restrictive as other aspects of life. By the 1900s, women of African descent were providing a variety of entertainment features. One notable example was Dorothy Darby, an African-American parachute jumper from Ohio who jumped from a plane into Jackson Park in Windsor, Ontario, in August 1938:

> The crowd dwindled as the dinner hour approached, but swelled again as the throb of an airplane motor was heard approaching from Detroit. All eyes strained upward, until a tiny white speck had grown into an airplane. Then a

Courtesy of Grey Roots Archival Collection, Owen Sound, Ontario, AF4.

Like other female auxiliaries, these women would have been involved in community outreach, providing help by way of financial support, finding housing and employment, aiding the sick and the elderly, and fundraising for various community causes. This is a photo of the ADAH Chapter No. 7 Scenic City Lodge 22 in Collingwood and Owen Sound, Ontario.

> dot of white fell from the plane, and plummeted toward earth. Its descent was halted suddenly when a white parachute opened and Miss Dorothy Darby, premier woman parachute jumper, completed her 38th jump, and landed on the grounds.[4]

Women also performed dance routines, acted in plays, and participated in the Miss Sepia International Beauty Pageant, a popular feature of "The Greatest Freedom Festival on Earth" initiated in Windsor.

The shift in social mores with each passing generation also impacted the visibility and participation of women in Emancipation Day commemorations. As the public sphere become more receptive to the female presence, women's involvement increased. Today, women are active in all aspects of August First celebrations, including headlining as speakers, artists, authors, storytellers, and musicians. Black and White women — like Lisa Scott of the Emancipation Festival in Owen Sound, Ontario; Daphney Laraque of the UNIA in Montreal, Quebec; and Anne Jarvis, Historical Interpreter at Griffin House/Fieldcote Memorial Park and Museum in Ancaster, Ontario — have taken on the role as organizers. The reach of freedom and liberation extended not only to people of African descent, but to the female gender as well. These examples are testament to how far Black women, and women in general, have come since emancipation during the Victorian Era.

11

Dissent and Diminution

Only through hardship, sacrifice, and militant action can freedom be won. The struggle is my life. I will continue fighting for freedom until the end of my days.

— Nelson Mandela, *The Struggle is My Life*, 1978.

In the immediate aftermath of the Emancipation Act, there was no general consensus among Blacks in Canadian cities and towns as to how Emancipation Day should be acknowledged or even if it warranted any recognition at all. African Canadians were not then, and are not today, a homogeneous group. They came from different social, economic, religious, and educational backgrounds, all of which influenced the organization of and participation in the celebrations. Even among those who agreed that the abolition of slavery of African people should receive some form of public observance, there was a divergence of opinion on what should be celebrated, how it should be celebrated, and on what should be remembered or forgotten.

While a portion of Blacks felt that no one should ever forget the horrors and atrocities of enslavement that their ancestors endured, another camp contended that the act of freeing enslaved Blacks should not be celebrated because the passing of that piece of legislation was the right, just, and moral thing to do. They wanted to forget pieces of the past, primarily the enslavement of Africans, because they felt that slavery was a degrading, painful experience that bred racial humiliation, fed the contempt of the larger society, and increased prejudice and contempt from Whites. The argument was made that the common history of people of African descent should not focus on the slave history. Instead this public platform should be used to remember and pay tribute to useful, positive experiences and contributions made by people of African descent.

Thousands, as evidenced by the attendance of these affairs, were in accordance that Emancipation Day should be commemorated by all people, inclusive of both Black and White citizens who admire liberty and justice, and not just an occasion for Blacks to thank Britain for a free life and opportunities in Canada.

Some African Canadians completely opposed any form of commemoration and boycotted Emancipation Day, because Blacks continued to face racial discrimination in all facets of their lives. This sentiment persisted well into the early 1900s, espoused by those who felt there was nothing to celebrate because Africans did not receive anything to be joyous about. There should be no celebration for justice. One person who held this view was Dr. Anderson Ruffin Abbott, who expressed there was not "any cause for jubilation" and provided a scenario to support his opinion: "if I am robbed by a highwayman and he afterwards returns my property, my first efforts would be directed towards bringing the thief to justice instead of jubilating over the recovery of what I had been wantonly deprived."[1]

In places that held regular commemorations, occasional boycotts were organized by individuals who wished to make a public statement about a particular grievance. An example of this would be the demonstrations in St. Catharines in 1871 to protest segregated common schools and in Chatham in 1874 when anti-Black racism was widespread.

Others saw Emancipation Day as a buyout, citing the £20 million compensation package slave masters in all British possessions, except Canada, received from the British government as merely another purchase of African slaves and not a "true victory of rights seized by those in held in bondage." As such, from this perspective no festivities were necessary.

Shortly after Confederation and the end of the American Civil War, there was an increase in complaints against Emancipation Day celebrations made by some members of the Black community, an increase that correlates with the decrease in Canada's Black population. In the 1870s there was a mass migration of Blacks moving back to the United States from centres that had high populations of people of African descent — especially from such towns in Ontario as Windsor, Chatham, and St. Catharines, and from Victoria, British Columbia. They were followed by Canadian-born Blacks in search of better prospects. There was growing objection to celebrating freedom when the democratic rights of Blacks were being blatantly infringed, with segregated schools, restricted public access, and the denial of jury duty. The decrease in African-Canadian residents in some areas resulted in the decline and gradual end of large Emancipation Day observances. Tied to this was the fact that many felt that the need to express gratitude to Britain had run its course. And there was yet another opposing point of view regarding these grand events. Some felt that the money spent to put on these often elaborate functions could be better spent in helping less fortunate, struggling workers who barely earned enough to sustain their families.

In the early 1900s there was a steady decline in the number of August First celebrations in particular towns and cities. Festivities occurred less frequently and interest began to wane, not only in Canada but in other regions in the United States and the Caribbean that acknowledged the anniversary.

Author Mitchell Kachun identifies several reasons for the downturn. The elders — those former freedom seekers who were able to provide vivid, first-hand accounts of the experiences of bondsmen and bondswomen or retell the stories connected to the anti-slavery movement — were few and far between. Consequently, the original meaning of the date being observed was fading away.

Secondly, once slavery was abolished in the United States, there was a decrease in interest from the White community in Black social issues. Another factor contributing to the decline in this type of celebration was the gradual disappearance of the communal experience as part of the fabric of life. It was being replaced by the proliferation of other social outlets and the rise of popular culture. When gambling and more alcohol consumption were integrated into Emancipation Day as acceptable social practices, the conduct of the "once well-ordered crowds" became negatively influenced. The speeches and lectures that previously educated and informed gatherers no longer captivated audiences as they preferred other ways of gaining knowledge about African history and were more interested in mass entertainment. Newer generations felt less of a need to maintain the level of social and political activism subscribed to by their forefathers and foremothers.[2] The increased social integration of African Canadians into mainstream society, including interracial marriages, also had an impact. As Colin McFarquhar surmised, an event that reminded "Blacks of their previous low positions as slaves and ... whites of their role in keeping them in servitude hardly seemed ... subjects to discuss continually."[3] This was not something that some people from either race wanted to attend, especially those in a personal interracial relationship.

While certain locations witnessed the demise of Emancipation Day, other sites continued to hold annual festivals, and others still experienced an expansion of participation. The end of the nineteenth century was the beginning of a period of transformation.

12

The Evolution of Emancipation Day

Freedom is a precious thing, and the inalienable birthright of all who travel this earth.

— Paul Robeson, *Born of the People*, 1953.

Over time the meaning and importance of Emancipation Day continued to evolve. In fact, the event has changed continuously over its 177-year history. The tone and focus of Emancipation Day celebrations have been influenced not only by local matters, but also by various provincial, national, and international factors affecting people of African origin. Tracing the development and evolution of Emancipation Day in Canada mirrors the African-Canadian community's struggle for equal rights: first through the abolition movement of the nineteenth century, then through the fight for equality and complete civil rights — a movement that lasted from the mid-1850s through to the 1960s with Martin Luther King.

Past Emancipation Day observances have embodied these differing civil rights movements. However, in the early 1900s festivities became more removed from their commemorative, educational, and political purposes that made August First such an integral institution in the African-Canadian community. The relationship between Blacks and the recognition of emancipation was heading in a new direction, focusing more on social gatherings featuring amusements and having a good time.

Blacks were being drawn to new forms of mass entertainment in the early twentieth century such as dance halls, vaudeville, amusement parks, nickelodeons, and movie houses, even though they did not always gain admission or were restricted to particular days, times, and seating. Several entertainment establishments began to compete for the attention, money, and attendance of Blacks. In response, Emancipation Day planning committees became creative and began to incorporate more recreation and leisure activities to keep their patrons, including beauty pageants, popularity contests, tugs-of-war, baseball games, boxing matches, and various skill competitions and races. Because mainstream culture was not fully accessible to Blacks, these added features to August First celebrations provided an opportunity for men, women, and children of African descent to socialize and showcase their talents. Along with the new predominant theme of enjoyment at Emancipation Day observances came an increase in the consumption of alcohol and gambling, now generally regarded as more socially acceptable activities across the broader spectrum of Canadian society.

Very little, if any, liquor was served at Emancipation Day gatherings during the 1800s as most adhered to the temperance principles prevalent during that era. Many people from all racial and social groups either completely abstained from drinking alcohol, or did not consume spirits but allowed some consumption of wine. Temperance organizations were formed to speak out against the excessive use of alcohol and to pressure different levels of government to pass anti-alcohol laws. At the 1835 commemoration in St. Catharines, "they drank water, the greater part being members of the Temperance Society," and the "Toasts were given … from excellent Port wine — no spirits being allowed."[1]

Temperance was a recurring theme among African Canadians in social settings and in the Canadian Black newspapers. In their article, John McKivigan and Jason Silverman explain: "The organizers of the Emancipation Day celebrations strove to ensure that the behaviour of blacks at the festivities would be exemplary so to make a favourable impression on the white public."[2] They point out that African-American abolitionist Frederick Douglass recognized the magnitude of this element of the celebrations: "If these occasions are conducted wisely, decorously, and orderly, they increase our respectability in the eyes of the world, and silence the slander of prejudice."[3] Living by temperance principles helped

Blacks display a respectable presence in mainstream society and was also regarded as a mark of racial advancement.

By the early 1900s the less-than sober conduct of Black and White celebrants at Emancipation Days in Essex and Kent counties was becoming unacceptable, so much so that local Black leaders like Pastor E.E. Thompson of the First Baptist Church publicly criticized the increasingly drunken behaviour. An article in a local newspaper described that when the crowd assembled to commemorate Emancipation, "At times the bars were lined five and six deep."[4] In 1911, Charles Hurst, a man of African descent, was charged with killing fifty-year old Thomas Brown, a White man, at a demonstration in Tecumseh Park. Hurst was accused of beating Brown to death over bad whisky.[5]

Opposition from the religious community had grown so strong by 1912 that a group of ministers formed an association and petitioned the Sandwich town council to ban the upcoming Emancipation Day. But the local politicians declined to side with the group that year because of the large amount of money the Emancipation Day festival brought into the town. Excessive drinking resulted in an upsurge of physical altercations, sometimes with deadly results. More and more people were being arrested.

Gambling, which was a major part of August First holidays in Windsor by 1900, became a growing problem. That year, a reporter said, gambling fakirs attracted more people than the sporting activities. In 1905 Clarence Mason, the mayor of Sandwich, issued orders that no gambling would be permitted and instructed police to arrest anyone who set up gambling operations. In 1912 at least five people were arrested for shooting craps on park grounds at Lagoon Park, but despite efforts of law enforcement, "crap game promoters did a flourishing business."[6] Even children were being enticed to gamble. Citizens who opposed the seemingly widespread "loose" conduct called the festivities in southwestern Ontario "orgies." These new inclusions of dubious repute were corrupting the original nature of Emancipation Day.

Such compromising activities also contributed to a change in the newspaper coverage. Up until the late 1800s the reports of Emancipation Day used more positive descriptive language such as "orderly," "a superior class of a race," "well-behaved citizens," and "conducted themselves in a model fashion." As Frederick Douglass feared, the increase in bawdy behaviour diminished White peoples' view of African-Canadian decorum and reinforced existing racial stereotypes. The writers for some mainstream papers, and in that region of Ontario it was primarily the Windsor papers, frequently used derogatory, stereotypical phrases to describe an African-Canadian crowd: "little darkies," "The chicken coops of Essex and Kent countries have suffered materially."[7] A few papers also referred to Black men as "boys." The clean image of Emancipation Day observers had become tarnished in the public eye, the rowdy behaviour of some being generalized to all.

After the turn of the twentieth century, celebrations were less racially mixed in the centres that continued to recognize August First. In his analysis of the annual event, Colin McFarquhar argues that "Emancipation Day seemed to pull Blacks and Whites apart more than it brought them together especially in the years after 1900,"[8] a shift that can be attributed to several social factors. For one, by the 1840s and 1850s the support of Whites for African-Canadian issues had decreased. The abolition of American slavery saw the general disappearance of White advocates of human rights in Canada. There was a division in the interpretation of Black's post-slavery experience, a division that became increasingly evident in the speeches delivered at Emancipation day assemblies.

White speakers did not acknowledge the prejudice and racism faced by Blacks, but instead highlighted the opportunities they had and should take advantage of. McFarquhar contends that some Whites held the sentiment that as long as people of African descent were no longer enslaved they had nothing to complain about. Hence, there was a disagreement on what constituted full equality. Also, with the end of slavery there was less White assistance in organizing events. Again, perhaps they believed that it was not necessary to mobilize for the cause of Black rights. Coupled with this is the fact that when fugitives became more settled in their new environment and were better able to work together they were able to exercise more control over the cultural traditions that were meaningful to them.

Although there was a decrease in their participation, Whites still attended Emancipation Day and were always welcome. Invitations in newspaper ads and notices from the organizing committees were extended to the general public, including White Canadians. By the beginning of the twentieth century, the involvement of Whites was limited largely to that of spectator, with only the occasional speaker. Whites participated in the cakewalks and sometimes a White baseball team played against a Black team, but they were not always included in sporting contests. The division of Blacks and Whites in relationship to Emancipation Day mirrored their separation in the larger society. They established and attended separate cultural institutions including churches, schools, lodges, and benevolent societies, and for the most part lived separately. White involvement in Emancipation Day shifted and was no longer always in a supportive role.

A portion of the conflicts at Emancipation Day commemorations were altercations precipitated by Whites. At the 1859 event in Brantford, "a number of whites, to their disgrace be it said, undertook to 'cut up dog' amongst the colored people, and created quite a disturbance. The fire bell was rung by some blackguard, who thought it no doubt a joke. This caused a stampede, and as order could not be restored, the meeting was unceremoniously broken up."[9] In Halifax, Nova Scotia, in 1867 a group of White hooligans attacked the Black celebrants on their way to the evening banquet and, "the few policemen in neighbourhood were powerless against the mob who seemed perfectly lawless and determined to resist authority."[10] At Windsor's observance in 1913, "A number of white persons stood outside and made things unpleasant for the celebrants."[11]

During the Depression era of the 1930s, Walter Perry, the organizer of the Windsor's huge August First anniversaries, took on the task of trying to transform the Windsor and Essex County's commemorations to its former level of esteem and to "plan an Emancipation Celebration which would be a credit to the race."[12] Through a sophisticated level of planning, organization, and coordination, Perry and the British American Association of Coloured Brothers of Ontario (BAACB) revolutionized the event into the three-day affair coined the "Greatest freedom show on earth." Their efforts proved successful in restoring Emancipation Day to its historic public calibre. As in the past, celebrations "… began with a sunrise service, followed by a parade, complete with marching bands … into the sixty-three acre Jackson Park with its imposing stadium and its bandstand."[13] Government officials and notable community leaders of both races from Windsor and Detroit addressed the audience. The crowd was treated to musical performances covering all genres and other forms of entertainment including skills demonstrations and various sporting games. A grand picnic and barbecue served as the communal feast.[14]

Another factor impacting on the evolution of Emancipation Day in Canada was the emergence of a Black middle class. As the years passed, the people with a personal connection to physical slavery disappeared and there was no longer a fugitive group. Education made social mobility possible and the contested interpretations of the slave experience evident in the nationwide celebrations altered the role that the memory of slavery played in the annual holiday. From the early 1900s, and arguably still today, African Canadians have been in pursuit of a new freedom, emancipation from mental slavery, an agenda immortalized in the words of Bob Marley in his lyrics for *Redemption Song*.[15] Marley's words originated from a speech delivered by Pan Africanist leader Marcus Garvey in Halifax, Nova Scotia, in 1937, in which he says:

> We are going to emancipate ourselves from mental slavery because whilst others might free the body, none but ourselves can free the mind. Mind is your only ruler, sovereign. The man who is not able to develop and use his mind is bound to be a slave of the other man who uses his mind, because man is related to man under all circumstances for good or ill.[16]

Garvey toured Canada, visiting several branches of the international organization named the Universal Negro Improvement Association (UNIA), including branches in Sydney, Nova Scotia; Toronto; and Montreal. He also fuelled the establishment of new branches. The aim of the formation of the UNIA was to provide a space in which Blacks could work cohesively to improve their social, political, and economic conditions; to address matters of concern to them locally and globally; and to foster racial pride. The UNIA has also participated in Emancipation Day Celebrations in Canada. Bertrand Joseph Spencer Pitt, the organizer of the "Big Picnic" in St. Catharines, was the president and attorney for the Toronto branch, who collectively played a role in the organization of the event. Additionally, the UNIA branch in Montreal has taken the initiative to renew Emancipation Day celebrations in that city. Marcus Garvey himself was a supporter of Emancipation Day commemorations. B.W. Higman briefly discusses Marcus Garvey's opinion on Emancipation Day and his endeavour to make the holiday "a sacred and holy day ... a day of blessed memory."[17] According to the social issues of the time, Emancipation Day served as a political tool as well, a role that changed in each successive generation. It shifted from opposing segregation in public spaces and obtaining suffrage to equal employment access.

The issue of reparations also has a close relationship with Emancipation Day. The occasion was the opportune moment to raise the debate about whether or not or what form of compensation the descendants of enslaved Africans in all former English colonies were entitled to from the British government. Many took the position that Britain should pay some form of damages for the free labour they benefitted from and for the brutal, inhumane discrimination the system imposed on Blacks. The matter is also very relevant not only to African Canadians who were the descendants of slaves, but also to the wrongfully displaced Black citizens who lived in places like Hogan's Alley in Vancouver, British Columbia, and in Africville, a community once in the northern part of Halifax, Nova Scotia.

With the passing of the years much of the old-time formality and ceremony disappeared from these freedom festivals. In particular, August First events had lost their original educational and political functions of memorializing African ancestors, teaching about Black history, forcing social change, confronting racial discrimination, and furthering Blacks' struggles for full citizenship and equal rights. Coupled with the outward migration of a significant segment of the African-Canadian population, this led to the eventual termination of some observances. Interestingly, however, in some centres today, such as the Owen Sound Emancipation Day event, more attention is being paid to incorporating education on African-Canadian history into the activities while retaining the more traditional family-style character of the day, including services in the now renovated BME church.

On the whole, celebrations have been and continue to be reflective of the perspectives and experiences of Blacks and of Canadian society, while showcasing the diversity of African-Canadian culture.

13

The Legacy of Emancipation Day Celebrations

Freedom is not free.
— Martin Luther King Jr., speech delivered in Montgomery,
Alabama, 1959.

The significance of Emancipation Day commemorations within the Canadian context is multilayered. Its initial meaning for a few decades after its inception was to celebrate the freeing of Africans enslaved in British colonies and the opportunities afforded to the new citizens on British soil. This would later extend to the abolition of slavery in the southern United States. It represented a victorious end in the ongoing struggle for the abolition of a brutal, inhumane practice that lasted for over three centuries. The annual occasion also served to pay respect to Britain and to Canada and the respective provinces through a public demonstration of loyalty, patriotism, and gratitude for the legal dissolution of the institution of slavery.

Another integral role of August First observances was the remembrance of the stories, experiences, and courage of enslaved ancestors, the recognition of the military role of African-Canadians, the honouring of their predecessors, and their tenacity in overcoming obstacles and barriers. For a time, the recognition of the central role of enslaved Africans, free Blacks, and Black abolitionists in the abolition movement was important when African-Canadians gathered together — the resistance of those in bondage and the way in which all Blacks engaged together to challenge the slave status imposed upon them. Simultaneously, respect and appreciation was paid to the White activists and sympathizers who worked and lobbied tirelessly for the cause.

The lasting impact of this African-Canadian cultural institution is reflected in the several purposes it served. From its onset it was an event by Blacks for Blacks. And while the social aspect of having a good time cannot be ignored, Emancipation Day was more than just a party. Throughout its 175-year recognition, the spirit and notion of freedom has remained constant, although its definition would change to meet the needs of a particular time. The notion of freedom as a continuous journey is captured succinctly in the words of poet Robert Frost, "The woods are lovely, dark, and deep, but I have promises to keep, and miles to go before I sleep." In this case, the attainment of liberty was a joyous occasion while simultaneously creating a realm of the unknown. Within a short time, former slaves found out that they had not achieved full citizenship with emancipation and arrived at the conclusion that there would be much more to do in the struggle for equality for themselves and their predecessors.

Emancipation Day served as an instrument to pass on the history and the memory of those who went before them and as a beacon for taking up the responsibility to carry on from where the ancestors left off. The public parades, marching through the principal streets of the towns and cities they lived in, are symbolic of the long, difficult, fulfilling journey of Africans in Canada, a journey for equality and justice in its many forms.

Emancipation Day has been an important tool in community building through fostering a sense of togetherness and unity in the Black community, a forum for education, and an opportunity to mobilize for a common purpose — a better future for the next generation. The communal experience was critical, especially in the early years, because for centuries Africans had been divided and separated from each other. The sense of unity that Emancipation Day provided nurtured the process of community building.

The August First celebration provided the venue to disseminate information and knowledge through the speeches, discussions, and literature such as pamphlets and newspaper coverage, especially since in the early years of commemorations a sizeable number of the fugitives who lived in Canada were illiterate. The event has always been used to advocate for education, with the aim of contributing to the community. Not only

A ribbon-cutting ceremony was held on August 1, 2008, in Windsor, Ontario, to mark the 175th anniversary of Emancipation Day commemorations, from left to right: the former United States Consul General John R. Nay; the mayor of Windsor, Eddie Francis; James Allen, North Star Community Centre; Justice Beth Allen; and Windsor city councillor, Ronnie Jones.

were Blacks educated during Emancipation Day events, White Canadians were, too. Here was a platform to bring awareness of the existence of Black populations in communities across the nation and of how people of African descent have enriched and contributed to the broader Canadian society. As well, the event stimulated a deeper awareness and appreciation of the contributions of African Canadians in the building of their local communities, encouraging Whites to assist Blacks and further the causes that are of benefit to all citizens. Within the observances, attention was also paid to the frustrations felt by Blacks.

Additionally, Emancipation Day played a crucial role in the ongoing redefinition of the meaning of being Black in places where Blacks once were enslaved or treated as second-class citizens. These were the people who escaped to Canada, the African-American fugitive slaves, Black Loyalists, and free Blacks who came to Canada, and included groups from the Caribbean and native-born African Canadians. Throughout the decades Emancipation Day was used to express and negotiate the various identities. The dynamic structure of the Black community — men, women, children, fugitives to free Blacks, American to Canadian-born, day labourers to wealthy business owners, and illiterate to university educated — became illuminated, and demonstrated the deep level of solidarity and support found within this diverse group.

On a more personal and intimate level for many African Canadians, the occasion evoked the courage of early Black settlers and African slaves who resisted. It revealed the hope and possibilities of a people and the convictions of Blacks, and affirmed the belief that Africans are survivors who endure, persevere, and must continue to do and to be better; a process that continues to this day.

A close examination of Emancipation Day activities informs observers of the social interactions between members of the Black community and of the interactions between Blacks and Whites. It reveals racial attitudes, racial stereotypes, and social issues of specific time periods, from the past to the present.

Evidence of the legacy of African Canadians and their commitment to their adopted country or land of birth is found in the images, records, reports, and commentary in newspaper articles, journals, speeches, and pamphlets in relation to Emancipation Day and its underlying themes. It is also found in the buildings, churches, homes, and schools they erected when they took advantage of the opportunities afforded them as a result of that piece of legislation that guaranteed Blacks, at least on paper, all the rights and privileges of a British subject. Additionally, the legacy of Emancipation Day is apparent in the social changes brought about by the protests of African-Canadians, the enactment of their vision and optimism for an equal and just future. The political and cultural agendas of African Canadians in the nineteenth and twentieth centuries were advanced at these yearly events ranging from the integration of public schools, to representation at the various levels of government, to land and property ownership.

While on one hand August First observances have been joyous expressions of a celebratory nature, they have been just as much "a remembrance of exclusion across time and space," an exclusion that has persisted since the inception of the African slave trade. Africans were first denied status as persons, an exclusion that later manifested into segregation and anti-Black racism. Exclusion is just as significant an issue today as it was back then as the African-Canadian narrative still remains separate and apart from national history. Emancipation Day has been a celebration of Blacks' fortitude in overcoming these circumstances and of their drive to participate fully in the social, cultural, political, and economic life of Canada. The anniversary of the achievement of freedom is about the ability to exercise full citizenship and the tenacity to challenge whatever impedes their rights and equality.

Interestingly, the examination of earlier Emancipation Day festivities in Canada illuminated the complex, interconnected, national, and continental networks that worked to uplift the community in their pursuit of common goals. Celebrants travelled long distances regionally and cross-country, and came from various parts of the United States to participate in events. At some point throughout the history of Emancipation Day, members of the numerous religious groups, benevolent societies, fraternal orders, literary societies, and veteran associations have all engaged in the organization and execution of commemorative affairs as planners, event chairpersons, and participants. Innumerable White supporters were also involved in some capacity in all the locales where commemorations happened. Speakers carried their messages to different areas of Ontario and some visited other provinces. A close relationship extended across the Canada-United States border. American abolitionists, lecturers, bands, and guests would come to partake in annual observances. The maintenance of these networks was essential to survival in everyday life, and provided the necessary support to counter social hostilities and to assist one another in furthering personal and collective aspirations. It shows the Black community possessed a global and pan-African perspective and awareness of the need to nurture racial solidarity and interest across political boundaries.

Freedom festivals have been much more than the remembrance of Canada's and America's slave past. It demonstrates how Canadian pioneers, Black and White, worked side by side for survival, success, and equality as well as how they trusted and believed in one another in their efforts. The legacy of Emancipation Day is an unforgettable cultural tradition.

Epilogue

The most rewarding freedom is freedom of the mind.
— Amy Garvey, *Garvey and Garveyism*, 1963.

The onset of the twenty-first century triggered a revival in the observance of Emancipation Day in locations that previously celebrated the holiday. From the 1990s onward, the celebrations have experienced a move to new venues and a change in format to attract a wide array of supporters. Celebrations in Toronto were revived in 1997 by the Ontario Black History Society, and in Windsor in 2008 by the Windsor Council of Elders and Emancipation Planning Committee with the support of several other community organizations and the City of Windsor. Uncle Tom's Cabin Historic Site in Dresden began commemorations in 2005. Owen Sound observances have persisted throughout the years, but have been restructured to retain relevancy for ongoing participants and to attract new visitors. A particular element is the renewed emphasis on education with a specific interest in the recognition of both local and general African-Canadian history. The current organizers of both Owen Sound and Windsor events have utilized a weekend-long festival format packed with many activities designed to draw huge audiences. In Quebec, the Universal Negro Improvement Association (UNIA) in Montreal hosted an Emancipation Day event in 2009.

Several reasons can be attributed to the resurgence of Emancipation Day observances. One is the surge in popularity of genealogy. The

Courtesy of Valerie Tillman Coon.

Strictly Rhythm Hip Hop dance performers from Guelph on stage at the Emancipation Festival in Owen Sound in 2007.

research of one's ancestors is attracting more and more African Canadians, and through familial investigation descendants of early Black pioneers have discovered important facts about their forebearers and about the social interactions of early Canadians. Secondly, there is a new cohort of people, White and Black, intrigued by the history of African Canadians and their contributions to the building of this nation. Canada has a sizeable population of Black citizens, but very few know about the nation's rich African heritage. Many are trying to understand how early Black Canadians dealt with such pressing issues as promoting education for their community, facing pervasive racism, encouraging integration, and creating an identity for themselves. All are issues that continue to be problematic for people of African descent living in this country, along with the need to engage in matters that affect Africans throughout the Diaspora. Many seek to draw from past knowledge and strength to solve these problems, and Emancipation Day has played an integral role in the past in tackling these issues.

Emancipation Day has come full circle, once again being employed to educate and mobilize new generations. There has been a resurgence in the "freedom movement" both personal and social in an attempt to liberate our society and ourselves from modern forms of social confinement — mental enslavement, materialism, commercialism, and violence.

Underground Railroad Cyclists at the Owen Sound Emancipation Day Celebration, 2007. The Adventure Cycling Association, in partnership with the University of Pittsburgh Center for Minority Health, retraced one of the escape routes from Mobile, Alabama, to Owen Sound following the "Drinking Gourd," the Big Dipper Constellation. Another tour called the Underground Railroad Celebration Ride cycled from Buffalo, New York, to Owen Sound.

Once again, advocates are seeking legal recognition of Emancipation Day. A provincial bill was passed into law in 2008 to officially recognize the first of August as Emancipation Day in Ontario. The Ontario Black History Society had petitioned different members of the provincial parliament and the premier of Ontario to implement a legal acknowledgement of Canada's history of enslavement and its role as a haven for fugitive American slaves.[1] There is also a push to internationalize the legal recognition of Emancipation Day by the National Joint Action Committee of Trinidad and Tobago in all territories of the former British Empire in the Caribbean, North America, and Africa. Emancipation Day is relevant to the continent of Africa in recognition of the loss of millions of people that ravaged the economic, political, and social development of villages, kingdoms, and nations in Africa, and because of the many Africans enslaved on the continent by the British in their possessions such as South Africa.

Coincidentally, in Ontario, Emancipation Day coincides with the August 1st Civic Holiday that honours Lieutenant John Graves Simcoe, who was instrumental in setting the wheels in motion to end slavery in Upper Canada. Individuals and community groups have suggested the two observances be officially merged. Evelyn Myrie, writing in the *Hamilton Spectator*, suggests that, "The idea of formally combining the Lord Simcoe Day with Emancipation Day should be given some consideration" because Simcoe's efforts "gave Upper Canada the distinction of being the first jurisdiction in the British colony to pass an anti-slavery act."[2] Joining the two observances would be a powerful educational tool for highlighting knowledge about Canadian slavery and the abolition movement. At commemorations at the Griffin House and Fieldcote Memorial Park and Museum in Ancaster, which began in 2002, Anne Jarvis, the historical interpreter there, said: "We are open on the holiday Monday so the Civic holiday in August seemed the obvious date for the recognition as it is the nearest date to Emancipation Day."[3]

How can Emancipation Day remain pertinent to African Canadians and the wider society in the twenty-first century? The nature of commemorations must stay true to its roots while incorporating innovative means of retaining and capturing the interest of its audience. Current approaches used by the organizations in localities mentioned, in an effort to be relevant to today's adult and youth, blend current forms of entertainment and urban culture such as cycling tours, basketball tournaments, walk-a-thons, hip-hop dance competitions, and art shows with traditional ones like storytelling, presentations, picnics, and parties. One suggestion is that plans to restore the celebrations should go one step further by creating a "commemoration circuit" whereby each of the established locations and any other sites planning to revitalize August First as recognition of the abolition of slavery might alternate with nearby communities to host larger-scale events.

Yet another approach could involve a promotional initiative linking existing Emancipation Day celebrations in the manner of the Underground Railroad African-Canadian Heritage Tours, which are growing in popularity. By partnering in this manner, long-established annual events — such as those at Owen Sound, Ontario, and newer smaller celebrations elsewhere — could, by working together, bring about greatly increased appreciation of the Black experience and the contributions of African Canadians to Canada's rich heritage.

Moving forward with co-operative planning would enable people to learn more about their province and country and its diversity, which in turn would assist in the process of the development of a Canadian identity for descendants of native-born African Canadians and for people like myself who are African Canadians with immigrant parents. It can encourage them to reclaim — and claim — their heritage and their nation. For new citizens it can foster an understanding of the people who came before them. Emancipation Day will continue to adapt to the people and the needs of Canada until Canada has achieved complete equality for all of its citizens.

Whatever new directions lay ahead, there is little doubt but that Emancipation Day celebrations will continue as an important cultural tradition with significance for all Canadians.

Appendix A

Letter to Queen Victoria, 1854

To Her Most Gracious Majesty, Queen Victoria

May It Please Your Majesty:

We, the Coloured Inhabitants of Canada, most respectfully, most gratefully and most loyally approach you Gracious Majesty, on this, the anniversary of our death to Slavery, and our birth to Freedom. With what feelings, or what words can we adequately express our gratitude to England for such a boon?

Our hearts are wholly your Majesty's; and if the time should ever come when your Majesty might need our aid, our lives would be as they are, at your service.

What a happy, what a proud reflection it must be to your Majesty, to know that the moment the poor crushed slave sets foot upon any part of your mighty dominions, his chains fall from him — he feels himself a man, and can look up. Can it be conceived that he would not on that same spot turn, and whilst defending the hallowed soil, that memory would not fire his brain, and gratitude nerve his arm! Can your Majesty, imagine that from such a people, loyalty could be an empty name, or devotion be a dream! Faults of commission may be urged against us by those who grudge us our Freedom; but we carefully watch that such faults shall be the exception and not the rule; at the same time, we pray your Majesty in your judgment of us, to remember that whilst the invigorating food of education was jealously withheld from us, the brutalization cup of slavery was forced between our lips until we drained it to the very dregs.

The effects, more or less, must have been a mortal stupor, for which the hand of time and kindness can alone provide the cure. But amid all our trials, we beg your Gracious Majesty to believe we yet thank the Most High that the God of battle may give victory to your Majesty's arms — that He will continue to bless your Majesty as a Queen, bless you as a wife, bless you as a mother; and that it will please Him in his infinite wisdom and mercy, long "to put back thee time" of removing you from your Earthly to your Heavenly crown. And as in duty bound, We will ever pray.

Toronto, Canada West
August 1st, 1854

Originally from the *Provincial Freeman*. August 5, 1854, taken from Peter C. Ripley *et al*, eds., *The Black Abolitionist Papers, Volume II: Canada 1830–1865* (Chapel Hill: University of North Carolina Press, 1986), 295–96.

Appendix B

Emancipation Song: "Get Off the Track!"

The lyrics of "Get Off the Track!" were written by Jesse Hutchinson, Jr. of the Hutchinson Family Singers in 1844. It was sung to the tune of "Old Dan Tucker."

Ho! The car Emancipation
Rides majestic thro' our nation,
Bearing on its train story,
Liberty! a nation's glory.
Roll it along, roll it along, thro' the nation,
Freedoms car, Emancipation!

Men of various predilections,
Frightened, run in all directions;
Merchants, editors, physicians,
Lawyers, priests, and politicians.
Get out of the way! Every station!
Clear the track of 'mancipation!

Let the ministers and churches
Leave behind sectarian lurches;
Jump on board the Car of Freedom,
Ere it be too late to need them.

Sound the alarm! Pulpits thunder!
Ere too late to see your blunder!

Politicians gazed, astounded,
When, at first, our bell resounded:
Freight trains are coming, tell these foxes,
With our votes and ballot boxes.
Jump for your lives! Politicians,
From your dangerous, false positions.

Railroads to Emancipation
Cannot rest on Clay foundation.
And the _tracks_ of 'The Polkitian'
Are but railroads to perdition!
Pull up the rails! Emancipation
Cannot rest on such foundation.

All true friends of Emancipation,
Haste to Freedom's railroad station;
Quick into the cars get seated,
All is ready and completed —
Put on the steam! All are crying,
And the liberty flags are flying.

On, triumphant see them bearing,
Through sectarian rubbish tearing;
The bell and whistle and the steaming,
Startle thousand from their dreaming.
Look out for the cars while the bell rings!
Ere the sound your funeral knell rings.

See the people run to meet us;
At the depots thousands greet us;
All take seats with exultation,
In the Car Emancipation.
Huzza! Huzza!! Emancipation

Soon will bless our happy nation.
Huzza! Huzza! Huzza!!!

See George Clark, *The Liberty Minstrel*, (New York: Levitt & Alden, 1845), 144–45.

Notes

Foreword

1. The province now named Ontario went through several name changes. It was first called Upper Canada, then Canada West, and finally Ontario.
2. For the longest while, August First was dubbed West Indian Emancipation because the largest numbers of enslaved people who were freed lived in the British West Indies.
3. Eighteenth-century streams of Black migration to Canada included the African captives who were held as slaves in New France and later British North America, the Black Loyalists who arrived after the American Revolutionary War, and the Trelawny Maroons who were deported by the British from Jamaica to Nova Scotia. For the seventeenth century, the majority of Black persons in Canada were slave captives. Mention must be made of the twentieth century. During the early decades, Blacks from the American Plain States settled on the Canadian Prairie. Likewise, during the second half of the century Black Caribbeans and continental Africans migrated to Canada in large numbers.
4. Examples of enslaved people rising against the British include Tacky's War, 1760 (Jamaica); the First Black Carib War, 1769 (St. Vincent); the Slave Rebellion of the British Virgin Islands, 1790 (Tortola); the Demerara Revolt of 1823 (British Guiana); and Bussa' Rebellion, 1816 (Barbados).

Introduction: Background on an African-Canadian Celebration

1. Excerpt from the unpublished poem, "The True Essence of Freedom," by Fitzroy E. Dixon.

2. For more on Charles Stuart, see Karolyn Smardz Frost *et al*, *Ontario's African Canadian Heritage: Collected Writings of Fred Landon, 1918–1967* (Toronto: Natural Heritage Books-Dundurn, 2009), chapter 18, "Captain Charles Stuart, Abolitionist," 215–30.

3. A fellow Presbyterian minister in Truro named Daniel Cock owned two slaves. Reverend MacGregor published and distributed a written criticism of Cock's slaveholding, argued the evils of the institution, and countered the popular arguments in support of slavery. Copies can be found at Dalhousie University, the Legislative Library of Nova Scotia, and the Saint John Free Library. Robin Winks, *The Blacks in Canada* (Montreal: McGill-Queen's University Press, 1997), 103 n15.

4. Jim Crow laws legalized racist practices that restricted the public lives of African Americans: where they could and could not go and what they could and could not do.

5. *Dawn of Tomorrow*, 1854. This African-Canadian newspaper was established in London, Ontario, in 1923 by James F. Jenkins and published until 1966.

6. The Fair Accommodations Practices Act of 1954 made it illegal for hotels, restaurants, theatres, and other businesses that served the public in Ontario to refuse service to individuals because of their race.

7. Black women from the English-speaking Caribbean — mainly teachers, office workers, and nurses — were recruited for emigration to Canada to work as domestic servants in White households. By 1965, almost three thousand women were admitted to work as domestics for a minimum of one year, after which they received landed-immigrant status and could sponsor family members. Ken Alexander and Avis Glaze, *Towards Freedom: The African-Canadian Experience* (Toronto: Umbrella Press, 1996), 178.

Chapter 1: Exploring the Meaning of Emancipation Day

1. *Voice of the Fugitive*, August 12, 1852.
2. *London Free Press*, August 4, 1896.
3. West India Day is another name that was sometimes applied to August First. Personally, I find it to be a misnomer, even though it was widely used at one time.

Chapter 2: From Enslavement to Freedom

1. For more information see Afua Cooper, *The Hanging of Angélique: The Untold Story of Canadian Slavery and the Burning of Old Montréal* (Toronto: HarperCollins, 2006).

2. After a year-long trial, there was a split decision from the judges. Therefore no judgment could be entered and Nancy Morton lost her case. She was returned to Jones as his property and was sentenced to serve fifteen years as a slave. Robin Winks, *The Blacks in Canada* (Montreal: McGill-Queen's University Press, 1997), 108.

3. Olaudah Equiano, a native African, was kidnapped as a young boy, enslaved, and sold to a plantation owner in Virginia. Equiano, also known as Gustavus Vassa, was later sold to Captain Pascal, a British naval officer. He was able to purchase his freedom, and then travelled throughout England lecturing about his experiences and the atrocities of slavery.

4. Frederick Douglass was an African-American abolitionist from Rochester, New York. He travelled internationally and gave speeches to inform the public on the inhumane enslavement of Africans and to motivate Blacks to mobilize and become self-sufficient.

5. The earliest recorded incident of slavery in Canada was a young African boy given the name Olivier LeJeune. David Kirke, an English merchant, was his original owner.

6. The case of Chloe Cooley was the impetus for Simcoe to push for a legal end to slavery in Upper Canada. For more information on Chloe Cooley, see Adrienne Shadd *et al*, *The Underground Railroad: Next Stop, Toronto!* (Toronto: Natural Heritage Books, 2002).

7. Under the Limitation Act of 1793, masters also had to provide food and clothing to their charges, including when they were manumitted. Also, owners had to secure some form of employment for slaves freed after the age of twenty-five.

8. The Fugitive Slave Law, passed by the United States Congress in 1793, permitted slave owners and slave catchers to pursue runaway slaves anywhere in America and return them to where they were held. Free Blacks could also be sold into slavery with little legal protection.

9. Robin Winks, *The Blacks in Canada*, 11.

10. Daniel Hill, *The Freedom Seekers: Blacks in Early Canada* (Agincourt: Book Society of Canada, 1981), 20; James Cleland Hamilton, *Osgoode Hall: Reminiscences of the Bench and Bar* (Toronto: Carswell Co., 1904), 162.

11. J.R. Kerr-Ritchie, *The Rites of August First: Emancipation Day in the Black Atlantic World* (Baton Rouge, LA: Louisiana State University Press, 2007), 18–20.

Chapter 3: Southwestern Ontario

1. Daniel Hill, *The Freedom Seekers: Blacks in Early Canada* (Agincourt: Book Society of Canada, 1981), 46.

2. "Common schools" were schools that received provincial funding as well as local tax support. It provided any student with a free education. According to the Common Schools Act of 1850, "separate schools" could legally be established for children of different religions and races. A misinterpretation of section XIX of this Common School Act, which made the pre-existing segregation legal, was imposed by many local school boards wanting segregated schools for Blacks and Whites.

3. Donald G. Simpson, *Under the North Star: Black Communities in Upper Canada* (Trenton: Africa World Press, 2005), 152.

4. Levi Coffin published his observations on his travels, including the visit to Amherstburg in *The Reminiscences of Levi Coffin: The Reputed President of the Underground Railroad* published in 1876.

5. See *Amherstburg 1796–1996: The New Town on the Garrison Ground* (Amherstburg Bicentennial Committee, 1996), 241.

6. Daniel Pearson (also spelled Pierson), lived at the corner of George and Gore Streets. For over thirty years, Pearson officiated over Emancipation Day celebrations in Amherstburg. *Amherstburg Echo*, August 9, 1889.

7. *Amherstburg 1796–1996*, 242.

8. Caldwell's Grove was located on the land of British Loyalist William Caldwell, at the mouth of the Detroit River off Pike Road about two kilometres east of town.

9. Delos Rogest Davis, a native of Colchester, became the second Black lawyer in Canadian history in 1885 and became the first African Canadian appointed to the King's Council in Canada. He established a law firm with his son on Gore Street in Amherstburg.

10. *Amherstburg Echo*, August 8, 1879.

11. Josephus O'Banyoun was born in Brantford, Ontario. He became the pastor of the Little Zion BME Church in Owen Sound in 1856. O'Banyoun had moved to Halifax, Nova Scotia, by 1860, where he was appointed minister of the BME church and was the first to organize a choral group called the Jubilee Singers. While there, he met his second wife, Mary Elizabeth Goosely of Liverpool, Nova Scotia. Upon his return to Ontario, O'Banyoun was the pastor at St. Paul's AME Church in Hamilton in 1878. During this time he formed an Ontario branch of the Canadian Jubilee Singers, which became a choral group that performed around the province. He was appointed as the first secretary of the AME Conference in Ontario serving in 1885, and again from 1887 to 1889. He passed away in 1905 while in charge of the AME church in Amherstburg.

12. *Amherstburg Echo*, August 9, 1889.

13. *Ibid.*

14. *Ibid.*

15. *Ibid.*

16. *Ibid.*
17. *Ibid.*
18. *Amherstburg Echo*, August 3, 1894.
19. John H. Alexander was the principal of the King Street School, the public school for Black children in Amherstburg for thirty years. He had been born in Anderdon, twelve kilometres north of Amherstburg on October 15, 1857. Alexander became a town councillor from 1923 to 1926 and was appointed town assessor in 1930.
20. The ministers included a Reverend L. Pierce, Reverend J.E. Allen, Reverend J.A. Holt, and Reverend C.P. Hill.
21. *Amherstburg Echo*, August 3, 1894.
22. *Ibid.*
23. Statement from the Alvin McCurdy Collection, Archives Ontario, F2076-3-34, Emancipation Day Clippings, B397059.
24. *Ibid.*
25. The North America Black Historical Museum was established in Amherstburg in 1975 through the efforts of Melvin "Mac" Simpson.
26. From the Emancipation Day Collection, North American Black Historical Museum.
27. In September 1792, Judge William Dummer Powell sentenced Joseph Cutten, a man of African descent, to death for stealing rum and furs. Cutten was executed by hanging. Powell also sentenced another Black man to death for his crimes, but the convicted man escaped before his sentence was carried out. Powell was later appointed chief justice of Upper Canada.
28. The Stone Barracks, the present-day site of General Brock School located at Sandwich and Brock Streets, was originally built as a school in 1808, then used as a military barrack during the War of 1812 and again in 1839 following the Rebellions of Upper Canada.
29. See Julia H. Roberts, *In Mixed Company: Taverns and Public Life in Upper Canada* (Vancouver: University of British Columbia Press, 2009), 111–12.
30. See J.R. Kerr-Ritchie, *The Rites of August First: Emancipation Day in the Black Atlantic World* (Baton Rouge, LA: Louisiana State University Press, 2007), 132. In 1857, Colonel Prince made some disparaging remarks against Blacks. He called them "animals" and "criminals," and stated they were only good as slaves. Prince argued they should be shipped to Manitoulin Island and argued that Blacks couldn't be good citizens just as the spots of a leopard couldn't be changed. See Robin Winks, *The Blacks in Canada* (Montreal: McGill-Queen's University Press, 1997), 214, and Daniel Hill, *The Freedom Seekers*, 106.
31. John Bull represented a typical Englishman, the personification of England, equivalent to Uncle Sam in the United States. Quote from the *Voice of the Fugitive*, August 13, 1851.

32. Samuel Ringgold Ward escaped slavery with his parents when he was three years old. They settled in New York, where Ward received his education. He became a Congregationalist minister, and when he moved to Windsor, Ontario, he founded the newspaper, the *Provincial Freeman* and became an agent for the Anti-Slavery Society of Canada.

33. *Voice of the Fugitive*, July 2, 1851; August 13, 1851.

34. *Ibid.*, July 30, 1851.

35. See "Windsor Communities" (*www.windsor-communities.com*) and "On the Road North" (*virtualmuseum.ca/blackhistory/OnTheRoadNorth.html*).

36. Levi Coffin, *Reminiscences of Levi Coffin*, 150–151.

37. *Ibid.*

38. *Liberator*, August 26, 1859.

39. Sandwich Mineral Springs operated as a park between 1866 and 1888. John Gauthier owned the property. He drilled for oil on his property, but found a mineral spring instead. Around 1902 it became Lagoon Park, which existed until 1910. A hotel that was still there was used by Emancipation Day visitors. The park featured a carousel, a dance pavilion, the Electric Theatre, the Meoloscope Parlour, and the Electric Tower. Mineral Springs and Prince's Grove Park were located at present-day Mic Mac Park at Prince and Carmichael Roads.

40. *Windsor Evening Record*, August 1, 1895.

41. Colin McFarquhar, "A Difference of Perspective: Blacks, Whites, and Emancipation Day Celebrations in Ontario, 1865–1919." *Ontario History* 92, no. 2 (Autumn 2000).

42. *Windsor Evening Record*, August 1, 1905.

43. *Ibid.*, August 1, 1913; August 2, 1913.

44. Mitchell Kachun, *Festivals of Freedom: Memory and Meaning in African American Emancipation Celebrations, 1808–1915* (Amherst: University of Massachusetts Press, 2003), 246.

45. Daniel Hill, *Freedom Seekers*, 48.

46. *Voice of the Fugitive*, August 12, 1852.

47. The North American League was created by James Theodore Holly, a Black abolitionist born in Washington, D.C., and raised in Brooklyn, New York. He had moved to Windsor in 1851 and was in attendance that day.

48. *Voice of the Fugitive*, August 12, 1852.

49. *Ibid.*

50. *Ibid.*

51. *Ibid.*

52. *Ibid.*

53. Windsor's first Black alderman was James Dunn, from 1887 to 1888. His brother Robert Dunn was elected alderman in 1893 and held the seat to 1903.

54. *Windsor Evening Record*, August 1, 1895.

55. Jack Johnson was the first Black world heavyweight boxing champion, a title he held from 1908 to 1915. He was born in Galveston, Texas, in 1878 and was the son of former slaves. He died in 1946.

56. *Windsor Evening Record*, August 2, 1907.

57. *Windsor Evening Record*, August 2, 1900; August 1, 1902; August 3, 1909; August 2, 1910; August 1, 1911; August 1, 1912; August 2, 1912; August 1, 1913; August 2, 1913; August 24, 1914.

58. The British American Association of Coloured Brothers (BAACB) was formed in Windsor in 1935. As an African-Canadian organization, the group aimed to actively challenge discrimination in the city and to organize the celebration of Emancipation Day.

59. Robert R. Moton was president of Tuskegee College in Tuskegee, Alabama, from 1915 to 1935. He was instrumental in the creation of the Tuskegee Veteran's Administration Hospital, the first and only such hospital staffed by Black professionals.

60. Walter Perry was born in Chatham in 1899, and moved to Windsor with his mother after his father died when he was eight years old. He lived in the McDougall Street corridor where a large number of Blacks lived. Perry passed away in 1967.

61. Peggy Bristow, "A Duty to the Past, a Promise to the Future: Black Organizing in Windsor — The Depression, World War II, and the Post-War Years." *New Dawn: The Journal of Black Canadian Studies* 2, no. 1 (2007): 3.

62. *Toronto Star*, July 29, 1947.

63. *Ibid.* July 29, 1947; August 2, 1948; August 2, 1949.

64. *Ibid.*, July 30, 1950.

65. An African-American female civil-rights activist and founder of the Bethune–Cookman College in Daytona Beach, Florida. President Franklin Delano Roosevelt appointed Mary McLeod Bethune to his "Black Cabinet," which was made up of various Blacks selected to advise his administration on concerns of African Americans.

66. Daisy Bates was a civil rights activist and advisor to the Little Rock Nine. She was the selected African-American student chosen to integrate Central High School in Little Rock, Arkansas, in 1957.

67. Fred Shuttlesworth was a Baptist minister and civil rights activist in Birmingham, Alabama. He formed the Alabama Christian Movement for Human Rights in 1956 to fight segregation and to lobby for voting rights for Southern Blacks.

68. Myrlie Evers was the wife of civil rights activist Medgar Evers, the field secretary for the North American Association for the Advancement of Colored People. He was gunned down in 1963 in his driveway in Jackson, Mississippi. His death left a widow and three sons.

69. Emancipation Day Collection, North American Black Historical Museum, FS-35.

70. "Windsor Communities" (*www.windsor-communities.com*), accessed on October 2009.

71. In 1938, African-American parachute jumper Dorothy Darby jumped from a plane for the thirty-eighth time onto the grounds of Jackson Park. Emancipation Day Collection, North American Black Historical Museum, FO-11.

72. Emancipation Day Collection, St. Catharines Museum.

73. Anderson Ruffin Abbott Papers, scrapbook 2, folder 1, 45–46, Baldwin Room, Toronto Reference Library, Toronto Public Library.

74. "Emancipation Celebration" (*www.emancipationday.ca*), accessed October 2009.

75. John Brown was the American leader of the Harper's Ferry Raid in Virginia that sought to take over the American government and eliminate slavery. The convention in Chatham was organized to recruit fighters, hold training sessions at Tecumseh Park, draw financial support from sympathetic Blacks living in the vicinity, and to receive assistance in the drafting and implementation of the constitution for the provisional government Brown planned to establish.

76. Mary Ann Shadd was a writer and first full-time editor of the *Provincial Freeman*. The paper's headquarters remained in Chatham until September 1857 when the last issue was published.

77. Nelson Hackett escaped from Arkansas and came to Chatham in September of 1841, where he was tracked down and uncovered a few months later by his master Alfred Wallace, and arrested. Fifteen Black soldiers tried to rescue him, but he was quickly moved to a jail in Sandwich. After court proceedings he was extradited to the United States, the first time a slave was returned from Canada West.

78. For more on Dr. Anderson Ruffin Abbott, see Catherine Slaney, *Family Secrets: Crossing the Colour Line* (Toronto: Natural Heritage Books, 2003).

79. In *Simmons vs. Chatham*, 1861, the judge's decision upheld segregation in Chatham's public schools. See Robin Winks, *Blacks in Canada*, 373–74.

80. Peter C. Ripley *et al*, eds. *The Black Abolitionist Papers, Volume II: Canada 1830–1865* (Chapel Hill: University of North Carolina Press, 1986.)

81. For more on William King, see Victor Ullman, *Look to the North Star: A Life of William King* (Toronto: Umbrella Press, 1994). Reprint.

82. *Provincial Freeman*, August 19, 1854; July 26, 1856; and the *Chatham Weekly Planet*, July 30, 1856.

83. At the eighteenth annual AME church conference and the first annual BME Conference held in Chatham on September 23, 1856, Reverend W.H. Jones moved that the Canadian AME churches separate from the general AME conference and establish their own church, the BME church.

84. *Liberator*, August 30, 1860.

85. Isaac Holden was the captain of the Victoria Company No. 3, Chatham's all-Black fire brigade that formed in 1857, and the first African-Canadian city councillor in Chatham.

86. *Chatham Weekly Planet*, August 3, 1871.

87. Anderson Ruffin Abbott Papers, scrapbook 2, folder 1, 45–46. Baldwin Room, Toronto Reference Library, Toronto Public Library.

88. *Ibid.*; *British Colonist* (Victoria), August 21, 1874.

89. Anderson Ruffin Abbott Papers, Baldwin Room, Toronto Reference Library, Toronto Public Library.

90. *Toronto Globe*, August 2, 1882; *Toronto World*, August 2, 1882.

91. *Chatham Tri-Weekly Planet*, August 5, 1891; Adrienne Shadd, "No Black Alley Clique: The Campaign to Desegregate Chatham's Public Schools, 1891–1893." *Ontario History* 99, no. 1, (Spring 2007): 77–96.

92. Colin McFarquhar, "A Difference of Perspective," 155.

93. *Ibid.*, 149; *Chatham Daily Planet*, August 2, 1893.

94. Mitchell Kachun, *Festivals of Freedom: Memory and Meaning in African American Emancipation Celebrations, 1808–1915* (Amherst: University of Massachusetts Press, 2003), 177.

95. *Chatham Daily Planet*, August 3, 1897.

96. *Ibid.*

97. *Chatham Daily Planet*, August 2, 1899.

98. Josiah Henson, a former slave from Maryland, escaped to Canada in 1830. He was a church minister and stalwart community activist, and founder of the Dawn Settlement.

99. In 1872, Frederick Douglass became the first Black to be nominated as a vice-presidential candidate, and the first Black presidential candidate at the Republican Convention in 1888. In 1889, Douglass was appointed the United States minister to Haiti. See Steve Anzovin and Janet Podell, *Famous First Facts About American Politics* (New York: H.W. Wilson, 2001), 226. Douglass penned his third and most known autobiography, *The Life and Times of Frederick Douglass* in 1881.

100. There were allegations that the funds raised on behalf of the colony were used by Josiah Henson and Hiram Wilson, abolitionist and Congregational missionary from Boston, for personal benefit while the debt accumulated at Dawn continued to grow.

101. *Provincial Freeman*, August 26, 1854; J.R. Kerr-Ritchie, *The Rites of August First: Emancipation Day in the Black Atlantic World* (Baton Rouge, LA: Louisiana State University Press, 2007), 159.

102. James Hollinsworth, brother-in-law of William Whipper, managed Whipper's Inn in Dresden.

103. Aaron Highgate was a teacher at the Princess Street School in Chatham in 1859. He was a supporter of John Brown's plan to attack Harper's Ferry and was on his way to join Brown's militia but turned back after receiving word that Brown had been caught.

104. William Whipper was a Black abolitionist and a well-known "stationmaster" of the Underground Railroad out of Columbia and Philadelphia. He used actual railroads to transport escaped slaves across the American-Canadian border to freedom, stowing them in secret compartments. Whipper was a wealthy businessman who ran successful lumber and coal businesses with his brother-in-law Stephen Smith in Columbia. He also invested money in the railroad company he used to smuggle slaves into Canada, and owned several railway cars. In 1853 on a visit to the Dawn Settlement, he purchased land, built a house and a warehouse, and established other companies in Dresden, including an inn. His sister's husband, James Hollinsworth, managed all of the Dresden companies.

105. *Provincial Freeman*, August 22, 1857.

106. *Ibid.*, July 25, 1857.

107. *Ibid.*

108. "Diary of Thomas Hughes," MS, Diocese of Huron Archives, London, Ontario.

109. *The Christian Recorder*, September 7, 1861.

110. *Ibid.*

111. *Ibid.*

112. *Ibid.*

113. *Ibid.*, September 7, 1861.

114. Robin Winks, *Blacks in Canada*, 373; James W.St.G. Walker, "African Canadians." Magosci, Paul, ed. *Encyclopedia of Canada's People* (Toronto: Multicultural History Society of Ontario, 1999): 139–76.

115. *British Colonist* (Victoria), August 6, 1890; *Hamilton Spectator*, August 2, 1890.

116. *Chatham Daily News*, August 8, 2006.

117. *Ibid.*, August 2, 2005.

118. Hugh Burnette, a second-generation African Canadian and a descendant of slaves, worked as a carpenter. He was a co-organizer of the Chatham-based National Unity Association, a Black community organization. For more on the life of Hugh Burnette, see John Cooper, *Season of Rage: Hugh Burnette and the Struggle for Civil Rights* (Toronto: Tundra Books, 2005).

119. *Hamilton Spectator*, August 2, 1890; *British Colonist* (Victoria), August 6, 1890.

120. Jane Rhodes, *Mary Ann Shadd Cary: The Black Press and Protest in the Nineteenth Century* (Bloomington: Indiana University Press, 1998), 132.

121. For more information on William Clarke, see the chapter on British Columbia in Robin Winks, *Blacks in Canada*, 280–82.

122. Alfred Jones and his brother, Aby Jones, arrived in London in 1833. Both had been slaves in Kentucky and had forged passes to escape slavery via the Underground Railroad. They both became some of the wealthiest men in London through various business ventures, such as a cooperative store, a pharmacy, and the acquisition of real estate. Daniel Hill, *The Freedom Seekers*, 158.

123. The original site of the school operated by Dillon, which opened in November of 1854, was the military barracks, somewhere on the lands of present-day Victoria Park.

124. The Second Baptist Church was located at the corner of Thames and Horton Streets. It was built on property that was purchased and donated by Aby Jones, who also gave money to help put up a temporary frame building on the site. Aby and his brother Alfred were church officers and deacons of Second Baptist. Benjamin Miller became the minister after Daniel Turner died in 1860.

125. Shadrach Martin was born in May 1833 in Nashville, Tennessee, to an enslaved mother and a free Black father who bought his future wife's freedom. After they died when Shack was young, he was adopted by a man who gave Shadrach his name. As a teenager, he became a barbering apprentice. He later settled in London. See *London Free Press*, March 26, 1910.

126. William McClure, Savage, David, ed., *Life and Labours of the Reverend William McClure by William McClure* (Toronto: James Campbell & Son, 1872), 342.

127. The Free Coloured Mission was operated by a missionary body called the Colonial Church and School Society, under the guardianship of St. Paul's Church, Reverend Marmaduke Dillon was the director and continued in that role until the summer of 1859. J.I. Cooper, "The Mission to the Fugitive Slaves at London." *Ontario History* 46 (Spring 1954): 131–39; *London Free Press*, August 1, 1862.

128. *Toronto Globe*, August 4, 1885.

129. *London Free Press*, August 1, 1895; *British Colonist* (Victoria), August 1, 1895.

130. *London Free Press*, August 4, 1896.

131. See Theda Skocpol, *What a Mighty Power We Can Be: African American Fraternal Groups and the Struggle for Racial Equality* (Princeton: Princeton University Press, 2008).

132. See Nina Mjagkij, *Organizing Black America: An Encyclopedia of African-American Associations* (New York: Garland Publishing, 2001).

133. *London Free Press*, August 4, 1896.

134. *Dawn of Tomorrow*, August 1935; July 25, 1938; *Dawn* owner James F. Jenkins and a man named J.W. Montgomery (of Toronto) established the Canadian League (afterwards Association) for the Advancement of Colored People (CAACP). The organization was created to fight racial discrimination and growing anti-

Black sentiment in various facets of society and to foster unity of Black cultural institutions in Canada. Branches opened in Toronto, Brantford, Niagara Falls, and Dresden. Their efforts proved most effective in London through helping Blacks continue their education, working with juveniles, and distributing food baskets in the winter. White executive members included Canadian anti-slavery historian Fred Landon (also a friend of Jenkins) and Canadian slavery scholar Justice William Renwick Riddell, both historians of African-Canadian history. For more on Fred Landon's writings, see Karolyn Smardz Frost, Hilary (Bates) Neary, and Bryan Walls, eds. *Ontario's Black Heritage: Collected Writings of Fred Landon, 1918–1967* (Toronto: Natural Heritage-Dundurn, 2009).

135. *The Dawn of Tomorrow* was a Black London-based newspaper founded in 1923 by owner and editor James F. Jenkins. It was the official voice of the Canadian League for the Advancement of Colored People and was published until 1966. Fred Landon, a fellow Londoner and personal friend who researched African-Canadian history, also wrote for *The Dawn*.

136. The Community Family Club held weekly meetings aimed at fostering closer relationships between parents and children as well as developing skills ranging from how to build, make, and use radios to woodworking, sewing, knitting, and music.

137. *The Dawn of Tomorrow*, July 1948; *London Free Press*, July 15, 1948, August 2, 1949.

138. Paul Lewis was the president of the CAACP in 1941 and 1942. Originally from Philadelphia, Lewis came from Detroit to London in 1913. He had come to visit friends, but never went back to the United States. Lewis worked in London as a porter and a shoeshine man, and was a member of Beth Emanuel BME Church.

139. *London Free Press*, August 6, 1968.

140. *London Free Press*, March 26, 1910; August 6, 1968; August 1, 1977; August 8, 1978; August 3, 1982; August 7, 1984.

141. Information for Oxford county is from Joyce Pettigrew, *A Safe Haven: The Story of the Black Settlers of Oxford County* (Otterville, ON: South Norwich Historical Society, 2006).

142. The cakewalk was a popular African-American dance that originated on southern plantations by enslaved Africans. They imitated the "high society" manners of their White masters and mistresses, bowing and bending while doing a high-step promenade, a basic dance move of walking steps and figures typically involving a high prance with backward tilt. The slaves dressed in handed-down dresses and suits. The dance became a White-sanctioned performance then competition. Dances were held at the master's house and he and his guests served as judges for the contest that awarded the winning couple with a cake, hence the phrase "take the cake."

143. Pettigrew, *A Safe Haven*, 92–94; *Ingersoll Chronicle*, August 21, 1907.
144. *Ibid.*

Chapter 4: Central Ontario

1. Sophia Pooley was owned by Joseph Brant from the time she was seven years until the age of twelve when she was sold to a White Englishman in Ancaster named Samuel Hatt. When freed by her owner, she moved to Queen's Bush Settlement. See Benjamin Drew, *The Refugee: Narratives of Fugitive Slaves in Canada* (Toronto: Dundurn Press, 2008), 184.
2. Robin Winks, *The Blacks in Canada* (Montreal: McGill-Queen's University Press, 1997), 367.
3. Daniel Hill, *The Freedom Seekers: Blacks in Early Canada* (Agincourt: Book Society of Canada, 1981), 100.
4. For more information on the trial, see Patrick Brode, *The Odyessey of John Anderson* (Toronto: Osgoode Law Society, 1990).
5. Peter Simeon O'Banyoun, Josephus' father, donated plot of land on the north side of Dalhousie Street at the corner of Murray Street for the purpose of erecting the BME church. The senior O'Banyoun was a runaway slave from Kentucky. He was a church minister and took the oath of allegiance to become a British citizen. Josephus was born about 1842. See note 7 in chapter 3 on Josephus O'Banyoun.
6. *Brantford Expositor*, February 10, 2007.
7. *Brantford Weekly Expositor*, August 5,1859; *Brantford Courier*, August 4, 1886.
8. *Brantford Expositor*, February 10, 2007; *Brantford Weekly Expositor*, August 4, 1865.
9. J. Lucas was one of the sons of Andrew Lucas, an escaped slave from Tennessee owned by General Andrew "Stonewall" Jackson. While living in the Niagara region, he fought in the Battle of Queenston Heights during the War of 1812. Lucas moved to Brantford in 1845 where he operated a livery business, taking care of the horses of several local White businessmen. He and his wife had fourteen children. *Brantford Expositor*, June 30, 1997.
10. *Brantford Courier*, August 2, 1894.
11. *Brantford Courier*, August 3, 1903; *Toronto Star*, August 4, 1903.
12. *Ibid.*
13. Charles F.W. Snowden worked in various positions such as as a soap maker, general labourer, stationary boilerman, and construction worker on local homes and buildings of Guelph University. He was born in Brantford in 1868, and was raised from an early age by his maternal grandmother, Martha Coleman, a former slave from Kentucky, after his mother passed away and

his father went to Chicago in search of work. Snowden was a member of the Grace Anglican Church and was a sought-after guitar and fiddle player for local house parties and community events.

14. These teams were part of the segregated baseball leagues in Ontario and Canada. At that time, African Canadians could not play in the White professional leagues. All-Black Canadian baseball teams included the London Colored Stars. See Bill Humber, *A Sporting Chance: Achievements of African-Canadian Athletes* (Toronto: Natural Heritage Books, 2004), 45.

15. *Brantford Courier*, August 1, 1912; *Toronto Star*, August 1, 1912; *Brantford Courier*, August 2, 1912.

16. *The Souls of Black Folks: Hamilton's Stewart Memorial Community*. Worker's Art and Heritage Centre and the Virtual Museum of Canada.

17. Nelson Steven was born in Virginia and escaped to Canada. Shortly after, he risked his life, returning to the United States to enlist with the Union Army (25th U.S. Colored Troops, Company B) in 1865. He returned to Canada in 1866, settled in Hamilton, was married, and worked as a cigar roller. He died in 1890 and was buried in a pauper's grave in Hamilton Cemetery. In August 2007, a grave-marker ceremony was held in Steven's honour and a Civil War veteran's headstone was placed at his burial site.

18. Daniel Hill, *Freedom Seekers*, 103.

19. *Ibid.*, 109.

20. Jesse Happy escaped slavery with the use of his master's horse. He was being sought after in Upper Canada by David Castleman from Kentucky, the owner of Solomon Moseby (another fugitive who sought refuge in Upper Canada). Castleman furnished legal papers asking the Canadian government to send Happy back to slavery. Happy was ordered released from the Hamilton jail on November 14, 1837, because it was determined that he did not steal the horse, but that he used the horse to flee enslavement, a practice deemed illegal under British law. See David Murray, *Colonial Justice: Justice, Morality, and Crime in the Niagara District, 1791–1849* (Toronto: Osgoode Society for Canadian Legal History, 2002), 198–203.

21. Paola Brown was part of the Black settlement in Woolwich, in the Queen's Bush, Peel Township, in 1832. By 1851 he was in Hamilton. He stated: "Slaveholders, I call God, I call Angels, I call Men, to witness, that your destruction is at hand, and will be speedily consummated, unless you repent." "Address Intended to be Delivered in the City Hall, Hamilton, February 7, 1851, on the Subject of Slavery, Hamilton, 1851," as cited by Robin Winks, *The Blacks in Canada*, 254; Daniel Hill, *Freedom Seekers*, 150, 154.

22. *Hamilton Spectator*, August 3, 1857.

23. Charles McCullough, *Essays on Canadian History: A Scrapbook of Clippings from the Hamilton Spectator*. Vol 1, Hamilton Public Library, Special

Collections; *Montreal Witness*, August 13, 1859; "Auchmar Estate Hamilton" (*www.auchmar.info*), accessed August 2009.

24. *Ibid.*; Daniel Hill, *Freedom Seekers*, 183.

25. Charles H. Drinkwater, *A short account of the manner in which Emancipation Day first of August was spent in the city of Hamilton, together with the sermon which was preached before the members of the Brotherly Union Society in the Church of St. Thomas, Hamilton by the Rev. C. H. Drinkwater, B.A., Rector* (Hamilton: A Lawson & Co., 1864), 10.

26. The Brother Union Society was a large African-Canadian benevolent society formed in 1862. The society helped Hamilton's Black community by paying for funerals and providing financial assistance to those in need. They celebrated their 23rd anniversary in 1885. Members included George B. Washington, Reverend J.B. Roberts of St. Paul's AME, Alexander Doston, and George Morton.

27. Josephus O'Banyoun had recently returned from Halifax, Nova Scotia, and become the minister of the AME church.

28. In the1860s, William Butler organized a church in Bronte, which became a BME church in 1875, eventually leading to the formation of the Turner AME Church in Oakville. It still stands today and is used as an antique shop.

29. *Toronto Globe*, August 2, 1878.

30. *Hamilton Spectator*, August 2, 1878.

31. *Ibid.*, August 2, 1884.

32. George Morton was born in Hamilton in 1859. He lived on Augusta Street and worked as a letter carrier for thirty-six years and for twenty-one of those years served as the treasurer for the local Letter Carriers' Association. He also was the secretary for the Brotherly Union Society. Morton passed away on August 20, 1927. From the *Hamilton Herald*, August 20, 1927.

33. *Toronto World*, August 2, 1884.

34. *Hamilton Spectator*, August 2, 1884.

35. *Ibid.*, August 2, 1902; *Toronto Star*, August 1, 1902.

36. *Hamilton Spectator*, August 2, 1890.

37. *Ibid.*, August 1, 1893.

38. *Ibid.*, August 2, 1906.

39. *Ibid.*, August 3, 1909.

40. Enerals Griffin was an African American born in Virginia, who came to Canada in 1829, along with his wife Priscilla. Enerals bought the Griffin House and eighteen-hectare property from George Hogeboom in 1834 for 125 pounds. For one hundred and fifty years his descendants lived and worked on the valley farm. It is not known if Enerals was escaping to freedom or had already been given his freedom and was journeying to Upper Canada in search of a better life. We do know that he could read and write because of his signature

on his naturalization papers. Descendants intermarried and their identity by colour disappeared, and by the mid-twentieth century their Black past was unknown to many descendants.

The Griffins are buried at St Andrew's Presbyterian Church on Sulphur Springs Road in Ancaster. A headstone marks their graves. In 1991, the Griffin House was designated by the Ancaster Local Architectural Conservation Advisory Committee for its unique historical and architectural significance, and, in 2008, the house received National Historical Site designation. Information from Anne Jarvis, Historical Interpreter. Griffin House/Fieldcote Memorial Park and Museum, personal communication through June to November 2009.

41. Hill's home is located at 457 Maple Grove Drive. It still stands today.

42. "Oakville's Black History," Oakville Museum at Erchless Estate, Deborah Hudson, curator, 2000. Canadian Caribbean Association of Halton (CCAH), parts of which were reproduced online on the CCAH website (*ccah.ca*), accessed on September 2009.

43. The Mariner's Home is located at 279 Lawson Street and is still standing today; see Hazel Mathews, *Oakville and the Sixteen: The History of an Ontario Port* (Toronto: University of Toronto Press, 1953), 248; C. Cross, curator of Collections, Oakville Museum at Erchless Estate, personal communication November 2009; Veronica Tyrrell, executive director of the Canadian Caribbean Association of Halton, personal communication, November 2009.

44. *Toronto Star*, August 2, 1929.

45. *Ibid.*

46. From Rachel Mendleson, "Alvin B. Aberdeen Duncan: 1913–2009." *Macleans* 56, March 2, 2009.

47. It took years of careful research by Ruby West Jackson of Madison, Wisconsin; Walter T. McDonald of Racine, Wisconsin; and Hilary J. Dawson of Toronto, Ontario, to uncover Joshua Glover's complete story. In 2007, this story came to public attention in *Finding Freedom: The Untold Story of Joshua Glover Runaway Slave*, by Ruby West Jackson and Walter T. McDonald, and published by the Wisconsin Historical Society Press.

48. The 1851 North American Convention of Coloured People was held in Toronto because it was decided that this city would be the safest location for a large meeting. This meeting was chaired by Henry Bibb, J.J. Fisher, Thomas Smallwood, and Josiah Henson. There were hundreds of people of African descent from the northern United States, England, and across Canada who had decided to encourage settlement to Canada rather than to Africa.

49. Daniel Hill, *Freedom Seekers*, 20.

50. *Ibid.*, 107.

51. J.R. Kerr-Ritchie, *The Rites of August First: Emancipation Day in the Black Atlantic World* (Baton Rouge: Louisiana State University Press, 2007).

52. *The Church*, August 11, 1838.

53. Based on his regular involvement in Emancipation Day commemorations in Toronto, Henry James Grasett is likely to have been an anti-slavery activist of the Anglican Church in Toronto. He participated in local Emancipation Day events for over twenty years, delivering speeches and sermons.

54. *Black Abolitionist Papers*, Vol. 2: 76–83.

55. *St. Catharines Journal*, August 6, 1840.

56. Thomas Smallwood was a former slave from Maryland. After arriving in Canada he assisted other fugitives to escape slavery and set up new homes. He operated a saw factory on Front Street. Smallwood self-published his personal story in 1851, the first slave narrative written in Canada. See Thomas Smallwood, *A Narrative of Thomas Smallwood (Coloured Man)* (Toronto: Mercury Press, 2000).

57. *Black Abolitionist Papers*, Vol. 2: 2, 295–96.

58. *Provincial Freeman*, August 5, 1854.

59. Daniel Hill, *Freedom Seekers*, 183.

60. *Brantford Semi-Weekly Expositor*, August 5, 1856.

61. *Owen Sound Comet*, August 2, 1860.

62. *Toronto World*, August 2, 1883; August 3, 1883.

63. *The Globe*, August 2, 1892; *Toronto Daily Mail*, August 2, 1892.

64. Donald G. Simpson, *Under the North Star: Black Communities in Upper Canada* (Trenton, New Jersey: Africa World Press, 2005), 122.

65. *Toronto Evening Star*, August 1, 1895.

66. *Toronto Star*, August 2, 1946.

67. *Toronto Star*, August 1, 1947; *Toronto Star*, July 30, 1951.

68. Donald Moore, *Don Moore: An Autobiography* (Toronto: Williams-Wallace Publishers, 1985), 182. The TEC developed its own colour guard and drill team, and supported several women's auxiliaries. Their slogan was "Equal rights for all, special privileges for none."

69. *Ibid*.

70. Donald Moore, *Don Moore*, 188.

71. Violet King graduated from the University of Alberta and became a member of the Alberta Law Society. She was a descendant of one of the African-American immigrants from Oklahoma who settled in the prairie provinces between 1908 and 1911. For more information, see Gwen Hooks, *The Keystone Legacy: Reflections of a Black Pioneer* (Edmonton, AB: Brightest Pebble, 1997).

72. *Toronto Star*, August 5, 1958.

73. *Globe and Mail*, July 27, 1964.

74. *Share*, July 31, 2008.

Chapter 5: The Niagara Region

1. In 1840, the militia under the command of Captain Alexander MacDonald attempted to rescue and free two enslaved African women from a small group of Southerners having dinner at a local hotel in Niagara, but were unsuccessful and withdrew. The corps disbanded in 1851 after the completion of the Welland Canal. These servicemen then settled around the Niagara Peninsula and some assisted in the movement of refugees on the Underground Railroad and helped to settle the newcomers.

2. In 1983 the BME Church was rededicated in honour of Robert Nathaniel Dett. Born in Drummondville, he was a composer, pianist, and music educator in both Canada and the United States. Dett was the church's organist from 1898 to 1903. In 1998 Brainerd Blyden-Taylor founded the Nathaniel Dett Chorale, named in honour of the talented Niagara-area musician. The choral group performs various forms of Afro-centric music. In 2009, they were invited to perform at the inauguration of United States President Barack Obama, the first African-American president.

3. The land for these two churches and other lots used for homes was sold to members of the community by William Hamilton Merritt, a White abolitionist in St. Catharines. He was a local politician, the chief engineer of the Welland Canal, and architect of the first Niagara Suspension Bridge.

4. The passage of the legislation on July 9, 1793, provided that Africans already enslaved in Upper Canada would remain the property of their owners for life, children born to slaves would be freed at age twenty-five, and their children would be free at birth. Also, the importation of slaves into the province was prohibited and any slaves entering into Upper Canada would be freed automatically. Lastly, owners of freed slaves had to provide for their security.

5. Michael Butler and Nancy Power, *Slavery and Freedom in Niagara*, 69. In the early nineteenth century, pamphlet writing was a form of public protest in the abolition movement. Pamphlets were used to conscript Blacks to fight slavery, to provide advice to fellow Africans, and to record history (speeches, sermons, etc.). See Richard Newman et al, eds., *Pamphlets of Protest: An Anthology of Early African American Protest* (New York: Routledge, 2001).

6. Henry Gray was very active in the organization and execution of Emancipation Day celebrations in St. Catharines. He hosted the communal meals for a time at his property on Cherry Street and was on the planning committee in 1843.

7. *St. Catharines Journal*, August 2, 1838; *The Church*, August 11, 1838.

8. Henry Garrett was one of the fugitives who gradually moved inland further from the border. After escaping enslavement in Virginia, he seems to have settled first in Drummondville, moved to Brantford briefly, then settled in London where he operated a bakery.

9. *Niagara Chronicle*, July 17, 1844.

10. *Liberator*, August 23, 1861.

11. Colin McFarquhar, "A Difference of Perspective: Blacks, Whites, and Emancipation Day Celebrations in Ontario, 1865–1919." *Ontario History* 92, no 2 (Autumn 2000):152.

12. B.J. Spencer Pitt appears to be the fifth Black lawyer in Ontario. He came to Canada in 1928 to attend Dalhousie University in Nova Scotia before going to London, England, to obtain his law degree in international law and constitutional history. He was called to the bar in 1928 and opened a law office on Dundas Street West in Toronto. Spencer Pitt was recalled as a mentor and an advocate by many. Lance C. Talbot, "History of Blacks in the Law Society of Upper Canada," The Law Society of Upper Canada Gazette 24, no. 1, March 1990: 67–68; Roy Vogt. *Whose Property? The Deepening Conflict Between Private Property and Democracy in Canada* (Toronto: University of Toronto Press, 1999), 376; Sheldon Taylor, "B.J. Spencer Pitt: A Forgotten Icon." *Share News*, February 21, 2002: 9.

13. "Emancipation Days: The 'Big Picnic.'" *Dalhousie Peer* 1, no. 7, (August 1997). Emancipation Day Collection, St. Catharines Museum.

14. Information from Wilda Hypolite, "The Big Picnic: Lakeside Park, Port Dalhousie," Emancipation Day Collection, St. Catharines Museum; this is a page of transcribed interview notes.

Chapter 6: Around the Northern Terminus

1. See Peter Meyler, ed., *Broken Shackles: Old Man Henson From Slavery to Freedom* (Toronto: Natural Heritage Books, 2001), Appendix "The Old Durham Road Pioneer Cemetery Committee," 201–04.

2. For a video on the story of this cemetery and the surrounding area, see *Speakers for the Dead*, produced by David Sutherland and Jennifer Holness, and distributed by NFB.

3. John Frost Jr., a member of one of the leading families of Owen Sound, recorded Henson's oral history, and put it together as a collection of anecdotes set in an historical context for publication in 1889. A new edition of *Broken Shackles* was edited for today's reader, annotated, and republished in 2001. See Peter Meyler, ed., *Broken Shackles*.

4. John Hall was born in Amherstburg, Ontario, in 1807. John, his mother, and ten siblings were kidnapped by slave hunters along the Upper Canada–Detroit border and sold into slavery in Kentucky. He escaped his enslavement, using the Underground Railroad to return to his native land.

5. "Presque Isle." *Northern Terminus: Northern Terminus: African Canadian History Journal* 5, (2008): 19–20.

6. Lisa Wodhams, "To Enlighten our Hearts: The 145th Emancipation Celebrations," *Northern Terminus: African Canadian History Journal*, Volume 5, 2008: xiii-xix; Amelia Ferguson. "146th Emancipation Festival: Community, Roots, and Culture." *Northern Terminus: African Canadian History Journal* 6 (2009): ix-xiii.

7. Research on the Queen's Bush Settlement was initiated by Linda Brown-Kubisch when she was the research librarian at the Kitchener-Waterloo Public Library. Her original work culminated in the publication of *The Queen's Bush Settlement: Black Pioneers 1839–1865* (Toronto: Natural Heritage Books, 2004). For names of Black pioneers, see pages 190–235.

8. "The Queen's Bush Settlement: 1820–1867." *Featured Plaque of the Month*, Ontario Heritage Trust, September 2008.

9. *Elmira Independent*, August 25, 1997; *Dumfries Reformer*, August 5, 1863.

10. *Elmira Independent*, October 26, 1992.

11. *Hamilton Spectator*, August 1, 1890.

12. Personal communication with Stacy McLennan, registrar/researcher, Doon Heritage Crossroads, Kitchener, August 2009.

13. Robin Winks, *The Blacks in Canada* (Montreal: McGill-Queen's University Press, 1997), 245; Daniel Hill, *The Freedom Seekers: Blacks in Early Canada* (Agincourt: Book Society of Canada, 1981), 58.

14. Daniel Hill, *Freedom Seekers*, 175)

15. *Ibid.*, 177, 226n42.

16. This account was written in 1885 by Marion Keith (real name Martha Graham), a novelist from Oro. See Tim Crawford, ed., *The Oro African Church: A History of the African Methodist Episcopal Church, Edgar, Ontario, Canada* (Oro, ON: The Township of Oro-Medonte, 1999), 28.

17. Joanna McEwan, *The Story of Oro* (Oro: Township of Oro, 1987).

18. Tim Crawford, *The Oro African Church*, 37.

19. John Nettleton was a tailor and opened a tailor shop on Main Street in 1857. He became involved in local politics.

20. John Nettleton, "Reminiscences, 1857–1870," *Papers & Records*, Huron Institute 2: 13–19.

21. Gary E. French, *Men of Colour: an Historical Account of the Black Settlement on Wilberforce Street in Oro Township, 1819–1949* (Stroud: Kaste Books, 1978), 56.

22. *Owen Sound Comet*, August 2, 1860; Daniel Hill, *Freedom Seekers*, 184.

23. *Collingwood Enterprise-Messenger*, August 4, 1898.

24. Personal communication with Janie Cooper Wilson, executive director of the Silvershoe Historical Society, ongoing June through November 2009.

Chapter 7: Quebec: Montreal

1. Article 47 of the Articles of Capitulation stated that: "Negroes and Panis of both sexes shall remain, in their status as slaves, in possession of the French and Canadians to whom they belong; they shall be at liberty to keep them in their service in the colony or sell them; and they may also continue to bring them up in the Roman religion." Robin Winks, *The Blacks in Canada* (Montreal: McGill-Queen's University Press, 1997), 24.

2. See Afua Cooper, *The Hanging of Angélique: The Untold Story of Canadian Slavery and the Burning of Old Montréal* (Toronto: HarperCollins, 2006.)

3. Dorothy G. Williams, *The Road to Now: A History of Blacks in Montreal* (Montreal: Véhicule Press, 1997), 26.

4. Anthony Grant came from New York City in 1830 at the age of twenty-nine. He was a self-employed launderer. He advertised his services (the earliest newspaper ad in Montreal for services by a Black person). Grant was very active in the local Black community in the movement against slavery and racial equality. On July 23, 1833, he hosted a meeting of twelve men of African descent at his house on St. Paul Street to discuss the implications of the passage of the Emancipation Act. They publicly endorsed the bill by publishing a statement of resolutions in the newspaper. Then, in May 1834, he wrote an open letter to Montrealers, both Black and White, to expose that African Canadians in the city were being denied certain rights, particularly serving on juries, because of their race. Grant died in 1838 following an accident. Frank Mackey, *Black Then: Blacks and Montreal 1780s–1880s* (Montreal: McGill-Queen's University Press, 2004), 92.

5. Frank Mackey, *Black Then*, 199.

6. *Ibid.*, 197.

7. *Montreal Gazette*, August 2, 1834.

8. Shadrach Minkins escaped slavery in Virginia and eventually arrived in Montreal in 1851. See Gary Collison, *Shadrach Minkins: From Fugitive Slave to Citizen* (Cambridge:Harvard University Press, 1998).

9. John Dougall was the editor of the *Montreal Witness* from 1851 to 1871. He was an executive member of the Anti-Slavery Society of Canada during the 1850s, acting as a "one-man corresponding society" for the group in Montreal. As a philanthropist he donated to the Refugee Home Society in the Windsor and Elgin areas. Dougall used his newspaper to attack American slavery. See Robin Winks, *The Blacks in Canada*, 222, 254, 258, 261–62.

10. D.S. Janes, a Montreal merchant, was a staunch abolitionist. A member of the American Presbyterian Church, Janes was very active in assisting African-American slaves who escaped using the Underground Railroad, so much so that he was called "the African consul." He was also one of fourteen

vice-presidents of the Anti-Slavery Society of Canada in the early years of the organization.

11. The YMCA in Montreal was formed in 1851. A motion against American slavery was first put forth in the winter of 1857. Then, a few months later when asked to place their vote on whether the upcoming North American conference should be held in Richmond, Virginia, the Montreal association unanimously adopted a resolution moved by Francis Grafton against holding the convention in Virginia. They also agreed to sever ties with affiliations in southern slaveholding states to express the group's opposition to slavery. Alfred Sanham, *History of the Montreal Young Men's Christian Association (the First Formed on the Continent), Also, an Account of the Origin of Men's Christian Associations, and Subsequent Progress of the Work in America* (Montreal: D. Bentley & Co., 1873).

12. *Montreal Witness*, August 7, 1861.

13. *Ibid.*, August 2, August 6, 1862.

14. *Montreal Witness*, August 2, 1862.

15. *Toronto Globe*, December 7, 1859.

16. *Ibid.*

17. Gary Collison, *Shadrach Minkins*, 216.

18. *Montreal Gazette*, August 1, 2009.

Chapter 8: The Maritimes

1. For information on Blacks in Nova Scotia, specifically in Yarmouth County, see Sharon Robart-Johnson, *Africa's Children: A History of Blacks in Yarmouth, Nova Scotia* (Toronto: Natural Heritage Books-Dundurn, 2009).

2. Richard Preston was an active church and community leader in the African-Canadian community in Nova Scotia. Preston escaped from slavery in Virginia as a young boy and settled in Nova Scotia. In 1832, he founded the African Baptist Church on Cornwallis Street in Halifax. The church is now known as the Cornwallis Street Baptist Church.

3. Amani Harvey Whitfield, *Blacks on the Border: The Black Refugees in British North America 1815–1860* (Burlington: University of Vermont Press, 2006), 1.

4. *Ibid.*; James W.St.G. Walker, "African Canadians." Paul Magosci, ed. *Encyclopedia of Canada's People* (Toronto: Multicultural History Society of Ontario, 1999), 154.

5. Robin Winks, *The Blacks in Canada* (Montreal: McGill-Queen's University Press, 1997), 129; "African Nova Scotians: In the Age of Slavery and Abolition." (*www.gs.ns.ca/nsarm/virtual/africanns*), accessed on August 2009.

6. *Morning Chronicle*, July 9, 1844.

7. Government House was the home of the lieutenant-governor of Nova Scotia, John Wentworth. It is the first official government residence in Canada. See *Novascotian*, August 9, 1847; Amani Harvey Whitfield, *Blacks on the Border*, 113.

8. *Morning Chronicle*, July 9, 1844: *Novascotian*, August 9, 1847.

9. *Ibid.*

10. The African School House opened in 1836 and was supported by Dr. Robert Willis, rector of St. Paul's (Anglican) Church on Argyle Street, Halifax.

11. *British Colonist* (Halifax), August 3, 1850.

12. *Ibid.*; *British Colonist* (Halifax), July 30, 1850; August 1, 1850; August 6, 1850; *Novascotian*, August 5, 1850.

13. Melville Island was the site of a former prison during the War of 1812. It was subsequently used as a receiving depot for incoming Black refugees between 1814 and 1816. Almost one thousand refugees were housed in the former prison during that time but were relocated once they obtained land grants.

14. *Novascotian*, August 9, 1852; August 15, 1853; *British Colonist*, August 4, 1855.

15. *Acadian Recorder*, August 5, 1867.

16. See Adrienne Shadd, "Where Are You Really From? Notes of an Immigrant From North Buxton, Ontario." Carl James, Adrienne Shadd, eds., *Talking About Identity: Encounters in Race, Ethnicity, and Language* (Toronto: Between the Lines, 2001) for a discussion and analysis based on personal experience.

17. According to Robin Winks, about 1,800 African Canadians resided here in segregation in the largest all-Black community in Canada. In 1879, this congregation was reorganized at the New Road settlement, now called North Preston. The parish became known as St. Thomas United Baptist Church. Robin Winks, *Blacks in Canada*, 456; Final Heritage Report, 56. See also Cam Robertson, *Report on Early History of the Preston Area: Cherry Brook, Lake Loon, Lake Major, East Preston, and North Preston* (Halifax Regional Municipality Department, 2004), 56.

18. The City of Saint John was the first incorporated city in Canada.

19. Becoming a "freeman of the city" required men to take an oath declaring loyalty to the British Crown, that they would obey the laws of the city, they owned land, and paid a collective. The "freeman" status allowed a person to trade freely and exercise their crafts.

20. *The Daily Sun*, February 26, 1885.

21. *Novascotian*, August 8, 1853.

22. See W.A. Spray, *The Blacks in New Brunswick* (Fredericton: Brunswick Press, 1972); "Heritage Resources Saint John" (*www.saintjohn.nbcc.nb.ca/Heritage*), accessed September 2009.

23. The Mechanic's Institute was located on Carleton Street in Saint John; *Novascotian*, August 15, 1859.

24. *Halifax Sun and Advertiser*, August 12, 1863.

25. Richard Crawford, *America's Musical Life: A History* (New York: W. W. Norton & Company, Inc., 2001); Richard Crawford, ed., *The Civil War Songbook: Complete Original Sheet Music for 37 Songs* (New York: Dover Publications, 1977).

26. "Get Off the Track!" was written in 1844 by Jesse Hutchinson Jr. of the Hutchinson Family Singers. The group was a professional quartet made up of three brothers and two sisters from New Hampshire. They engaged social issues such as slavery through song. "Get Off the Track!" remained popular into the 1860s and became an anti-slavery anthem. John Hutchinson sang over Frederick Douglass's grave when he died in 1895. See Appendix B.

Chapter 9: British Columbia

1. See Leland Donald, *Aboriginal Slavery on the Northwest Coast of North America* (Berkeley: University of California Press, 1997). Donald provides an in-depth examination of Native slavery along the Northwest coast; Barry Gough, *Gunboat Frontier: British Maritime Authority and Northwest Coast Indians* (Vancouver: University of British Columbia Press, 1984), 85–94; James Edward Fitzgerald, *The Examination of the Charter and Proceedings of the Hudson Bay Company* (Vancouver: Trelawney Saunders, 1849); John Adams, *Old Square Toes and His Lady: The Life of James and Amelia Douglas* (Victoria, BC: Horsdal & Schubart, 2001), 48–49.

2. Barry Gough, *Gunboat Frontier*, 85–94.

3. For more information on James Douglas, see Julie H. Ferguson, *James Douglas: Father of Confederation* (Toronto: Dundurn Press, 2009). The Quest Series.

4. See James Edward Fitzgerald, *The Examination, The Examination of the Charter and Proceedings of the Hudson Bay Company* (Vancouver, BC: Trelawney Saunders, 1849).

5. John Adams, *Old Square Toes and His Lady*, 122.

6. Several landmarks were named after John Giscome and Henry McDame e.g. Giscome Portage, Giscome Rapid, Giscome Canyon, McDame Creek, Mount McDame; Giscome's detailed journals of his prospecting expeditions were published in the *British Colonist* newspaper, see the *British Colonist*, December 14, 1863, 3.

7. Robin Winks, *The Blacks in Canada* (Montreal: McGill-Queen's University Press, 1997), 281.

8. *Ibid.*, 280–82.

9. *British Colonist*, October 24, 1859.

10. Sherry Edmunds-Flett, "Abundant Faith: 19th Century African Canadian Women on Vancouver Island," in *Telling Tales: Essays in Western Women's History*

edited by Catherine A. Cavanaugh and Randi R. Warne (Vancouver: University of British Columbia Press, 2000), 273.

11. Malcolm Edwards, "The War of Complexional Distinction: Blacks in Gold Rush California and British Columbia." *California Historical Quarterly* 56, no. 1, (Spring 1977): 43.

12. Also known as the African Rifles, these Black men organized themselves, with financial support from Vancouver Island's African-Canadian community, to protect against Native attacks and American expansion threats. They trained at the Drill Hall or on Beacon Hill and were the only armed forces in Victoria for almost one year. They remained in operation until 1864, then disbanded because of lack of financial support from the new governor.

13. *British Colonist,* August 2, 1861; August 2, 1862; August 1, 1863.

14. *Ibid.,* December 31, 1866.

15. Lynne Bell, "Artist's Pages: Decolonizing Tactics in Writing Space." *The Future of the Page,* edited by Peter Stoicheff and Andrew Taylor, eds., (Toronto: University of Toronto Press, 2004), 255–69; Andrea Fantona, "In the Presence of Absence: Invisibility, Black Canadian History, and Melinda Mollineaux's Pinhole Photography." *Canadian Journal of Communication* 31, no. 1 (2006): 227–38.

16. Crawford Killian, *Go Do Some Great Thing: The Black Pioneers of British Columbia* (Vancouver, BC: Douglas & McIntyre, 1978).

Chapter 10: The Role of Women in Emancipation Day Celebrations

1. *St. Catharines Journal,* November 12, 1835.

2. Jim Bearden and Linda Jean Butler, *The Life and Times of Mary Shadd Cary* (Toronto: NC Press, 1977), 150; Jane Rhodes, *Mary Ann Shadd Cary: The Black Press and Protest in the Nineteenth Century* (Bloomington: Indiana University Press, 1998), 93.

3. *Hamilton Spectator,* August 2, 1884.

4. Emancipation Day Collection, North American Black Historical Museum, Amherstburg, Ontario.

Chapter 11: Dissent and Diminution

1. Anderson Ruffin Abbott Papers, Baldwin Room, Toronto Reference Library, Toronto Public Library, scrapbook 2, folder 1:17.

2. See Mitchell Kachun, *Festivals of Freedom: Memory and Meaning in African American Emancipation Celebrations, 1808–1915* (Amherst: University of Massachusetts Press, 2003).

3. Colin McFarquhar, "A Difference of Perspective: Blacks, Whites, and Emancipation Day Celebrations in Ontario, 1865–1919." *Ontario History* 92, no 2 (Autumn 2000): 152.

Chapter 12: The Evolution of Emancipation Day

1. *St. Catharines Journal*, October 15, 1835.
2. McKivigan, John R. and Jason H. Silverman, "Monarchial Liberty and Republican Slavery: West Indies Emancipation Celebrations in Upstate New York and Canada West." *Afro-Americans in New York: Life and History* 10, no. 1 (January 31, 1986): 14.
3. *Ibid.*, 14.
4. *Windsor Evening Record*, August 2, 1912.
5. *Chatham Evening Record*, August 2, 1911.
6. *Windsor Evening Record*, August 2, 1912.
7. *Ibid.*, plus other Ontario newspapers, the *Brantford Expositor*, etc.
8. Colin McFarquhar, "A Difference of Perspective: Blacks, Whites, and Emancipation Day Celebrations in Ontario, 1865–1919." *Ontario History* 92, no 2 (Autumn 2000): 155.
9. *Brantford Expositor*, August 5, 1859.
10. *Acadian Recorder*, August 5, 1867.
11. *Windsor Evening Record*, August 2, 1913.
12. Peggy Bristow, "A Duty to the Past, a Promise to the Future: Black Organizing in Windsor — The Depression, World War II, and the Post-War Years." *New Dawn: The Journal of Black Canadian Studies* 2, no. 1 (2007): 17.
13. *Ibid.*, 16.
14. *Ibid.*
15. Written by Bob Marley, 1980, and published by Island Records Inc. 1980.
16. MacDougall, Paul. "Marcus Garvey and Nova Scotia: Birth of a Movement, Birth of a Religion, Birth of a Church." *Shunpiking Magazine* 5, no.32 (February/March 2000).
17. B.W. Higman, "Remembering Slavery: The Rise, Decline, and Revival of Emancipation Day in the English-speaking Caribbean." *Slavery and Abolition* 19, no.1, (1998): 93.

Epilogue

1. Bill 111 was the first bill co-sponsored by members of two different political parties in the provincial Legislature, Wellington-Halton Conservative MPP

Ted Arnott and Lambton-Kent-Middlesex Liberal MPP Maria Van Bommel; Emancipation Day Collection, Ontario Black History Society.

2. *Hamilton Spectator*, August 2, 2007.

3. Personal communication with Anne Jarvis, Historical Interpreter, Griffin House/ Fieldcote Memorial Park and Museum, June through November 2009.

Bibliography

Primary Sources

"Alvin McCurdy Collection." Archives Ontario.

"Anderson Ruffin Abbott Papers." Baldwin Room, Toronto Reference Library, Toronto Public Library.

"Black Settlement in Wellesley and Peel Townships Collection." Elmira Public Library, Elmira, Ontario.

Drinkwater, Charles H. *A short account of the manner in which Emancipation Day first of August was spent in the city of Hamilton, together with the sermon which was preached before the members of the Brotherly Union Society in the Church of St. Thomas, Hamilton by the Rev. C. H. Drinkwater, B.A., Rector.* A Lawson & Co., 1864. Monograph at Library and Archives Canada.

"Emancipation Day Collection." St. Catharines Museum at the Welland Canal, St. Catharines, Ontario.

Secondary Sources

Adams, John. *Old Square Toes and His Lady: The Life of James and Amelia Douglas.* Victoria: Horsdal & Schubart, 2001.

Alexander, Ken and Avis Glaze. *Towards Freedom: The African Canadian Experience.* Toronto: Umbrella Press, 1996.

Amherstburg 1796–1996: The New Town on the Garrison Ground. Amherstburg: Amherstburg Bicentennial Committee, 1996.

Bearden, Jim and Linda Jean Butler. *The Life and Times of Mary Shadd Cary.* Toronto: NC Press Ltd., 1977.

Bell, Lynne. "Artist's Pages: Decolonizing Tactics in Writing Space." *The Future of the Page*, edited by Peter Stoicheff and Andrew Taylor. Toronto: University of Toronto Press, 2004.

Black, Clinton V. *History of Jamaica*. Kingston, Jamaica: Longman Caribbean, 1983.

Butler, Michael and Nancy Power. *Slavery and Freedom in Niagara*. Niagara-on-the-Lake: Niagara Historical Society, 1993.

Bristow, Peggy. "A Duty to the Past, a Promise to the Future: Black Organizing in Windsor — The Depression, World War II, and the Post-War Years." *New Dawn: The Journal of Black Canadian Studies* 2, no. 1 (2007): 15–59.

Brown-Kubisch, Linda. *Queen's Bush Settlement: Black Pioneers 1839–1865*. Toronto: Natural Heritage Books, 2004.

Carnochan, Janet. *History of Niagara: In Part*. Toronto: William Briggs, 1914.

Coffin, Levi. *Reminiscences of Levi Coffin: The Reputed President of the Underground Railroad*. New York: Arno Press, 1968.

Collison, Gary. *Shadrach Minkins: From Fugitive Slave to Citizen*. Cambridge: Harvard University Press, 1998.

Cooper, John Irwin. *Montreal: A Brief History*. Montreal: McGill-Queen's University Press, 1969.

_____. "The Mission to the Fugitive Slaves at London," *Ontario History* 46 (Spring 1954): 131–39.

Coxson, Doug, ed. *Catch the Culture in Wilmot and Wellesley Townships*. New Hamburg, Ontario: New Hamburg Independent, 2008.

Crawford, Richard. *America's Musical Life: A History*. New York: W.W. Norton & Company, Inc., 2001.

_____, ed. *The Civil War Songbook: Complete Original Sheet Music for 37 Songs*. New York: Dover Publications, 1977.

Crawford, Tim, ed. *The Oro African Church: A History of the African Methodist Episcopal Church, Edgar, Ontario, Canada*. Oro-Medonte, Ontario: The Township of Oro-Medonte, 1999.

Donald, Leland. *Aboriginal Slavery in the Northwest Coast of North America*. Berkeley: University of California Press, 1997.

Drew, Benjamin. *The Refugee: Narratives of Fugitive Slaves in Canada*. Toronto: Dundurn Press, 2008.

Edmunds-Flett, Sherry. "Abundant Faith: 19th Century African Canadian Women on Vancouver Island." *Telling Tales: Essays in Western Women's History*. Catherine A. Cavanaugh and Randi R. Warne. eds. Vancouver: University of British Columbia Press, 2000.

Edwards, Malcolm. "The War of Complexional Distinction: Blacks in Gold Rush California and British Columbia." *California Historical Quarterly* 56, no. 1 (Spring 1977): 34–45.

Fantona, Andrea. "In the Presence of Absence: Invisibility, Black Canadian History, and Melinda Mollineaux's Pinhole Photography," *Canadian Journal of Communication* 31, no. 1 (2006): 227–38.

Ferguson, Amelia. "146th Emancipation Festival: Community, Roots, and Culture." *Northern Terminus: African Canadian History Journal* 6, (2009): ix–xiii.

Files, Angela E. M. *African Hope Renewed: Along the Grand River 1400s-1800s.* Brantford, Ontario: privately published, 2004.

Fitzgerald, James Edward. *The Examination of the Charter and Proceedings of the Hudson Bay Company.* London: Trelawney Saunders, 1849.

French, Gary E. *Men of Colour: An Historical Account of the Black Settlement on Wilberforce Street in Oro Township, 1819–1949.* Stroud, Ontario: Kaste Books, 1978.

"From Slavery to Freedom." Heritage Matters, Ontario Heritage Trust, August, 2007.

Gleaner Company. *The Gleaner Geography and History of Jamaica.* Kingston, Jamaica: The Gleaner Company, 1995.

Gough, Barry. *Gunboat Frontier: British Maritime Authority and Northwest Coast Indians.* Vancouver: University of British Columbia Press, 1984.

Hahne, Debbie. "The History of the Owen Sound Emancipation Day Picnic." *Northern Terminus: The African Canadian History Journal* 2 (2007): 12–16.

Hamilton, James Cleland. *Osgoode Hall: Reminiscences of the Bench and Bar.* Toronto: Carswell Co., 1904.

Higman, B.W. "Remembering Slavery: The Rise, Decline, and Revival of Emancipation Day in the English-speaking Caribbean." *Slavery and Abolition* 19, no.1 (1998): 90–105.

Hill, Daniel G. *The Freedom Seekers: Blacks in Early Canada.* Toronto: Book Society of Canada, 1981.

Hudson, Deborah. *Oakville's Black History.* Oakville, Ontario: Oakville Museum at Erchless Estate, 2000.

Humber, William. *A Sporting Chance: Achievements of African-Canadian Athletes.* Toronto: Natural Heritage Books, 2004.

Ibbotson, Heather. "Celebrations took the cake." *Brantford Expositor*, February 10, 2007, D1.

Jackson, John N. *The Mighty Niagara: One River, Two Frontiers.* Amherst, Massachusetts: Prometheus Books, 2003.

Jackson, Ruby West and Walter T. McDonald. *Finding Freedom: The Untold Story of Joshua Glover, Runaway Slave.* Madison, Wisconsin: Wisconsin Historical Society Press, 2007.

Jeffers, Toby, A. "A History of Blacks in Hamilton." *Hamilton Spectator.* February 18, 1993, A11.

Kachun, Mitchell. *Festivals of Freedom: Memory and Meaning in African American Emancipation Celebrations, 1808–1915.* Amherst, Massachusetts: University of Massachusetts Press, 2003.

Kerr-Ritchie, J.R. *The Rites of August First: Emancipation Day in the Black Atlantic World.* Baton Rouge, Louisiana: Louisiana State University Press, 2007.

Killian, Crawford. *Go Do Some Great Thing: The Black Pioneers of British Columbia.* Vancouver, British Columbia: Douglas & McIntyre, 1978.

Klinck, George. "The Development and Progress of Education in Elmira and Vicinity." *Elmira Signet* (1938).

Knowles, Paul. *Niagara and Southwestern Ontario: A Colour Guide.* Halifax, Nova Scotia: Formac Publishing, 1998.

Latta, Maureen. "Fugitive Slaves Found Temporary Refuge in Peel Township." *Elmira Independent,* October 26, 1992, 26.

Lewis, James. *Religious Life of Fugitive Slaves and Rise of Coloured Baptist Churches 1820–1865, In What is Now Known as Ontario.* New York: Arno Press, 1965. Published from an original B.D. thesis, McMaster University, 1965.

"London Public Library Scrapbook." Vol. 10, 116; Vol. 37, 5, 116.

McClure, William. David Savage, ed. *Life and Labours of the Reverend William McClure by William McClure.* Toronto: James Campbell & Son, 1872.

McCullough, Charles R. *Essays on Canadian History: A Scrapbook of Clippings from the Hamilton Spectator,* Vol. 1. Hamilton Public Library Special Collections.

McEwan, Joanna. *The Story of Oro.* Oro, Ontario: Township of Oro, 1987.

McFarquhar, Colin. "A Difference of Perspective: Blacks, Whites, and Emancipation Day Celebrations in Ontario, 1865–1919." *Ontario History* 92, no. 2 (Autumn 2000): 147–60.

McKivigan, John R. and Jason H. Silverman. "Monarchial Liberty and Republican Slavery: West Indies Emancipation Celebrations in Upstate New York and Canada West." *Afro-Americans in New York Life and History* 10, no. 1 (January 31, 1986): 7–15.

Mackey, Frank. *Black Then: Blacks and Montreal 1780s–1880s.* Montreal: McGill-Queen's University Press, 2004.

Mathews, Hazel. *Oakville and the Sixteen: The History of an Ontario Port.* Toronto: University of Toronto Press, 1953.

Mendleson, "Rachel. Alvin B. Duncan 1913–2009." *Maclean's.* February 25, 2009.

Mjagkij, Nina. *Organizing Black America: An Encyclopedia of African American Associations.* New York: Garland Publishing, 2001.

Myrie, Evelyn. "Emancipation Day is Lord Simcoe's Legacy." *Hamilton Spectator.* August 2, 2007, A15.

Nettleton, John. "Reminiscences, 1857–1870." *Papers & Records,* Huron Institute 2 (1914): 13–19.

Newman, Richard *et al,* eds. *Pamphlets of Protest: An Anthology of Early African*

American Protest. New York: Routledge, 2001.

O'Brien, Robert. "Victoria's Negro Colonists 1858–1866." *Phylon* 1st quarter (1942): 15–18.

The Preserver: The Black Cultural Centre for Nova Scotia Newsletter 20, no. 5, (August 2009).

_____ 20, no. 6, (September 2009).

"Presque Isle." *Northern Terminus: African Canadian History Journal* 5 (2008): 19–20.

Pettigrew, Joyce A. *A Safe Haven: The Story of Black Settlers of Oxford County.* Otterville, Ontario: The South Norwich Historical Society, 2006.

Quarles, Benjamin. *Black Abolitionists.* Cambridge: Da Capo Press, 1991.

Riddell, William R. "The Slave in Canada." *The Journal of Negro History* 5, no. 3, (July 1920): 261–377.

Riddell, William R. "Interesting Notes on Great Britain and Canada in Respect to the Negro." *Journal of Negro History* 13, no. 2 (April 1928): 185–198.

Riendeau, Roger *et al. An Enduring Heritage: Black Contributions to Early Ontario.* Toronto: Dundurn Press, 1984.

Ripley, C. Peter *et al,* eds. *The Black Abolitionist Papers, Volume II: Canada 1830–1865.* Chapel Hill, North Carolina: University of North Carolina Press, 1986.

Roberts, Julia. *In Mixed Company: Taverns and Public Life in Upper Canada.* Vancouver: University of British Columbia Press, 2009.

Robertson, Cam. *Report on early History of the Preston Area: Cherry Brook, Lake Loon, Lake Major, East Preston, and North Preston.* Halifax Regional Municipality Department (September 2004): 56.

Russell, Hilary. "Frederick Douglass in Toronto," *Cultural Resource Management* 4 (1998).

Shadd, Adrienne. "No 'Black Alley Clique': The Campaign to Desegregate Chatham's Public Schools, 1891–1893." *Ontario History* 99, no 1 (2007): 77–96.

_____. Cooper, Afua, Smardz Frost, Karolyn. *The Underground Railroad: Next Stop, Toronto!* Toronto: Natural Heritage Books, 2002.

_____. "Where Are You Really From? Notes of an Immigrant From North Buxton, Ontario." *Talking About Identity: Encounters in Race, Ethnicity, and Language.* Carl James, Adrienne Shadd, eds. Toronto: Between the Lines, 2001.

Shadd-Evelyn, Karen. *I'd Rather Live in Buxton.* Toronto: Simon & Pierre Publishing, 1993.

Shipley, Robert. *St. Catharines: Garden on the Canal.* Burlington, Ontario: Windsor Publications, 1987.

Simpson, Donald. *Under the North Star: Black Communities in Upper Canada.* Trenton, New Jersey: Africa World Press, 2005.

Skocpol, Theda *et al*, eds. *What a Mighty Power We Can Be: African American Fraternal Groups and the Struggle for Racial Equality*. Princeton, New Jersey: Princeton University Press, 2008.

Smardz Frost, Karolyn *et al*, eds. *Ontario's African Canadian Heritage: Collected Writings by Fred Landon, 1918–1967*. Toronto: Natural Heritage Books-Dundurn Press, 2009.

Sousa, Paul M. *"Orderly Manners: Nineteenth Century Street Processions in Hamilton."* Unpublished research paper. McMaster University, 1993.

Spray, W. A. *The Blacks in New Brunswick*. Fredericton, New Brunswick: Brunswick Press, 1972.

Talbot, Lance C. "History of Blacks in the Law Society of Upper Canada." *Law Society of Upper Canada Gazette* 24, no. 1 (March 1990): 65–70.

Taylor, Sheldon. "B.J. Spencer Pitt: A Forgotten Icon." *Share News*. February 21, 2002, 9.

Vogt, Roy. *Whose Property? The Deepening Conflict Between Private Property and Democracy in Canada*. Toronto: University of Toronto Press, 1999.

Walton, Jonathan W. *Blacks in Buxton and Chatham, Ontario, 1839–1890: Did the 49th Parallel Make a Difference?* Unpublished PhD Dissertation, Princeton University, 1979.

Walker, James W.St.G. "African Canadians." Magosci, Paul, ed. *Encyclopedia of Canada's People*. Multicultural History Society of Ontario, 1999, 139–176.

Whitfield, Harvey Amani. *Blacks on the Border: The Black Refugees in British North America 1815–1860*. Burlington, Vermont: University of Vermont Press, 2006.

Williams, Dorothy G. *The Road to Now: A History of Blacks in Montreal*. Montreal: Véhicule Press, 1997.

Winks, Robin. *The Blacks in Canada*. Monteal: McGill-Queen's University Press, 1997.

Wodhams, Lisa. "To Enlighten our Hearts: The 145th Emancipation Celebrations." *Northern Terminus: African Canadian History Journal* 5 (2008): xiii–xix.

Wright, Richard. *Centennial Encyclopaedia of the African Methodist Episcopal Church*. Philadelphia: Book Concern of the AME Church, 1916.

Newspapers

Amherstburg Echo
Brantford Courier
Brantford Expositor
British Colonist (Halifax)
British Colonist (Victoria)

Chatham Daily Planet
Chatham Evening Record
Chatham Tri-Weekly Planet
Chatham Weekly Planet
Collingwood Enterprise-Messenger
Daily Sun
Dawn of Tomorrow
Halifax Sun and Advertiser
Ingersoll Chronicle
Liberator
London Free Press
Montreal Gazette
Montreal Witness
Niagara Chronicle
Novascotian
Owen Sound Comet
Provincial Freeman
Toronto Globe
Toronto Star
Voice of the Fugitive
Windsor Evening Record

Websites

"African Nova Scotians: In the Age of Slavery and Abolition." Nova Scotia Archives and Records Management. *www.gs.ns.ca/nsarm/virtual/africanns.*

Auchmar Estate Hamilton. *www.auchmar.info/.*

Black History in Guelph and Wellington County. *guelph.ca/museumsites/BlackHistory/index.htm.*

"Black Loyalist 175 / Freedom Schooner Amistad Public Events in Halifax." Maritime Museum of the Atlantic. *museum.gov.ns.ca/mma/Events/Amistad.html.*

"Oakville's Black History," Canadian Caribbean Association of Halton. *www.ccah.ca.*

"Closed Canadian Parks." *cec.chebucto.org/ClosPark/CCPIndex.html.*

Doyle, Stuart. "Fraternal Lodges: Developing and Expanding the Village in Rural Southern Virginia," 2009. *Nathanielturner.com/blackfraternalorders.html.*

Glavin, Terry. "History of Slavery Far From Black and White." April 12, 2007. *straight.com.*

Grey Roots Museum & Archives. *www.greyroots.com/.*

Heritage Resources Saint John. *www.saintjohn.nbcc.nb.ca/Heritage.*

Lerech, Deborah. "The Underground Railroad." *www.oakvilletrails.ca*

Niagara Falls Museum. *www.niagaramuseum.com.*

"On the Road North: Black Canada and Journey to Freedom." Virtual Museum of Canada. *virtualmuseum.ca/blackhistory/OnTheRoadNorth.html.*

Owen Sound Emancipation Festival. *www.emancipation.ca.*

"Souls of Black Folks: Hamilton's Stewart Memorial Community." Worker's Arts and Heritage Centre/Virtual Museum of Canada. *virtualmuseum.ca/pm.php?id=exhibit_home&fl=0&lg=English&ex=236.*

Windsor Communities. *www.windsor-communities.com.*

Windsor Emancipation Celebration. *www.emancipationday.ca.*

"Worker's Art and Heritage Centre. The Souls of Black Folks: Hamilton's Stewart Memorial Community." The Virtual Museum of Canada. *virtualmuseum.ca/pm.php?id=exhibit_home&fl=0&lg=English&ex=236.*

Index

About the Author

Natasha Henry is the director of programs and an elementary teacher at a private school in the Greater Toronto Area. She is also a curriculum consultant and speaker, specializing in the development of learning materials that focus on the African experience. Natasha has developed the educational programs for two innovative exhibits on African Canadian history: *...and Still I Rise* and *Enslaved Africans in Upper Canada*. Natasha lives in Mississauga, Ontario.

Of Related Interest

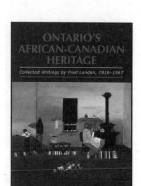

Ontario's African-Canadian Heritage
Collected Writings by Fred Landon, 1918–1967
by Karolyn Smardz Frost, Bryan Walls, Hilary Bates Neary, and Frederick
H. Armstrong
978-1-55002-814-0
$28.99 £15.00

Ontario's African-Canadian Heritage is composed of the collected works of
Professor Fred Landon, who for more than sixty years wrote about African-
Canadian history. The selected articles have, for the most part, never been
surpassed by more recent research and offer a wealth of data on slavery,
abolition, the Underground Railroad, and more, providing unique insights
into the abundance of African-Canadian heritage in Ontario. Though
much of Landon's research was published in the Ontario Historical Society's
journal, Ontario History, some of the articles reproduced here appeared in
such prestigious U.S. publications as the Journal of Negro History.

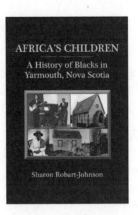

Africa's Children
A History of Blacks in Yarmouth, Nova Scotia
by Sharon Robart-Johnson
978-1-55002-862-1
$28.99 £16.99

Chronicling the history of Black families of the Yarmouth area of Nova Scotia, *Africa's Children* is a mirror image of the hopes and despairs and the achievements and injustices that mark the early stories of many African-Canadians. This extensively researched history traces the lives of those people, still enslaved at the time, who arrived with the influx of Black Loyalists and landed in Shelburne in 1783, as well as those who had come with their masters as early as 1767. Their migration to a new home did little to improve their overall living conditions, a situation that would persist for many years throughout Yarmouth County.

Available at your favourite bookseller.

 **DUNDURN PRESS**
www.dundurn.com

What did you think of this book?
Visit www.dundurn.com for reviews, videos, updates, and more!

Marquis Book Printing Inc.

Québec, Canada
2010